RAY SIMPSON

His Complete Celtic Prayers

MINNEAPOLIS

RAY SIMPSON
His Complete Celtic Prayers

© Copyright 2011 Ray Simpson.
Original edition published in English under the title RAY SIMPSON by Kevin Mayhew Ltd, Buxhall, England.

This edition published in 2020 by Fortress Press. All rights reserved. Except for brief quotations in critical articles or reviews, no part of this book may be reproduced in any manner without prior written permission from the publisher. Email copyright@augsburgfortress.org or write to Permissions, Fortress Press, PO Box 1209, Minneapolis, MN 55440-1209.

Cover image: © iStock 2020: Old stone carved Celtic design symbol, Celtic knot stock photo by vetas
Cover design: Emily Drake

Print ISBN: 978-1-5064-6019-2

I dedicate this book to Helen who initially
and most faithfully typed and pasted prayers
from twenty of my books.

Contents

	Page
About the author	10
About this book	11

	Prayer Nos
Christian seasons	
Advent	1–20
Christmas	21–43
New Year	44–51
Epiphany	52–63
Lent	64–73
The Passion and Holy Week	74–105
Palm Sunday	76–79
Good Friday	80–89
Saturday (Easter Eve)	90–95
Easter	96–105
Easter Eucharist	104–105
Ascension	106–118
Pentecost	119–143
Pentecost Eucharist	140–143
Trinity	144–164
Trinity Eucharist	163–164
Harvest	165–168
Harvest Eucharist	166–168
Michaelmas/Angel season	169–185
Remembrance of saints, loved ones, forebears and war dead	186–187
Remembrance	188–192
All Saints	193–219
All Saints' Eve (Halloween)	193–203
All Saints' Day	204–208
Unknown saints	209–219
All Souls	220–230
All Souls' Eucharist	230

Liturgy, Eucharist and special services

Preparation	231–233
Opening prayers	234
Confession and lament	235–258
Thanksgiving and praise	259–266
Praise	260–266
Making peace	267
Intercession	268–272
General prayers of blessing and consecration	273–276
Eucharist	277–299
Closing blessings	300–301
Saints' days and holy days	
(including Eucharist prayers)	302–353
1, 2 February, Festival of Light, St Brigid, Candlemas,	
Imbolc	302–304
11 February, Caedmon	305
14 February, St Valentine's Day	
(Quinquagesima – love)	306–308
23 February, St Polycarp	309–310
2 March, St Chad, St Cedd	311–313
Rogation	314–317
1 May, Beltane: Midsummer	318–319
21–22 June	320
24 June, St John the Baptist, summer solstice	321–324
28 July, St Samson and Wilberforce	325–328
31 July, Joseph of Arimathea, Ignatius Loyala,	
Lammas Eve	329–333
1 August, Lammas	334–336
6 August, Transfiguration	337–339
25 August, St Ebbe	340
28 August, Augustine of Hippo	341
8 September, the Birth of the Blessed Virgin Mary	342–345
14 September, Holy Cross Day	346–351
11 November, St Martin of Tours (Remembrance)	352–353
Special Services	354–432
Wedding	354–361
Renewal of wedding vows	362–371
Baptism of believers	372
Baptism and dedication of infants	373

Infant blessing	374–379
Blessings for homes and other buildings	380–396
Dying, funerals and wakes	397–412
Earth blessing	413–417
Summer solstice	414–415
Winter solstice	416–417
Healing	418–429
Healing of places	430–432

Daily rhythm

Waking/morning	433–488
Midday	489–513
Evening	514–525
Night	526–593
Children's prayers	594–609
School	610–612

Saints and other companions 613–755

God with us

Awareness of the Presence	756–798
Compassion	799–807
Love for all	808–809
Work	810–830
Healing: physical and spiritual	831–857
Hospitals	850
Grace of God	851–857
Seeking God's help	858–901
Discipleship	868–876
Truth	877–879
Contentment	880–882
Appreciation and awareness	883–901
Authenticity	902–910
Led by God	911–920
Peace	921–930
Holy Spirit/spiritual gifts	931–950
Renewal and recreation	951–980
Simple lifestyle	981–1026
Justice	985–997
Mission and witness	998–1026

Growing, exploring, listening, discerning	1027–1091
Guidance for the journey	1092–1097
The Soul Friend	1098–1104
Times of trial	1105–1122
Journeying, pilgrimage	1123–1166
Arriving in a new place	1164–1166
Church	1167–1184
Government	1185–1190
Stillness	1191–1197
Forgiveness	1198–1202
Sorrow and loss	1203
Home and families	1204–1221
Vehicles	1222–1225
Leisure	1226–1230
Loving friendships	1231–1235

God's World

Thanksgiving and praise	1236–1249
Blessings	1250–1256
Blessings on food	1257–1279
Garden	1280–1282
Sport	1283–1285
Money	1286–1291

Prayers for others and the world

Caring for God's world	1292–1312
The human family	1313–1350
God's care for creation	1351–1362
All creation	1363–1367
Peace on Earth	1368–1380
Unity	1381–1387
The cosmos	1388–1389
All humanity	1390–1391
Those who are suffering	1392–1396
Battered families	1397–1404
Serving others	1405–1410
Anniversaries	1411–1413
Family members	1414–1418
When away from home	1419–1420

Personal prayers
Computer	1421–1422
Journeys	1423–1424
The ordinary and the extraordinary	1425–1435
Retreats	1436–1440
Self and others	1441–1443

Circling prayers
1444–1456

Seasons
Spring	1457–1464
Summer	1465–1478
Autumn	1479–1490
Winter	1491–1506

Indexes
Index of first lines
Subject index

About the author

Ray Simpson is the founding guardian of the international Community of Aidan and Hilda and the principal tutor of its Celtic Christian Studies programme. He lives on the Holy Island of Lindisfarne where many pilgrims come to the Community's Retreat House, library and Spirituality Centre, the Open Gate. An Anglican priest, he was previously also a Free Church minister in a new church plant sponsored by six church streams at Bowthorpe, Norwich. Ray is the author of numerous bestselling books on Celtic Spirituality, published by Kevin Mayhew Ltd. He writes a daily prayer tweet on Twitter@whitehouseviews and a weekly blog on http://www.aidanandhilda.org/public_html/web/blog_simpson.php

About this book

This is a book of contemporary prayers. In what sense can it claim to be Celtic, let alone complete? Such claims are indeed debatable.

There is a good selection of 'I arise' prayers, which echo the ancient Irish loricas such as Saint Patrick's Breastplate. The circling prayers have roots as far back as Saint Ninian. Some of the prayers for homes, healing and journeys echo those in Alexander Carmichael's nineteenth-century collection of ancient oral prayers from Scotland's islands and highlands, *The Carmina Gadelica*; and there are a good many prayers inspired by the lives of Celtic saints.

Of course, no collection of prayers can be fully complete, but this collection is comprehensive. It is complete, or holistic, in the sense that all created and human life is included. The circle in the Celtic Cross is a symbol of creation and of the primal: nothing is excluded from God's embrace. These prayers reconnect us with the seasons and the streets, the Scriptures and the saints, the struggles and the silence. Finally, the music of life and the poetry of words, which are so often squeezed out of liturgy books compiled by committees, hopefully flow here more freely.

The prayers are selected from over twenty of my published titles, and many new ones have been composed for this publication.

This book may be useful alongside a Bible lectionary or anthology as an aid to personal devotion. It is a rich resource for those who lead church or group worship or offer pastoral care. The exhaustive index at the back indicates prayers suitable for hundreds of occasions. May your praying be enriched.

Ray Simpson, White House, Holy Island of Lindisfarne

Christian seasons

Advent

1   Calm us to wait for the gift of Christ.
Cleanse us to prepare the way for Christ.
Teach us to contemplate the wonder of Christ.
Anoint us to bear the life of Christ.

2   Christ, wake us to your summons, urgent in our midst,
to truth we cannot hide from – your power alone will last.
The worlds that now so scorn you will vanish like a dream.
When you take back your own; all good will be one stream.
Echoes a prayer of George McLeod

3   In the wasteland may the Glory shine.
In the land of the lost may the King make his home.

4   All-knowing God,
parents-in-God picture and pattern your ways;
forgive us for following idols and illusions.
All-seeing God,
prophets shine like candles in the night;
forgive us for staying in the dark.
All-holy God,
front runners like John clear obstacles from your path;
forgive us for blocking your way.
All-giving God,
people like Mary offered their all as bearers of your life;
help us to be bearers of your life.

5   Lord, though we may laugh
at failed end-of-world predictions,
may we live this day
as if you will come
and find us doing our duty with joy,
alert and ready to meet you.

6   Help us to prepare a way for you:
by our thoughtfulness towards others;
by our care in little things;
by our upholding of the oppressed.

7   Help us to prepare a way for you:
by our thoughtfulness towards creatures;
by our care of crops and kitchens;
by our upholding of creation.

8   The Earth is becoming a wasteland:
Breath of the Most High, come and renew it.
Humanity is becoming a battleground:
Child of Peace, come and unite it.
Society is becoming a playground:
Key of Destiny, open doors to our true path.
The world is becoming a no-man's-land:
God with us, come and make your home here.

9   Christ, Light of the world,
meet us in our place of darkness.
Christ, Light of the world,
meet us in our place of longing.
Christ, Light of the world,
meet us in our place of working.

10   Among the hungry,
among the homeless,
among the friendless,
come to make things new.
Among the powerful,
among the spoilt,
among the crooked,
come to make things new.
In halls of fame,
in corridors of power,
in forgotten places,
come to make things new.
With piercing eyes,
with tender touch,
with cleansing love,
come to make things new.

11   Come to us, Wisdom,
     moving in the flux and flow of the cosmos
     to bring worlds into being.
     Come to us, Wisdom,
     permeating all creation,
     the life of soil and seed and seasons.
     Come to us, Wisdom,
     shaping nations and ensouling peoples.
     Come to us, Wisdom,
     encompassing the mysteries of the unseen world
     and the mysteries of the soul.
     Come to us, Wisdom,
     the seeing eye of art and science,
     the ear of all that breathes.
     Come to us, Wisdom,
     the light of our darkness,
     the reconciler of that which is divided.
     Come to us, Wisdom,
     the weaver of Earth's destiny,
     the completer of our call.

12   Wisdom, permeating creation and informing all peoples,
     come and bring us the mind of God.
     Shaper of peoples,
     who through Moses
     gave guidance that would make a people great,
     guide us into the ways of true greatness.
     Bedrock, Sign of community,
     come to places of instability
     and root them in realities that nothing can destroy.
     Key to Destiny,
     unlock our potential
     and our capacity to befriend and serve others,
     that we may be mentors and soul friends
     amid a needy people.
     Light-bringer,
     illumine places of darkness, despair and disease.
     True Fulfiller of Desire, harness our deepest longings
     to your infinite purpose of love.
     God with us – the Presence that cannot be taken from us –
     may we live with you and may you live in us for ever.

13   Great Spirit, swirling in the elements,
      you brought to birth a world.
      Mighty Father, swirling in the elements,
      you brought to birth a Son.
      Eternal Christ, swirling in the elements,
      you stride towards us now.
      Glory to God in the highest.

14   You are holy, you are whole.
      Let Earth give praise from pole to pole.
      You are coming, coming here
      to bring your hard-pressed people cheer;
      bringing to them human birth
      born of heaven, born of Earth;
      bringing to them bread and wine,
      giving hope of life divine.
      You are coming, you are whole –
      let Earth give praise from pole to pole.

15   Desire of every nation,
      we bring to you those who are empty
      and who long to find meaning.
      Come to them, Lord Jesus.
      Desire of every nation,
      we bring to you those who are overlooked
      and who long to know their worth.
      Come to them, Lord Jesus.
      Desire of every nation,
      we bring to you those who are exploring,
      but who do not know what they search for.
      Come to them, Lord Jesus.

16   Lord, you keep us waiting for signs of hope.
      You keep us looking for ways in which you come.
      The pain of the world, the anguish of the people
      cry out to you.
      Come, Lord Jesus, come.

17 Son of the prophets, on our longings
    let your light shine.
    Son of Mary, on our littleness
    let your light shine.
    Son of Eternity, on our lying down
    let your light shine.

18 We wait in the darkness, expectantly, longingly;
    come, O God Most High.
    In the darkness we can see the splendour of the universe –
    blankets of stars, the solitary glowing of the planets.
    Come, O God Most High.
    In the darkness of the womb mortals are nurtured
    and the Christ child was made ready
    for the journey into light.
    Come, O God Most High.
    In the darkness the wise three
    found the star that led them to you.
    Come, O God Most High.
    In the darkness of dreams
    you spoke to Joseph and the wise ones
    and you speak still to us.
    Come, O God Most High.
    In the darkness of despair and distress
    we watch for a sign of hope from the Light of lights.
    Come, O God Most High.
    Echoes a Maori prayer from New Zealand

19 God be with us on our journey towards Christmas.
    Help us to go deeper into what is real
    until we are brought to the wonder of your incarnation.
    Dear Son of God, you took flesh to redeem us.
    Forgive our hardness.
    Dear Son of Mary,
    with sacrifice of love you came to us.
    Forgive our selfishness.

20 With Abraham and Moses,
    waiting to be led to a place of promise,
    we wait.

With Amos and Hosea, Isaiah, Micah,
and all the prophets believing
that you are a God of justice,
we wait.
With Paul and Silas,
and all God's people imprisoned and persecuted
for acting on their faith,
we wait.
With Naaman and Jairus,
Bartimaeus and the Syro-Phoenician woman,
longing for an end to pain and rejection,
we wait.
With Zaccheus in his tree
and the Samaritan widow at the well,
keen to be liberated from a half-life,
we wait.
With Sarah and Hannah, Elizabeth and Mary,
looking forward to new life and new beginnings,
we wait.
With Jesus in the desert,
and in the garden because he asks us to,
we wait.

Echoes a prayer of The Wild Goose Resources Group

Christmas

21 Jesus, born in a stable,
    make here your home.
    Jesus, born of a peasant girl,
    make here your home.
    Jesus, searched for by wise seekers,
    make here your home.
    Jesus, reared at a carpenter's bench,
    make here your home.
    Jesus, risen from the wintry ground of death,
    make here your home.

22 Homemaker God,
who made yourself at home in a cowshed,
come to all who are sleeping rough.
May the light of the Bethlehem family
be a light for the homeless in our world.

23 May we journey with you,
Jesus, Mary and Joseph,
to your birthplace at Bethlehem,
firm in the faith,
loyal to the truth,
obedient to your Father's will
along the path that leads to life.

24 Universal Child,
we will welcome you when you call.
We will open the long-shut parts of our lives.
We will become young again with you.

25 Babe of heaven, Defenceless Love,
you had to travel far from your home.
Strengthen us on our pilgrimage of trust on Earth.
King of Glory, you accepted such humbling;
clothe us with the garments of humility.
Your birth shows us the simplicity of the Father's love;
keep us in the simplicity of that love.
Your coming shows us the wonder of being human;
help us to cherish every human life.
Echoes a prayer of George Appleton

26 Now is born Christ the king of greatness.
Glow to him stars and streets;
glow to him churches and trees.

27a Thank you for the holy family,
Mary, Joseph and the others.
May families reflect their dedication to put your will first;
may purity, love and trust grow strong in our households.

27b Thank you for the prophetess Anna
who, honed in daily attunement to you
in the offering of praise,
discerned your presence
in an ordinary but significant moment.
Take our senses, hone our intuition,
steep us in the disciplines of the Spirit,
that we may see your hand at work
in the events of today and tomorrow.

27c Thank you for the sanctuaries of Egypt
that were offered to the holy family,
for their acquaintance with God-honourers
of another land and religion,
for the hermits and holy people of the deserts.
We pray for God-honourers
who seek to welcome your servants
in Egypt, in Muslim lands and everywhere;
for refugees, for hermits and others who pattern
an alternative way to that of our acquisitive society.

27d Thank you for the home in Nazareth,
and for the boy Jesus
growing in skills of carpentry
and in the confidence of puberty.
We pray for young people who are confused,
deskilled, orphaned,
and who know neither themselves nor their calling:
may they find affirming adults to be alongside them.

27e Thank you that even at the death of Jesus,
the holy family grew through the adoption of John
into Mary's family.
We pray for those who have died,
and for those who face loss of life or limb or hope.
May the healing light of Christ shine upon them,
and may they come to know that there is
a family more wonderful than they have ever known.

CHRISTIAN SEASONS

28 Lord of time and eternity,
    prepare our minds to celebrate with faith
    your birth on Earth.
    Fill our hearts with wonder
    as we recall the precious moment
    when you were born as our brother.

29 May every lone parent and child
    be cherished as Mary cherished you.
    May those who are out in the cold
    find a stable place as warm as yours.
    May those who work on the land
    be as responsive to your presence as were the shepherds.

30 Let the cares of the past grow dim,
    let the skies and our hearts grow clear,
    until the Son of God comes striding towards us
    walking on this Earth.

31 Jesus, proclaimed by angels;
    light up our darkness.
    Jesus, worshipped by shepherds;
    light up our darkness.
    Jesus, adored by wise men;
    light up our darkness.
    Jesus, God who is with us now;
    light up our darkness.

32 Jesus, you are the glory of eternity shining among us,
    the tenderness of God here with us now.
    Jesus, you are the Healing Person, the pattern of goodness,
    fulfilling among us the highest human hopes.
    Jesus, you are the champion of the weak,
    the counsellor of the despairing,
    the brother of us all, who knows our every need.
    Jesus, you are the splendour of the Father, the Son of Mary,
    our Bridge between Earth and the world beyond.

33 Angels' Lord, who for nine months
was hidden in love's furnace, Mary's womb –
you who stole down to Earth, humbler than all –
take us to yourself, and make us like you.

34 The Earth gave you a cave,
the skies gave you a star,
the angels gave you a song;
may we give you our love.
Echoes an Orthodox prayer

35 The love that Mary gave her Son
may we give to the world;
the love that you give us through your Son
may we give back to you.

36 Son of the elements, Son of the heavens,
Son of the moon, Son of the sun,
Son of Mary of the God-mind,
Son of God, firstborn of all creation,
dwell with us today.

37 Jesus Christ, Son of glory,
who for love comes among us,
bless to us this day of joy.
Open to us heaven's generous gates.
Strengthen our hope.
Revive our tired souls
till we sing the joys of your glory
with all the angels of heaven.
Hold also those who are sleeping rough,
those who feel shut out of society,
those who are cold and hungry,
and these we name before you now.

38 Bless, O Lord, this Christmas tree,
all that goes on to it
and all that goes on around it.

May the needles that point upwards
lead us to worship the Creator
who came from heaven to be born as a child.
May the needles that fall to the ground
remind us of the needs of the poor
and those at the bottom of the social pile.
May the decorations that brighten this dark season
prompt us to celebrate it with thoughtfulness and joy.

39   Child of Glory, Child of Mary,
at your birth you were proclaimed the Prince of Peace.
You came to remove the wall
that divides one people from another;
may walls of hostility and fear come tumbling down.

40   O Saviour Christ,
you existed before the world began.
You came to save us and we are witnesses of your goodness.
You became a tiny child in a cot
showing us the simplicity of our parents' love.
You chose Mary as your mother
and raised all motherhood to a divine vocation.
May all mothers be bearers of life and grace
to their husbands, their children
and to all who come to their homes.

41   Today, O Lord,
as we contemplate Mary and Joseph,
may we live in the wonder of your divine conceiving;
may we live in the wonder of our divine receiving.

42   Child of Glory, Child of Mary,
born in the stable,
King of all,
you came to our wasteland,
in our place suffered
Come to us now with your call.

43   Birther, Father, Mother of the cosmos,
breathing through all creation,
breathing your life through a woman's womb
into a human form:
bring new birth to us who gather
at this time of the Birth.
Bring birth to our nation,
to this ailing, ageing world,
and bring to birth in us,
who are your people,
the new creation
which we stand on tiptoe to see.

New Year

44   God bless to us this year,
never vouchsafed to us before.
It is to bless your own presence
that you have given us this moment, O Lord.

       Bless to us our eyes
and everything they shall see.
Bless to us our neighbours;
may our neighbours be a blessing to us.

       Bless to us our households
and all our dear ones.
Bless to us our work
and all that belongs to our provision.

       Give to us clean hearts
that we may not need to hide from you
one moment of this new year.

45   Lord of the years,
we will ring out the old year,
the lust to gain,
the craze to destroy,
we will ring in the new year,
the joy of being,
the will to transform.

46 God of the years,
    at the gate of the year we put our hands in yours.
    As the old tide recedes,
    may we plant your footsteps in fresh sands.
    May we travel with less baggage and more wisdom
    and learn from you how our journey should be.

47 *For use at a Eucharist*
    Lord of the year behind us,
    Lord of the year before us,
    as Mary and Joseph named Jesus in the temple,
    may we name him in our hearts,
    receive him in this Eucharist
    and journey with him through this year.

48 Bless to us this time of threshold,
    when we pass from the old to the new.
    Bless to us this bread,
    made from grains of wheat that pass away,
    that it may become for us
    the food that nurtures new life.
    Bless to us this wine,
    made from grapes that pass away,
    that it may become for us
    the drink of heaven's ever-renewing life.

49 Lord, with joy and for love of you
    we commit ourselves to seek and do
    your perfect will in this coming year.
    We are no longer our own but yours.
    Put us to what you will;
    place us with whom you will;
    let us be put to work for you or put aside for you;
    let us be full, let us be empty;
    let us have all things, let us have nothing.
    We freely and with all our heart
    give you all things for you to use.
    May we walk with you through this year
    in unity with our fellow Christians,

feeding upon your Word,
honouring all people,
serving our neighbour,
responsive to the leading of your Holy Spirit.
Echoes the words from The Methodist Covenant Service

50 You have given your all to us.
    May this food and drink of angels
    fortify us to give our all to you
    in all whom we shall meet
    and in all that we shall do
    throughout the coming year.

51 Holy Father, Holy Jesus, Holy Guide,
    be a smooth way before you,
    a guiding star above you,
    a keen eye behind you;
    this day, this year, for ever.

Epiphany

52 We welcome your light that glints in the rising sun.
    We welcome the light that dawns through your only Son.
    We welcome your light that gleams through growing earth.
    We welcome the light that you kindle in our souls.

53 The Magi searched for an infant king;
    Christ, lead us into your presence.
    They offered incense as their prayer;
    Christ, we bow in awe before you.
    Myrrh they gave to mourn your death;
    Christ, to you we pour out our suffering love.

54 Purify our lives like gold
      that we may be royal priests to you.
    Sanctify our hearts like incense
      that we may be adorers of your presence.
    Beautify our hearts like myrrh
      that we may be your fragrance on Earth.

55 May your presence draw people across the world
    and reveal your mother heart of compassion.
    Pour into the empty cups of the world
    the beauty and blessings of Christ
    and gather together your children.

56 You who became poor to make many rich:
    transform our dullness with radiant light;
    transform our drabness with vibrant joy;
    transform our shallowness with deepening wisdom;
    transform our suffering with growing trust.

57 As once you changed water into wine,
    change our drear day into sweet rest in you.
    Change the drudgery of the old and worn
    and of all for whom life's sparkle has gone.

58 Infant Jesus,
    truly God, truly human,
    truly infinite, truly frail,
    your greatness holds the universe;
    your face attracts our hearts;
    your goodness beckons all that is good in us;
    your wisdom searches us;
    your truth reshapes us;
    your generosity enriches our poverty;
    your hand fills us with blessings;
    your mercy brings forgiveness.
    Your glory fills the world.

59 O Christ, you entered the stream of human life:
    immerse us in the divine life.
    Immerse us in the waters that cleanse.
    Immerse us in the waters that overwhelm evil.
    Immerse us in the waters of creativity.
    Immerse us in the waters of life everlasting.

60 Christ, splendour of the Father's glory,
    sustaining all the worlds by your Word of power,
    renew your presence in our lives.

Christ, child of Mary, rich in wisdom,
Prince of Peace, God with us,
renew your presence in our homes.
Christ, begotten of the Father before time,
born at Bethlehem in time,
renew your presence in your Church.
Christ, truly God, truly human,
fulfilling the desires of the peoples,
renew your presence in the people.

61 Great God,
in creation you commanded the light
to shine out of darkness.
As the season of darkness recedes
may the incoming light be to us the true Light
in whose presence no unworthy thought,
no deed of shame,
may stubbornly remain.

62 Shed light upon our brow
and on what we grow.
Shed light upon our cheek
and on what we seek.
Shed light upon the seeds
and on our deeds.

63 May you be
lit by the glory of God,
drawn by the light of God,
warmed by the fire of God.

After Brian Frost

Lent

64 O Christ, you took the tree in your hands,
allowed nails to pinion you to it
until it became the tree of death.
The sun hid its sight and all creation wept.

CHRISTIAN SEASONS

> We pray for trees. Have mercy on them.
> We pray for the places where drought and flood now prevail
> because the trees have been torn from the earth.
> May trees be planted again, and become trees of life.

65 Lead us into the desert of purging,
    that through reflection and prayer
    we may leave behind the things that tie our spirits down
    and learn again to be your pilgrim people.
    Through fasting from the frenzied feeding of false desires,
    through study of your Word, meditation and acts of service,
    restore the clearness of our seeing
    and free us to share your generous love with all.

66 Help us to tread in the steps of Christ,
    in the steps of Christ our Champion and King.
    Show us the way when strong, when weak;
    be our Guide in everything.

67 O Holy Fire,
    O Holy Grace,
    O Overflowing Silent One:
    by your birth
    enable us;
    by your overcoming of spirits
    arm us;
    by your integrity
    make us true;
    by your fortitude in trials
    establish us;
    by your self-giving in death
    change us;
    by your mission to unquiet spirits
    raise us.

68 Teach us to leave behind prejudice and meanness of spirit.
    Incite us to generous giving.
    Help us to create space for you
    and play our part in the kingdom of your love.

69 Humility of God,
   who bowed your head upon the cross,
   bend our necks low
   that we may be led by you.
   Arm of God,
   you allowed your arms to be stretched out
   on the wood of the cross.
   Stretch out our arms in love of all through you.

70 Christ, you are the refined molten metal
   of our human forge.
   Purge our desires,
   strengthen our resolve,
   sharpen our minds,
   shape our wills.

71 Christ of the scars,
   into your hands we place the broken, the wounded,
   the hungry and the homeless.
   Christ of the scars,
   into your hands we place
   those who have been betrayed or bereaved;
   those who have suffered loss of family or friends,
   employment or home.
   Christ of the scars,
   into your hands we place neighbours defamed,
   lovers spurned, spouses deserted.
   Christ of the scars,
   into your hands we place victims of war and crime.

72 Saving God,
   by your incarnation and birth in poverty
   set us free.
   By your prayers and self-discipline
   set us free.
   By your tender works of mercy
   set us free.
   By your struggle for truth and justice
   set us free.

By your nobility in persecution
set us free.
By your self-giving even in death
set us free.

73 *Prayer after Communion*
Bearer of pain and Maker of love,
steep our souls in yours,
that we may walk in your steps
through the pain to glory.

The Passion and Holy Week

74 Christ, save us from a cheap Easter that lacks the waiting,
the pruning, the longing that gives it its worth.
May we not become tortured souls
like those who tried to remove you
from their puny empires in your last days on Earth.

75 You began your last week on Earth
by weeping over the city,
we weep with you for the blindness of pride,
the mad rush to consume,
the lust to control that drives you from among us.
You upturned the tables of the temple crooks,
and began to turn the world around.
Do it again through us.
On your last fateful Thursday
you made bread and wine immemorial:
may we never cease to remember you.
You chose what is weak in the world
to shame the strong:
may we not be ashamed
to be vulnerable and available.
King of Friday, as you die
all creation weeps amid earthquake and eclipse.
Your death will not be in vain:
we will lay down our lives for you.

Palm Sunday

76 Noble Christ, may we not become tortured souls
    like those who tried to remove you from their puny
    empires during your last weeks on Earth.
    As we retread the last week of your earthly life,
    may we so follow you in our hearts
    that you will enter our hearts.

77 O God, when the ride is bumpy
    and the world passes us by,
    you pour out your life for us,
    right to the very end.
    When we are edged aside
    and doors are shut in our face,
    you pour out your life for us,
    right to the very end.
    When others are out to get us
    and our home is not secure,
    you pour out your life for us,
    right to the very end.
    When our lives are but a flicker
    in the darkness that encroaches,
    you pour out your life for us,
    right to the very end.

78 The One who created us
    comes willingly to suffer for us;
    let us spread our resolves before him
    like branches of palm.
    The Almighty comes to us
    as one gentle and lowly of heart;
    let us put on clothes of humility and praise.
    The spirit is willing but the flesh is weak;
    let us watch and wait with him.

79 As your trial drew near, you looked upon
    the city and wept over it, because it did not
    recognise its salvation.

Open our eyes, that we may weep with you.
May we weep with you for the blindness of pride that
corrodes the dignity of human life . . .
Open our eyes, that we may weep with you.
We weep with you for the mad rush to consume
that tramples down on the Earth and its children . . .
Open our eyes, that we may weep with you.
We weep with you for the lust to control that
imprisons the soul and fragments community . . .
Open our eyes, that we may weep with you.

Good Friday

80   You saw a widow give what she had;
help us to give our money with love.
You taught us to work like those who tend vines;
help us to tend the planet with love.
You taught that the poor are your family;
help us to serve the poor with love.
Through your defenceless love,
teach us the grace of self-offering.
Through your weakness,
teach us the grace of acceptance.
In your betrayal,
teach us the grace of forgiveness.
In your trials,
teach us the grace of trust.

81   Lord Jesus, you taught that your chosen people
can only fulfil their calling
if they become like a seed that dies,
buried in the earth, in order that many new ones may grow.
We pray that our brothers and sisters in Christ,
Palestinians and people of every race,
may know that they are now at the heart of your purposes
on Earth and in heaven.

Lord Jesus, as you are lifted up on a tree placed in the earth,
the rulers and empires of this world are exposed
for what they are – cheap and short-lived substitutes
for true government.

You become the way for true unity in the human family;
all who are buried, humbled and earthed
become your common ground.
So may it be.

82   May we carry your cross
in our hearts through this day.
Your cross be in our eyes and in our looking.
Your cross be in our mouths and in our speaking.
Your cross be in our hands and in our working.
Your cross be in our minds and in our thinking.

83   You who lift the lowly and strengthen the frail,
who in your weakness raised a fallen world
and let sinners lift you on to a cross,
we thank you.
Lift each of us on to your shoulders
like a shepherd who does not neglect one lost sheep.
Lift us from Earth to heaven.

84   Kind Father, faithful Saviour,
with head bowed your spirit passed across.
We thank you.
Receive us, at our end, into the hands of the Father.
Breathe your last for us and hold us up,
then raise us from the dead.
Cause the powers and principalities to fall back
that we may come swiftly to you.
Echoes prayers on the passion from the Anglo-Saxon Convent of Nunnaminster, Winchester, about AD 900, which combine Irish and Roman elements

85   Dearest Christ, you have given love, given it exquisitely.
In your tiredness you washed your friends' tired feet.
In your generosity you gave bread to your betrayer.
In your all-seeing provision you bequeathed
a sacrament of bread and wine
that makes you constantly present to us.

In your anguish in the garden
you fought with demons and with doubt.
In your prayers you ever place your people
in the divine heart.
You call us to watch and pray.
Out of love for you we will watch and we will pray.

86   Crucified Christ, Son of the Father,
conceived by the Holy Spirit,
born of the Virgin Mary,
we adore you.
Crucified Christ, bearing contempt,
forgiving your enemies,
remaining always true,
we adore you.
Crucified Christ, treasure house of wisdom,
champion of justice, fount of love,
we adore you.
Crucified Christ, faithful to the end,
gatekeeper of paradise, eternal friend,
we adore you.

87   O King of the Friday,
whose limbs were stretched on the cross;
O Lord who did suffer
the bruises, the wounds, the loss;
we stretch ourselves beneath the shield of your might.
Some fruit from the tree of your passion
fall on us this night!
Echoes an early Irish prayer

88   Father, look upon your family,
for whom our Lord Jesus Christ was willing to undergo
betrayal and torture.
Forgive our unfaithfulness.
Cure us of our sins.
Restore our unity.
Strengthen us to walk the way of the cross.
Bring us to the place of resurrection.

89 The angel passed over the homes of the Godfollowers.
　　The fleeing people passed over the sea.
　　In their extremity you reached down to them, Lord.
　　Blessed be the God of eternal covenant.
　　The Christ walked the land doing works of mercy.
　　The tyrants dragged him to the gate of death.
　　In his extremity he called out to you
　　and you heard him.
　　Blessed be the God of eternal covenant.
　　O Christ, help us to become one with you.
　　In your weakness, teach us the grace of acceptance.
　　In your betrayal, teach us the grace of forgiveness.
　　In your trials, teach us the grace of trust.
　　In your defenceless love, teach us the grace of self-giving.

Saturday (Easter Eve)

90 We bless you for Mary
　　who with sorrow-pierced heart stayed with her son
　　at the foot of the cross.
　　We bless you for Joseph
　　who asked for the Life of all
　　to be laid in his garden of graves.
　　We bless you for the women
　　who adorned your grave with spices
　　and witnessed your resurrection.

91 O Christ, like the seed that falls into the ground
　　and yet bears fruit,
　　may we yet see the fruit of eternal life on Earth.

92 We thank you for Joseph,
　　who came to the governor by night
　　and asked for the Life of all to be laid
　　in his garden of graves.
　　We thank you for Mary, who with sorrow wept
　　as she saw her son hanging on the tree,
　　her heart pierced with sorrow.

We thank you for the women,
who went to the grave to watch,
to weep and offer fragrant spices of devotion.
We too will watch and weep and offer you
our tears,
our memories,
our tenderness,
our faith.

93   Into our place of darkness,
into our place of strife,
into our fears and worries,
come with eternal life.
Into those who are dying,
into those weary of life,
into those lost and despairing,
come with eternal life.

94   O Christ, you remembered those
who forgot your words about the sign of Jonah,
who after three days was delivered from the fish;
remember, too, those in our world who have lost hope.
O Christ, you remembered those
who went to their tombs without knowing you.
O Christ, go through the grave and the gates of death;
open to us the gate of glory.

95   *For Easter Eve at the tomb/for devotion at the cross any time*
Lord, we offer you,
like the women who came to your tomb,
our tears, the memories of your life, the spices of our faith,
the ointment of our tenderness,
the flowers of our personality –
all, Lord, for you.

Lord, we offer you,
like the angels all gathered round your throne,
our songs of awe-struck devotion,
our shouts of your great victory,

our bowing low in reverence,
our joyful surrender of all we are –
all, Lord, for you.

Lord we offer you,
like your faithful disciples down the years,
our ears to listen to your every word,
our eyes to spot the needy ones,
our hands to touch with tenderness,
our hearts to embrace any hurting lives,
all, Lord, for you.

Easter

96 Jesus, who stopped the wind and stilled the waves,
grant you calm in the storm times.
Jesus, victor over death and destruction,
bring safety on your voyage.
Jesus of the purest love, perfect companion,
bring guarding ones around you.
Jesus of the miraculous catching of fish
and the perfect lakeside meal,
guide you finally ashore.
From 'The First Voyage of the Coracle', Community of Aidan and Hilda

97 Risen Christ,
you burst from the grave;
help us to burst into life.
You breathed on your disciples;
breathe your life into us.

98 In our baptism, O Lord Christ,
our self-centred life is buried
and we rise up with your new life in us.
Day by day may we be buried;
day by day may we rise with you.

99 Risen Lord, you revealed yourself
to Mary in the garden at dawn.
Reveal yourself to us in the dawnings of our lives.
Risen Lord, you revealed yourself
to the fisherfolk as they toiled in vain at their work.
Reveal yourself to us in the long hours of our toil.
Risen Lord, you revealed yourself
to the walkers as they welcomed you into their home.
Reveal yourself to us as we walk
and make welcome our homes.
Risen Lord, you revealed yourself
to Thomas when he felt the scars in your body.
Reveal yourself to us
as we reach out to the scars of the world.
Risen Lord, you revealed yourself
to many as they met beneath the skies.
Reveal yourself to us in the wonder of your creation.

100 Christ Jesus, in the light of your risen presence
and in union with your first frail apostles, we say sorry:
for not weighing your words,
for not sharing your trials,
for not believing your promises.

101 Risen Christ, you turned Mary's tears into joy;
turn our tears into joy.
Risen Christ, you turned the travellers' despair into hope;
turn our despair into hope.
Risen Christ, you turned the disciples' fears into boldness;
turn our fears into boldness.
Risen Christ, you turned an empty catch into fullness;
turn our empty routines into fullness.
Risen Christ, you turned Thomas' unbelief into trust;
turn our unbelief into trust.

102 May Christ rise in glory,
scattering the darkness before your path.
The Sun of suns,
the eye of the great God,
the eye of the King of hosts,

is rising upon us,
gently and generously.
Welcome, glorious Son,
dawn of a new day.

103 Through the resurrection of your Son you overcame
the hold of sin and death.
Transform us in all our ways.

Easter Eucharist

104 Risen Christ,
you called Peter to love you and feed your flock.
We, too, accept your call to love you
and nourish those who hunger for you.
Risen Christ,
you burst from the grave.
Now burst into life through us.

105 Risen Christ,
as you appeared to your disciples
in the breaking of bread,
come to us afresh in this Eucharist.
You call us to be open to the coming of your Spirit.
Give us receptive, waiting and eager hearts
to receive all that you wish to give us.

Ascension

106 Sovereign of the universe,
a cloud hid you from sight,
yet your mortal humanity has been raised to life in God.
We pray for those whose life is clouded:
raise them to life in you.
For those clouded by fear:
raise them to life in you.
For those clouded by worry:
raise them to life in you.

For those clouded by hostility:
raise them to life in you.
May tiny infants in the womb be raised to life in you;
may those ailing or with disabilities be raised to life in you;
may bronzed and brave adventurers be raised to life in you;
may thinkers and researchers be raised to life in you;
may the battle-scarred and weary be raised to life in you.

107   Beautiful Christ,
you may depart from our sight,
but the fragrance of your love shall
ever linger in our hearts.
You have conquered death.
The fullness we long for we shall now receive.

108   You came down
to lift us up.
You descended to Earth
that Earth might ascend to heaven.
You descended to the dead
that the dead might rise to life
in the heat of the day.

Lift us up
in our fretting cares.
Lift us up
in our difficulties.
Lift us up
in our tiredness.
Lift us up
in disappointment.
Lift us up.

Lift us, Lord,
out of darkness into light,
out of despair into hope.
Lift us, Lord,
out of sadness into joy,
out of failure into trust.

ASCENSION

> Lift us, Lord,
> out of anger into forgiveness,
> out of pride into freedom.

109 Risen Christ,
you embraced our humanity
and now take it in to the heart of God.
May your glory be seen in humans fully alive.
In stony places may flowers grow.
In ugly faces may smiles show.
In hurting hearts may trust flow.
Ascended Christ,
even if we are in hellish places
we need despair no longer.
Alleluia!

110 Victor in the race,
you call us to follow you.
High Priest,
you understand our every need.
Eternal Giver,
you shower your gifts on every soul.
Head of the Church,
you wish no one to be separate from your Body.
Sender,
you promise us your Holy Spirit.

111 Ascended Lord,
you have made us living stones of the temple
you are to build.
We offer to you all that we are and all that we have.
King of Glory: ennoble us.
King of Grace: cherish us.
King of Life: renew us.
King of Promise: surprise us.

112 Lord, before you left this Earth
you urged your friends to immerse all peoples in your life.
We pray for parched and hungry people:
immerse them in your life.

We pray for torn and exiled people:
immerse them in your life.
We pray for lonely and unloved people:
immerse them in your life.
We pray for unjust and oppressive people:
immerse them in your life.

113 May the Eternal Glory shine upon us.
May the Son of Mary stay beside us.
May the life-giving Spirit work within us.

114 Promised Spirit,
come as the dew in the night,
come as the rain on dry land.
Come, renew our tired frames,
turn our deserts into pools of water,
renew in us your image of love.

115 Exalted One,
as haze rises from the mountain tops,
raise our souls from the granite of death.
Lift from us our anguish and our empty pride.
Having communed with heaven,
let us, transfused with joy, get down to the duties
that demand our attention.

116 Come, O Holy Flame.
Come as the heat in our hours of cold.
Come as the light in our hours of dark.
Come as the sun in our hours of gloom.
Holy Spirit in us, about us, above us, everywhere.

117 We offer you ourselves.
May our hands be your hands.
May our eyes be your eyes.
May our lips be your lips.
May our feet be your feet.

118 All-powerful One,
    a cloud hid you from sight,
    yet your mortality was raised to heaven.
    When our lives are clouded,
    raise us to life in you.
    May those whose lives
    are clouded by hostility, fear and addiction
    be raised to life in you.

Pentecost

119 Breath of God, blow away all that is unclean.
    Breeze of God, refresh withered lives.
    Wind of God, propel us to places you have prepared.

120 Holy Spirit,
    come as a gentle breeze
    that cools in the heat of the day.
    Come as the calming presence
    that restores stillness to our being.

121 Inflaming Spirit, come,
    kindle our hearts anew.

122 Spirit of God, rest on your people:
    waken your song deep in hearts.

123 Come, O Spirit of Love
    that goes to any lengths,
    that breaks through a lifetime's crippling habits,
    that wells up from the depths.
    Come, O Spirit of Joy
    that brings a song into haggard lives,
    a serenity into our roots
    and a sparkle into our eyes.
    Come, O Spirit of Peace
    that heals mistrust
    and brings us into harmony
    with the still centre of the universe.

Come, O Spirit of Kindness
that delights to sweeten the lives of others
and do beautiful things for God.
Come, O Spirit of Goodness
that opens the heart to Christ in friend and stranger.
Come, O Spirit of Gentleness
that bears all things without harshness or hardness.
Come, O Spirit of Fire
that burns away lust and double-minded ways.
Come, O Spirit of Wisdom
that teaches us to see into the nature of things
in order to know, speak and do what is right.
Come, O Spirit of Power
that snaps the chains of fear
and casts out the demons of hell and hopelessness.

124 Great Spirit, Wild Goose of the Almighty,
be our eyes in the dark places,
be our flight in the trapped places,
be our host in the wild places,
be our brood in the barren places,
be our formation in the lost places.

125 Spirit of God, among the wheels of industry,
renew the face of the Earth.
Spirit of God, among the computers of commerce,
renew the face of the Earth.
Spirit of God, among crime-infested neighbourhoods,
renew the face of the Earth.
Spirit of God, among tired and broken families,
renew the face of the Earth.
Spirit of God, among the lonely and the sick,
renew the face of the Earth.
Spirit of God, among the drugged and disillusioned,
renew the face of the Earth.

126 Spirit of the living God,
anoint our creativity, ideas and energy
so that even the smallest tasks
may bring you honour.

When we are confused,
guide us.
When we are weary,
energise us.
When we are burned out,
infuse us.

127 Release in us the power of your Spirit
that our souls may be free to roam
your boundless stretches of space.
May we soar high like the eagle,
see horizons yet undreamed of,
glow with fires of compassion,
flow with streams of creativity.

Breath of God, blow away all that is unclean.
Breeze of God, refresh our tired frames.
Wind of God, blow us where you will.
Dew of God, refresh our tired routines.
Rain of God, revive our withered lives.
River of God, flow through us and heal our land.

128 Holy Spirit, refine us, that we may be true.
Sending Spirit, release us, that we may touch lives for you.
Disturbing Spirit, recharge us, wasted lives to new.

129 O King of the Tree of Life,
the blossoms on the branches are your people;
the singing birds are your angels;
the whispering breeze is your Spirit.
O King of the Tree of Life,
may the blossoms bring forth the sweetest fruit,
may the birds sing out the highest praise;
may your Spirit cover all with her gentle breath.
Echoes Carmina Gadelica

130 God whose breath gives energy for struggle,
set us free to grow as the children of God.
Open our ears that we may hear the weeping of the world.
Open our mouths that we may be a voice for the voiceless.

Open our eyes that we may discern your just and gentle ways.
Open our hearts that we may bring courage and faith to life.

131 Come, Holy Spirit,
from heaven shine forth with your glorious light!
Most kindly, warming Light,
enter the inmost depths of our hearts.
Thaw that which is frozen,
kindle our apathy,
illumine our path.

132 Come like the fire and kindle love in our hearts.
Come like the winds and breathe fresh life into our frames.
Come like the tides and immerse us in your presence.
Come from the earth, sustain and nourish our being.

133 Spirit of the quiet earth,
Spirit bringing hope to birth,
bring forth in us the fruit of life.
Spirit, kindling flame that darts,
Spirit, wakening song in hearts,
bring forth in us the fruit of love.

134 O God, we see your story
in flowing streams, in people's dreams, in sporting teams.
As the water in the stream makes its journey to the sea,
so we will flow with your Spirit and with your saints,
on to you.
Echoes New Zealand/Aoroteara prayers

135 May the Spirit pour upon us as we sleep,
work in us as we dream,
take the frowning from our brows
and wake us up refreshed.

136 The blessing of the perfect Spirit be ours.
The blessing of the Three be pouring on us
graciously and generously,
hour by hour.

137 Spirit of God,
the breath of creation is yours.
Spirit of God,
the groans of the world are yours.
Spirit of God,
the wonder of communion is yours.
Spirit of God,
the fire of love is yours,
and we are filled.

138 Come to us with your anointing power.
Anoint us as you will for the ministries you will.
God of the call, God of the journey,
thank you for your anointing of Barnabas, Columba
and so many other of your saints
from the Day of Pentecost until now.
Holy Spirit, our strong tower, may your fibre grow in us.
Rain of God, revive our withered lives.
Wind of God, blow us where you will.
Breeze of God, refresh us in your love.
River of God, flow through us and heal our land.
River of God, flow through us and heal our land.

139 Deep peace of the Creator
be between you and all creatures.
Deep peace of the Saviour
be between you and all Christians.
Deep peace of the Spirit
be between you and all that is within you.

Pentecost Eucharist

140 Creator Spirit, come,
renew the face of the Earth.
Kindling Spirit, come,
inflame our waiting hearts.
Anointing Spirit, come,
in this Eucharist pour into our lives afresh.

141 Holy Spirit of God,
       you are the source of all that lives,
       of all that grows,
       of all that provides us with food.
       May we know your presence with us
       as we share this meal.

142 Spirit of God, be wild and free in me.
       Batter my proud and stubborn will.
       Blow me where you choose.
       Break me down if you must.
       Refashion me as you will.
       Move me powerfully away
       from the games I play
       in order to try and tame you.
       Lead me into the wild places,
       the places of dream or scream,
       the new frontiers or the total quiet,
       the long, dark tunnels
       or the wide, sunny vistas,
       to speak to lions,
       to move mountains,
       to bear tragedy,
       to mirror you.

143 Wind, wind blow on me.
       Blow away the cobwebs that clog the spirit.
       Blow up the suffocating airs of unbelief.
       Blow me near the things that are pure and good.
       Blow me along the path of your choice.
       Blow through me the breath of God's presence.

Trinity

144 God who is One,
       you create us in diversity.
       God who is Three,
       draw us into unity.

145 We grieve that we who are made
to reflect your three-fold love
have violated our nature and yours.
We have not reflected the Father's heart of the Creator.
We have not reflected the Mother's heart of the Saviour.
We have not reflected the Soul-friend's heart of the Spirit.
Holy and immortal One, have mercy upon us.

146 We arise today in a mighty force:
the God who is one, the God who is Three,
creating all through love.
We arise today
in the strength of the Father,
in the gentleness of the Son,
in the flow of the Spirit,
affirming all through love.

147 Open our eyes to see you reflected all around us:
in the sun that is fire, light and warmth;
in the water that is stream, ice and drink;
in parents who make love and conceive.

148 For our shield this day we call:
a mighty power, the Holy Trinity;
faith in the Three, trust in the One
creating all through love.
In faith we trust in the Father of all:
he's our refuge, a very strong tower.

For our shield this day we call:
Christ's power in his coming,
Christ's power in his dying,
Christ's power in his rising.

For our shield this day we call:
the mighty Spirit who breathes through all;
faith in the Three, trust in the One
making all through love.
Echoes part of St Patrick's Breastplate

CHRISTIAN SEASONS

149   We bless you for the sun:
      its source of fire,
      its beams of light,
      its rays of warmth.
      We bless you for water:
      when it is ice,
      when it is steam,
      when it is flowing free.
      We bless you for a human being:
      the thinking being,
      the doing being,
      the feeling being.
      We bless you for the Triune God:
      the Triune who creates,
      the Triune who takes flesh,
      the Triune who empowers.

150   Thank you for the little trinities
      that reflect to us your nature:
      for lovemaking, conceiving and nurturing;
      for body, mind and soul;
      for the fellowship of races, airwaves and sport.

151   Birther who brought worlds into being,
      bring your purpose to birth in us.
      Saviour who reconnected an estranged world to its Source,
      reconnect us to our Source.
      Spirit who breathes through everything that lives,
      breathe fully through us.
      Triune God who delights to bring diversity in unity,
      bring unity to our diversity.

152   May the life of the Three give birth to new creativity.
      May the yielding of the Three give birth to a new society.
      May the love of the Three give birth to new community.

153   God above us,
      God beside us,
      God beneath us.

Maker, cherish us;
Saviour, cherish us;
Spirit, cherish us;
Three all-kindly.

154 Glory to the Birther,
glory to the Son,
glory to the Spirit
ever Three in One.
Father who sought us,
Christ who bought us,
Spirit who taught us,
hold us in Trinity's clasp.

155 Power of powers
we worship you.
Light of lights
we worship you.
Life of lives
we worship you.

Source of life
we turn to you.
Saviour of life
we turn to you.
Sustainer of life
we turn to you.

Love before time
we adore you.
Love in darkest time
we adore you.
Love in this time
we adore you.

156 The Three who are over our head,
the Three who are under our tread,
the Three who are over us here,
the Three who are over us there,

the Three who in heaven do dwell,
the Three in the great ocean swell,
pervading Three, Oh be with us;
pervading Three, Oh be with us.
Echoes Carmina Gadelica

157 Into the Sacred Three we immerse you.
Into their power and peace we place you.
May their breath be yours to live;
may their love be yours to give.
Into the Sacred Three we immerse you.

158 As we enter into sleep,
keep our souls, O Father, keep.
As we enter into rest,
renew our frames, O Saviour blest.
When we wake with work to do,
Holy Spirit, see us through.
Holy Three, our shield, our wall,
be our rest, our joy, our all.

159 Eternal Love Maker,
eternal Love Mate,
eternal Love Messenger,
Three of Limitless Love,
we can glimpse your reflection in
a tender kiss,
a warm embrace,
sporting comradeship,
an adult affirming a child,
a meal shared,
two people listening to each other,
a group making music,
hospitality,
young people serving the old,
black and white people celebrating.
Three of Limitless Love,
may we reflect more of you
in whose likeness we are made.

160 Thrice holy God,
strengthen the hands that holy things have taken.
Bring us to life.
Call us to freedom.
Move between us with your love.
Today may we so participate in the dance of your Trinity
that our lives resonate with yours.

161 We thank you for revealing yourself
as Birther in majesty unbounded,
as only Son our Saviour,
as Spirit, our life and our Guide,
three Persons, equal in worth,
undivided in love,
flowing through us
till we reflect your three-fold friendship.

162 The blessing of the Three be upon you:
the blessing of peace for your journey;
the blessing of strength for your work;
the blessing of wisdom for your relationships.
And may the Three of Limitless Love
pour generously and always upon you.

Trinity Eucharist

163 We arise today in the vast might of the Trinity,
in the creating joy of the Father,
in the sustaining joy of the Spirit,
in the suffering and redeeming joy of the Saviour
who comes to us now in bread and wine.

164 Triune God,
you are neither monochrome nor narcissistic –
you make room for the other.
You are Divine Hospitality.
That is why we give you glory.
Triune God, you make room for the Big Bang,

for flux and flow in the cosmos,
and for a myriad evolutions.
That is why we
make room for you.

Harvest

165 May God
who clothes the flowers
and feeds the birds of the sky,
who leads the lambs to pasture
and the deer to water,
who multiplied loaves and fishes
and changed water into wine,
lead us,
feed us,
multiply us
and change us,
until we reflect
the glory of our Creator
through all eternity.

Harvest Eucharist

166 Provider God,
as autumn light ripens the grain,
ripen too our souls.
As brown leaves fall and sheaves are stored,
help us to fall into your ground
and store up deepening compassion.

167 As the grains of wheat
were scattered on a thousand fields
and now become one in this loaf,
so may we,
who are scattered in a thousand directions,
become one body in Christ.

168 You are the Food from which all souls are fed.
You who gave birth to the universe
are born again in us.
Alleluia!

Michaelmas/Angel season

169 At creation the angels sang in delight;
open our ears to their song today.
At the birth of your Son they proclaimed your praise;
open our eyes to their praise today.
As day follows night they follow your will;
open our hearts to their movements today.

170 Have mercy on us, O God, for our sins.
May these and the things of this day
which have displeased you
now fall away from us.
The light of the angels be ours.
The joy of the angels be ours.
The peace of the angels be ours.

171 O angel guardian of our right hands,
attend to us this night.
Rescue us in the battling floods;
clothe us, for we are naked;
succour us, for we are feeble and forlorn;
steer our vessels in the tempests of life.
Guide our step in gap and in pit;
guard us in the treacherous turnings
and save us from the harm of the wicked.
Save us from the harm any wish upon us
and protect us this night from a poisoned spirit;
encompass us till Doom from evil.
O kindly angel of our right hands,
deliver us from the wicked this night.
Echoes Carmina Gadelica

172 Good angels, messengers of God,
    protect us from all that would plague our bodies;
    protect us from all that would plague our souls.

173 We will start this day
    in the presence of the holy angels of heaven,
    without malice, without jealousy, without envy,
    without fear of anyone under the sun –
    the holy Son of God to shield us.

174 The angels delight to do your will;
    forgive us for denying and defying your will.
    The angels move freely unchecked by sin;
    forgive us for the holdbacks caused by our sin.
    The angels support the children of God;
    forgive us for discouraging the givers of love.

175 Have mercy on little ones abused;
    may tender angels draw them to your presence.
    Have mercy on those in black trial;
    may healing angels lift them into your presence.
    Have mercy on souls at death's door;
    may holy angels escort them to your presence.
    Have mercy on we who remain;
    may smiling angels radiate to us your presence.

176 In the name of the angelic force of the living God,
    we stand against the rulers, authorities and powers of evil,
    seen and unseen.
    God of hosts, deliver us from the powers of evil
    that have entrenched themselves in the structures
    of our society.
    Deliver us from
    racial and religious prejudice,
    exploitation and greed,
    abortion and euthanasia,
    sexual immorality and pornography,
    family breakdown and isolation,
    violence and crime,
    abusive witchcraft and channelling.

177 In the midst of dark powers
we magnify the greatness of heaven.
In the midst of foul deeds
we magnify the greatness of heaven.
In the midst of fearful thoughts
we magnify the greatness of heaven.
In the midst of a blighted land
we magnify the greatness of heaven.
In our time of need
we magnify the greatness of heaven.
May angels watch over our dreams and guard our sleep.
May the seven angels of the Holy Spirit
and the two guardian angels
shield us this and every night
till light and dawn shall come.

178 Almighty One,
who out of your love
has ordained the services of angels for our good,
through Michael, chief of angels,
save us from all that would bring harm.

179 Our Father in heaven,
send your angels to those
who need to be alerted to your presence;
attune us to the angelic harmonies that we cannot see
and help us to do on Earth as the angels do in heaven.

180 Fire of God,
kindle in us a love for you so great that we,
like the seraphim,
may blaze for ever in your presence.

181 Holy Raphael,
bring healing to those scarred by illness.
Holy Salathiel,
bring healing to those scarred by bad memories.
Holy Jegudiel,
bring healing to those scarred by fear of spirits.
Holy Barachiel,
bring healing to those scarred by fear of people.

CHRISTIAN SEASONS

     Holy Jeremial,
     bring healing to those scarred by mistreatment.
     Holy Gabriel,
     bring healing to those scarred by dark deeds.

182 Help us, O God, to lay aside the cares of the day
     that we, like the angels, who neither fret nor fear,
     may offer true worship, and rest in you.

183 We lie down this night with the nine angels
     from the crowns of our heads to the soles of our feet.
     We lie down this night
     under the protection of the angel Michael.
     We lie down this night
     under the healing of the angel Raphael.
     We lie down this night
     under the promise of the angel Gabriel.
     We lie down with guardian angels to right and left.

184 Angel of God, sent from the Fragrant Father of Mercy,
     the Encompassing Sacred Heart,
     the Spirit of the Deeps,
     make whole our souls this day.
     Ward off all that would harm.
     Pilot us safely across the ocean of life.
     Lift us above the tempests that would break us.

185 O bright, beautiful angel,
     by the unerring light of purity
     illumine every obstacle
     and beckon us on to the place beyond destruction.

Remembrance of saints, loved ones, forebears and war dead

186 Gatherer of souls,
     may we, with our forebears,
     commune with you.

Ennobler of souls,
may we, with the world's shining personalities,
reflect your glory in the world.
Comforter of souls,
may we, with those who have fallen in war,
be fulfilled in you.

187 Immortal God,
as leaves fall to the ground
we recall the fallen in war.
In the barrenness of trees without leaf
may they and we turn to you.

Remembrance

188 To those who were snatched from Earth by violent death,
Holy Jesus, grant rest eternal.
To those whose sleep is stolen by the ravages of memory,
Holy Jesus, grant rest eternal.
We pray for an end to the injustices
that become breeding grounds of war.
We pray for the restoration of fellowship
and the building of integrity.

189 Creator God,
who brings one day to a close and a new day to dawn,
we remember those who gave their today
that we might have a tomorrow;
when the lights went out in two world wars
and in many lesser conflicts;
when millions died in foul trenches or mass genocide;
when six million died in gas chambers;
when many died from acts of terror or revenge.

We mourn for the goodness and wisdom
that died with them;
for the skill and wit that perished,
the learning, the laughter and the leadership that were lost.

> The world has become a poorer place
> and our hearts become cold
> as we think of the splendour that might have been.
> *Echoes a Reform Jewish prayer*

190   We remember the waste of life and wit and learning.
We remember the love that was never shared.
We remember the torture of body and mind.
We remember those who died
without understanding or valour.
We remember those who have no grave
to mark their sacrifice.
Still stands your Eternal Sacrifice.
Lord God of hosts, be with them yet.

191   Saviour God, as we,
the communion of the living,
salute the communion of the dead,
heal the ancient wound that festers in humanity's heart.
Release compassion in places
where much blood has been shed.
Heal those
who can barely live with memories of injury or loss.
Salvage hope from the wrecks of time.

192   Christ, linking us across the shores of treachery and time,
we give you thanks:
for the heroism of those who served in armed services
or on the home front
to provide relief, medical care or supplies;
for the patient suffering of the inhabitants
through the time of scarring;
for the dedication of those
who kept alight the torch of freedom
and sustained hope in others
for the reconstruction of communities
and the reconciliation of peoples
of different nationality and creed
following the years of destruction.

We pray for commitment to the unending struggle
against selfish ways and violation of human dignity.
We pray for that peace
which is the full blossoming of our life together.

All Saints

All Saints' Eve (Halloween)

193   Lord Jesus Christ,
to whom the spirits are subject,
cast off the works of encroaching darkness
and bring us all under
your serene and victorious reign.

194   *In the northern hemisphere only*

We pray for children
who play Halloween games and Trick or Treat.
May they come to see the Light of the World.
We pray for witches, satanists
and those who dabble in the occult.
May they come to see the Light of the World.
We pray for people who suffer disorders
of the season of dark.
May they come to see the Light of the World.

195   For our shield today we call to us
strong powers of the angels obeying,
shining presence of the holy and risen ones,
prevailing prayers of godly fathers and mothers.
For our shield today we call to us
the truths of apostles,
the visions of prophets,
the victories of martyrs.
For our shield today we call to us
the vigils of hermits,
the innocence of virgins,
the deeds of heroes.

Around us today we gather these forces
to save our souls and bodies
from dark powers that assail us,
from false devisings,
from evils within and without.
Echoes part of St Patrick's Breastplate

196 Be with us now, Lord.
Keep us in your presence, power and peace
and may the saints and the angels watch over us.
Compassionate God of heaven's powers,
screen us from people with evil intentions.
Compassionate God of freedom,
free us from curses and spells.
Compassionate God of eternity,
free this place from bad influences of the past.

197 God of the ages,
God of the ancestors,
you preside over the spirits:
the spirits of the evil one
and the spirits of our forebears,
the spirits who do your will
and the spirits who are confused.
We entrust ourselves to you
as musicians entrust themselves
to the conductor of an orchestra.

198 All-powerful God,
circle the places where dark or distracting forces now gather.
Circle the groups in thrall to phantoms and ghouls.
May fears diminish and peace increase,
for yours is the kingdom, the power and the glory,
for ever and ever. Amen.

199 May your cross come between us and all things fearful;
your cross between us
and all things coming darkly towards us;
your cross be our sure way from Earth to heaven.

200　May your cloud of witnesses who shine so brightly
　　　enfold us through this night;
　　　the saints of God to will us,
　　　the peace of God to still us,
　　　the love of God to fill us
　　　for ever.

201　The shield of Christ be over us,
　　　the shield of the powers to guard us,
　　　the shield of the saints to hearten us.

202　The God of life go with us
　　　to protect us from ill,
　　　to keep our hearts still,
　　　to strengthen our will.

203　God of time,
　　　God of dark,
　　　God of Earth,
　　　God of heaven,
　　　you are
　　　stronger than the elements,
　　　stronger than the shadows,
　　　stronger than the fears,
　　　stronger than human wills,
　　　stronger than the spirits,
　　　stronger than magic spells.

　　　Your presence be our shield.
　　　The love of God to enfold us,
　　　the peace of God to still us,
　　　the Spirit of God to fill us,
　　　the saints of God to inspire us,
　　　the angels of God to guard us
　　　this night, this winter, for ever.

All Saints' Day

204　In the darkness of this passing age
　　　your saints proclaim the glory of your kingdom.
　　　Chosen as lights in the world, they beckon us on
　　　as we journey towards the greater light of Christ.

205 On this day of the saints of life
establish your vibrancy in our beings.
On this day of the saints of power
establish your strength in our frames.
On this day of the saints of virtue
establish your goodness in our hearts.

206 Blest are you, Sacred One, for those who
shine in the world and light up our way,
bring faith to birth as spiritual midwives,
accept death rather than deny God,
seek the dignity of life and labour,
foster appreciation of diverse cultures,
shepherd their people in sincerity of heart,
say yes to your callings.

207 We thank you for those who give their all
in the service of others,
for those who overcome heroic odds with nobility of spirit,
for those who are gracious in defeat
and magnanimous in triumph,
for those who are content with the little things,
for those who show us how to truly love.
Furnish our memories with these noble attributes
and inspire us also to give our utmost for your highest.

208 Saviour of us and the saints,
in the heat of the day
may the overcoming ones be with us.
When dark clouds assail us
may the undaunted ones be with us.
When the world goes grey
may the shining ones be with us.
When the flowers all fade
may the everlasting ones be with us.
When the birds cease to sing
may the singing ones be with us.
When people lie in the dust
may the risen ones be with us.

Unknown saints

209 Divine Upbringer,
who calls each of your children by name,
we remember with gratitude your many faithful servants
who, though they are neither known to us
nor great in this world's eyes,
are like precious jewels to you.

210 The glorious company of the holy and risen ones,
the prayers of prophets and steadfast believers,
the friendship of spiritual mothers and fathers
be with us today.

211 Great-hearted God,
as the saints do in heaven,
may we do on Earth:
in using our gifts,
in caring for others,
in holy dying.

212 May we do on Earth
as the saints do in heaven.
May we cheer drooping spirits
and smile on a frayed world.

213 Light up the fire in us, O Lord,
the fire that burned in your saints,
the fire of your presence,
the fire that can never go out.

214 Saint Fursey saw four fires –
may we put out the fires of falsehood, covetousness, discord
and cruelty.
Lord, graciously hear us.
Saint Brigit lit a fire of resurrection outside the Church –
may we keep the fire of resurrection in our hearts.
Lord, graciously hear us.

May we, like Saint David, gather bundles of souls.
Lord, graciously hear us.
May we, like Saint Chad,
show that a true leader is a servant.
Lord, graciously hear us.
May we, like Saint Patrick,
have enthusiasm to enable us to surmount trials of all kinds.
Lord, graciously hear us.
May we, like Saint Cuthbert,
seek to storm the gates of heaven
until the unseen godless powers are dethroned.
Lord, graciously hear us.
May we, like Saint Brendan,
realise the importance of living in community.
Lord, graciously hear us.
As Saint Columba left his homeland as a sign of repentance,
may we turn from selfish ways.
Lord, graciously hear us.
As God's Spirit sent Saint Samson
to spread the good news of the kingdom,
may we feel the urge to do the same.
Lord, graciously hear us.
As Saint Oswald,
may we be people of prayer, compassion and valour.
Lord, graciously hear us.
As Saint Ninian's community at Whithorn became
'Candida Casa',
a shining, glistening, white house,
may we become a lighthouse of the world.
Lord, graciously hear us.
As Saint Aidan was understood by the people,
may we by our example and words be understood.
Lord, graciously hear us.
As Saint Hilda brought out the creative
and spiritual gifts of people,
so may we seek to make people whole.
Lord, graciously hear us.
May we, by following you, be counted among your saints.
Lord, graciously hear us.

215 We arise today
   in the glorious company of the risen and shining ones,
   in the warming prayers of the fathers and mothers,
   in the blazing deeds of apostles,
   in the fiery faith of martyrs,
   in the kindling love of spiritual fathers and mothers,
   in love with the King of Life.

216 Light-creator, evil cannot make its home
   where you are welcomed in.
   Forgive us for the places where your light has been shut out.
   Light-giver, fear and fault-finding
   have no place where your love is invited in.
   Forgive us for the places where your love has been shut out.
   Light-conductor, loneliness and self-sufficiency
   have no place where your saints are welcomed in.
   Forgive us for the places where we have shut them out.

217 God of time; God of eternity;
   God of the saints; you are
   stronger than the elements,
   stronger than the shadows,
   stronger than the fears,
   stronger than the magic, spells and phantoms
   that assail us.

218 Keep us worthy of our calling,
   that we may come with your saints
   to glory everlasting.

219 We thank you that in your saints
   we see the many-splendoured facets
   of human lives flowing in their fullness.
   Spurred on by them we offer you
   our talents;
   our temperaments;
   our tasks;
   our trials;
   our triumphs.

All Souls

220 Eternal God, who mothers us all,
sinners find mercy in you and saints find joy.
You hold all souls in life;
the dead as well as the living are in your care.
Thank you for the wonder and variety of human lives.
We remember in your presence and give you praise:
for wise souls in our land;
for those who brought wit, invention or music;
for those whose work or care enriched others;
for the frail and those frustrated in their hopes;
for those who disappointed even themselves;
for the quiet and faithful ones;
for those who showed courage in triumph or trial;
for forgotten souls remembered now by you alone.

221 Jesus, Mediator between Earth and heaven,
through you we share with these our love.
We entrust them to you
because you alone are trustworthy
and your compassion knows no end.

222 Immortal God, we remember before you
our fathers and mothers;
those we were closely bound to
and those more distant who touched us through them;
friends and relations;
those who served you faithfully in their lives;
those who hurt or harmed us;
those who suffered untimely deaths;
those whose faith is known to you alone;
brothers and sisters in Christ;
those who inspire us through their lives, their writings,
their deeds of love –
holy and healing souls.

223 Sovereign of seas and stars,
hear us for ourselves and our forebears:
may your love never fail us,

may your friendship never desert us,
may paradise open its doors to us,
but always may your will be done.

224 God of eternity,
from you we come;
to you we go.
Have mercy on those who have gone.
Give peace to we who remain.

225 Guardian of the dark night of death,
guide those we love but see no longer on their voyage.
Be a guiding star above them;
illumine each rock and tide.
Guide their ships across the waters
to the waveless harbourside.

226 Since it was you, O Christ,
who bought each soul –
at the time it gave up its life,
at the time of severing the breath,
at the time of returning to dust
at the time you delivered judgement –
may your peace be on your ingathering of souls.
Jesus Christ, Son of gentle Mary,
your peace be upon your own ingathering.
Echoes Carmina Gadelica

227 When shadows lengthen
and the departed return to our thoughts,
Lord of the dark night of death, be with us yet.
As we linger with the shades of memory,
may heaven's praises pierce graveside tears.
Recall us to your presence,
touch us with your hope
and charge us with your glory.

228 The peace of Christ be there at the ingathering of souls.
The peace of Christ at our own soul's ingathering.
The peace of Christ be in this gathering.

229 O Christ, may the benefits of your passion
 be there for every soul
 at the time of returning to clay,
 at the time of giving account.
 Lead us, with all souls, to the Three of Limitless Love.
 Yes, to the Three of Limitless Love.

All Souls' Eucharist

230 Lord, as you were there at the shaping of all souls,
 so, too, you are there at each life's close;
 come in this sacrament through which your life flows.

Liturgy, Eucharist and special services

LITURGY, EUCHARIST AND SPECIAL SERVICES

Preparation

231 *When lighting a candle*

Candlelighter Lord, this candle that we have lit –
may it be Light from you
to lighten our way through difficulties and decisions.
May it be Fire from you to burn up our selfishness,
our pride and all that is impure within us.
May it be Flame from you to warm our hearts
and teach us love.
Lord, we cannot stay long in your house.
This candle is a little bit of ourselves that we offer to you.
Help us to continue our prayer in all that we do this day.

232 We come into your presence, restful Father.
We come into your presence, calming Son.
We come into your presence, peaceful Spirit.
May we and God be one.

233 Open our eyes to your presence.
Open our ears to your call.
Open our hearts to your mercies,
that you may be all in all.

Forgive our sins of omission:
our pride and our thoughtless ways;
forgive our sins of commission:
the tongues that lead others astray.

Take from us sloth and apathy,
all spirit of blame or despair.
Give us eyes for fresh ventures,
that we may sweep through the air.

Thank you for this family of Christians,
for the marvellous ways you have led.
Thank you for your hand now guiding us
to good challenges further ahead.

Give us this day your wisdom
and love for each and all.
Help us to learn to listen
and together respond to your call.

Opening prayers

234 Jesus, you are the glory of eternity shining now among us,
the tenderness of God here with us now.
God who is with us, we adore you.
Jesus, you are the Healing Person,
the pattern of goodness,
the fulfilment of the highest human hopes.
God who is with us, we adore you.
Jesus, you are the champion of the weak,
the counsellor of the despairing,
the brother of us all.
God who is with us, we adore you.
Jesus, you are the splendour of the Father,
the Son of Mary,
our Bridge between heaven and Earth.
God who is with us, we adore you.
Jesus, you are the source of life, the goal of the universe,
the people's friend, the world-pervading God.
God who is with us, we adore you.
Jesus, you are one of the human family,
Joy of Angels, Prince of Peace.
God who is with us, we adore you.

Confession and lament

235 Fountain of goodness,
form of true humility,
you bent your holy neck
and let a cross be placed upon you.
We thank you.
We bend the necks of our hearts low
and ask you to forgive us.

236 Intimate, merciful Saviour God,
you who lit up with all virtue the pure and the strong,
you who keep in your heart
the Spirit's seven gifts and your eight blessings,
you who offer them without demanding a return,
we thank you.

LITURGY, EUCHARIST AND SPECIAL SERVICES

      Take from our hearts the eight great sins.
      Cleanse our bodies and souls
      and light us up.

237   Eternal Creator of day and night,
      cleanse us by your refining fire.
      Kindle in us the Pentecostal flame
      and make our hearts burn with heavenly desires.

238   Sorry, Lord, for the sins committed by Christians
      during the Age of Pisces;
      for being corrupted by power,
      for not listening to you.

239   Sorry, Lord,
      for the shabbiness of my living and my working.
      Sorry, Lord,
      for the shallowness of my praying and my giving.
      Sorry, Lord,
      for the fickleness of my feeling and my speaking.
      Sorry, Lord, for the slowness of my hearing and my sharing.
      Sorry, Lord, for the dullness of my thinking and my loving.
      Sorry, Lord, for my deafness to the cries of the people;
      for not honouring your presence in creation,
      in the simple things all around.

240   Sorry, Lord,
      for the shabbiness of our living;
      for the shoddiness of our working;
      for the shallowness of our praying;
      for the selfishness of our giving;
      for the fickleness of our feeling;
      for the faithlessness of our speaking;
      for the dullness of our hearing;
      for the grudgingness of our sharing;
      for the slothfulness of our thinking;
      for the slowness of our serving;
      for the coldness of our loving.

241 For putting personal preferment
before the needs of the people, Lord forgive.
For becoming sour-faced
when laughter is called for, Christ forgive.
For living like a machine
rather than your masterpiece-in-the-making, Lord forgive.

242 For living in our comfort zones,
mindless of what goes on outside,
Lord have mercy.
For taking without asking what we can give,
Christ have mercy.
For being defensive when we are hurt,
and not reaching out to others,
Lord, have mercy.

243 Three of forgiving love,
we lay the broken bits of our lives at your feet:
promises we have broken;
trust we have broken;
your patterns we have broken;
above all, hearts of love we have broken.

244 Lord, we mourn
for a life of such goodness, cut down in its flower;
for a people who forfeited the flowering of their destiny;
for a city which turned away from its Saviour;
for a planet which rejected its Maker;
for ourselves, who languish, alone and lost.

245 For the ways we have marred your image in us, forgive us.
For resentment, rush or lack of trust, forgive us.
Now we open ourselves in love and faith
to your healing presence.

246 Lord Spirit, show me the things that are crooked in my life.
Lord Judge,
spare me from things that could be crooked in my life.
Lord Christ,
straighten out the things that are crooked in my life.

O my God, light up my darkness
and deliver me this day from temptation.

247 God of the fray, God of the bumps,
cool us down, because we are frayed.
Lift us up,
because we have come down with a bump.
Help us to accept the duties that confront us.
Help us to assimilate
the experiences that have enriched us
and to become aware of your presence,
now in the present moment.

248 We confess with shame
the loss in the Church of integrity, humility and patience;
the crushing of spontaneity,
the caging of the wild Spirit,
the breaking off of relationships,
the bruising of the crushed reeds,
the arrogance of the intellect,
the pride of empire-building.
We accept our share of responsibility for these sins,
and seek to shed them
on behalf of ourselves and our churches.
Lord, have mercy upon us and forgive us.

249 Most merciful God, we confess to you
before the company of heaven and one another
that we have sinned in thought, word and deed
and in what we have failed to do.
Forgive us our sins,
heal us by your Spirit
and raise us to new life in Jesus Christ.

250 From false desires and selfish deeds,
all-knowing God, deliver us.
From unworthy thoughts and prideful claims,
all-seeing God, deliver us.
From unclean hearts and petty ways,
all-cleansing God, deliver us.

251   Holy Jesus, hanged on a tree, victorious over death,
forgive us for our selfish deeds,
our empty speech
and the words with which we have wounded.
Forgive us for our false desires,
our vengeful attitudes
and for what we have left untended.

252   Father, the good things of your Earth
shout out your praise;
forgive us that our lives so seldom speak of gratitude.
Father, have mercy.
Lord, these good things are denied
to people in other parts of your Earth;
forgive us for pollution, neglect and greed.
Christ, have mercy.
Spirit, these good things would not be here
unless their seeds of life had first lain still
in the rhythms of winter's soil;
forgive us for trying to be what we are not
and for resisting your rhythms.
Spirit, have mercy.

253   You called humans to tend and bless your creation.
We confess with shame
that we have neglected and misused it.
Forgive us.
You gave laws that enable us to live
in mutual respect and well-being.
We confess with shame
that we have fallen prey to prejudice,
greed and dishonest ways.
Forgive us.
You showed us authentic ways to live in your loved Son.
We confess with shame
that we are slow to learn from and emulate him.
Forgive us.

254 For the rainforests gone,
and the deserts caused by human destruction,
dear God, we grieve with you.
For polluted seas, dirty streets and litter,
dear God, we grieve with you.
For not being content to savour the simple gifts of creation,
dear God, we grieve with you.

255 Creator, we have raped and spoiled your world:
forgive.
Saviour, we have ignored your teachings and warnings:
forgive.
Spirit, we have tried to live without you:
forgive.
Every sin we have ever thought or done:
forgive.
Every thing we sought outside your love:
forgive.
Every wasted moment:
forgive.
Every ill intent towards another:
forgive.
Every failure of love towards your creation:
forgive.
For the ways we have marred your image in us:
forgive.
For resentment, rush and lack of trust:
forgive.

256 We recall the things that stain our memories:
the complaining and grasping spirit,
the me-first attitude,
the unfair practices,
the hostility towards others,
the contempt for divine laws and humane values.

257 We are sorry, God of goodness, for
dis-ease in our eyes –
we have been driven in our looking;
dis-ease in our ears –

we have been driven in our listening;
dis-ease in our tongues –
we have been driven in our speaking;
dis-ease in our heart –
we have been driven in our actions;
dis-ease in our pockets –
we have been driven in our purchases.

Give us tears that the jewels of the nature
you've given us have become defaced,
and chastity's precious robe has been torn.
Give us tears for greed-driven bankers,
consumers who can't say no,
and those caught in the resulting trail of wreckage.
Give us tears for the squandering of talent,
the prostitution of love, the spawning of wastelands.
Give us tears for those displaced and those maimed by war,
and for those immune to the stranger at the door.

258 Creator and Saviour,
we have exploited Earth for our selfish ends,
turned our backs on the cycles of life
and forgotten we are your stewards.
Now soils become barren,
air and water become unclean,
species disappear
and humans are diminished.
In penitence we come to you.

Thanksgiving and praise

259 For earth and sea and sky in the harmony of colour,
we give you thanks, O God.
For the air of the eternal seeping through the physical,
we give you thanks, O God.
For the everlasting glory dipping into time,
we give you thanks, O God.
For nature resplendent, growing beasts,
emergent crops, the energies of the city,
we give you thanks, O God.

For the Person you sent to restore us
when we fell away from the goodness of your creation,
we give you thanks, O God.
For harmony restored through your Spirit
moving upon the turbulent waters of our lives,
we give you thanks, O God.
For the honour you give us
of lives flowing in the rhythm of your tides,
we give you thanks, O God.
For setting each of us,
like the stars upon their courses,
within the orbit of your love,
we give you thanks, O God.

Echoes a prayer of George McCleod

Praise

260   Now let us praise the Maker of heaven,
the Crafter of the starry skies,
the Keeper of Eternity.
Now let us praise the Birther of Glory,
the Guardian of the human race,
Uncreated Beauty
who binds the universe in one free bond of love.

261   May desks and treetops praise you.
May garments and lambs praise you.
May transport and fuel praise you.
May scents and sounds praise you.
May flowers and trees praise you.
May skies and roads praise you.
May neighbours and lovers praise you.
May gardens and sports praise you.
May swans and elegant music praise you.
May friendship and enterprise praise you.
May strength and beauty praise you.
May everything that lives praise you.

262 All that moves on the Earth,
bless your God.
All that swims in the water,
bless your God.
All that flies in the air,
give glory to God who nurtures us all.
Parents and children,
bless your God.
Friends and lovers,
bless your God.
Musicians and sports folk,
give glory to God who nurtures us all.
Parks and play areas,
bless your God.
Streets and shops,
bless your God.
Homes and gardens,
give glory to God who nurtures us all.

263 Ebb tide, full tide, praise the Lord of land and sea.
Barren rocks, darting birds, praise God's holy name!
Poor folk, ruling folk, praise the Lord of land and sea.
Pilgrimed sands, sea-shelled strands,
praise God's holy name!
Fierce lions, gentle lambs, praise the Lord of land and sea.
Noble women, mission priests, praise God's holy name!
Chanting boys, slaves set free,
praise the Lord of land and sea.
Old and young and all the land, praise God's holy name!

264 Praise the God of all the people.
Praise the All-compassionate One.
Praise the All-merciful One.
Praise the All-mighty One.
Praise the God who fathers and mothers us in our distress.
Praise the God who saves us when we stray.
Praise the Great Spirit who shapes the destiny of the world.
Praise the God of all the people.

265 We will sing to you, Almighty God,
for you are our strong Defender.
You are our forebears' God
and we will praise your greatness.
Holy and Mighty One,
who among the gods is like you?
Who is like you in holiness?
Who is like you in glory?
You rule in glory for ever.
Echoes Moses' song at the Red Sea, from Exodus 15

266 Creator Spirit, may air and elements praise you.
May flowers and fabrics praise you.
May floor and desktop praise you.

Your people praise you at the dawn of the day.
May birds and buses praise you.
May work and heat praise you.
May grass and growth praise you.

Your people praise you in the middle of the day.
May eating and talking praise you.
May thoughts and actions praise you.
May male and female praise you.

Your people praise you at the end of the day.
May night and day praise you.
May the seven days of the week praise you.
May all the good that has been done praise you.

Making peace

267 We are the Body of Christ.
Let us use what we have to build the common good,
and make a start by offering peace to one another.

Intercession

268 Protecting Father, stalwart Steersman, guiding Spirit,
we pray for friends in a sea of troubles.
We pray for households in a sea of troubles.

We pray for workplaces in a sea of troubles.
We pray for communities in a sea of troubles.
May your inspiration flow to them
and come to them like oil on troubled waters.

269 We pray for believers.
May their lives be signs of joyful service.

We pray that our churches may bring honour to you
and healing to the people.
May they be places of renewal and welcome.

We pray for people in authority.
May they strive for justice and peace.

We pray for our communities.
May refreshment be found by all who work.

We pray for our homes.
May they be places of hospitality and hope.

270 Jesus, broken on the cross,
we bring to you those suffering from broken dreams,
broken relationships and broken promises.
Jesus, have mercy on them.
Jesus, who lost everything,
we bring to you
those who have suffered loss of work, mobility
and well-being.
Jesus, have mercy on them.
Jesus, defenceless victim,
we bring to you
those who are victims of violence, abuse
and false accusation.
Jesus, have mercy on them.
Jesus, alone and destitute,
we bring to you
those who are lonely, homeless and hungry.
Jesus, have mercy on them.
Jesus, you died that we may be brought back to you.
Save and raise up
those who have none but you to turn to.
Jesus, have mercy on them.

271 Christ forsaken, have mercy on all who are forsaken.
Christ afraid, have mercy on all who are afraid.
Christ betrayed, have mercy on all who are betrayed.
Christ unnoticed, have mercy on all who are unnoticed.

272 Christ who comes with justice and peace,
we pray for victims of oppression and violence.
At your birth you were proclaimed the Prince of Peace.
You came to remove the wall
that divides one people from another.
May walls of hostility and fear come tumbling down.
You call the peacemakers blest.
Strengthen peacemakers in places torn apart
by the ravages of sin.

General prayers of blessing and consecration

273 The eternal Creator keep us,
the beloved Companion beside us,
the Spirit's smile upon us.

274 With these hands we bless the lonely,
the forgotten and the lost;
with these hands we shield your messengers
from attacks within, without;
with these hands we dispel darkness
and rebuke the evil forces;
with these hands we pray your victory
for those who fight for right.

275 May the God of gentleness be with you,
caressing you with sunlight and rain and wind.
May his tenderness shine through you
to warm all those who are hurt and lonely.
May the blessing of gentleness be upon you.

276 Uncreated Beauty,
you are worthy of our best devotion.
May we worship you with all our being.

May we worship you with all our senses.
May we worship you with all our temperaments.
May we worship you with all our talents.
May we worship you with all shades of colour.
May we worship you with all kinds of music.
May we worship you with treasures old and new.

Eucharist

277 Risen Christ, we welcome you.
You are the flowering bough of creation.
From you cascades music like a million stars,
truth to cleanse a myriad souls.
From you flee demons, omens and all ill will;
around you rejoice the angels of light.
Father, send us the tender Spirit of the Lamb;
feed us with the Bread of Heaven;
may we become drunk with your holiness.

278 Living God, change these elements of bread and wine
and the elements of our lives
with the transforming power of your presence,
that this Communion may become
a foretaste of your new creation.

279 Merciful God, send now, in kindness,
your Holy Spirit to settle on this bread and wine
and fill them with the fullness of Jesus.
And let that same Spirit rest on us,
converting us from the patterns of this passing world,
until we conform to the shape of him
whose food we now share.

280 This precious nectar is our delight.
From this cup flows warmth for our darkest night.
From you we drink in poise and power,
though we are broken, in a needy hour.
And cup-sharing with us are rich and poor,
folk of all kinds, all thirsty for more.

281 When your blood was spilled on the soil,
Earth was transformed
and the tree of death became the tree of life.
Through this Eucharist may we be
instruments of your transforming love.

282 As we share this foretaste of the heavenly feast,
generous be our hearts,
open be our hands;
justice be our benchmark,
thanksgiving be our call.

283 O Christ,
whose presence was revealed
through the multiplying of shared bread,
renew your presence among us in this bread.
O Christ,
whose presence was revealed
through the multiplying of shared water
that became like sparkling wine,
renew your presence among us through this wine.

284 In this Eucharist you have become one with us.
May the benefits of your passion
so flow into our lives
that we become one with you in all people.

285 May we rise from the holy table
with our senses no longer beguiled by trifles,
with our tongues set free from hollow talk
and with our bodies keen to live in eternal life.

286 God make us holy.
Christ make us holy.
In the name of the Spirit holy,
God, the Three all-holy,
we confess our sins to you,
Father, Son and Spirit holy.
Compassionate God of life,
your kindly pardon give:

EUCHARIST

for our careless talk,
our broken promises,
our empty speech,
for all that we have left undone,
for all that we have done amiss.

287 Jesus, tender Lamb of the tears and the piercings,
as we receive your forgiveness
enshield us, encircle us,
each day, each night.
Uphold us, be our treasure,
our triumph everlasting,
strong Son of our God most high.

288 We bless you, High King of creation,
for these gifts of bread and wine
that your Earth has brought forth
and human hands have made.
You will transform them into our spiritual food and drink,
blessed by God for ever.

289 As the grain once scattered on the fields
and the grapes once dispersed upon the hillside
are now reunited on this table in bread and wine,
so, Lord, may your whole Church
soon be gathered from Earth's four corners
as one at the feast in your coming kingdom.

290 With this bread we offer to you
the yeast of life rising,
the creativities and possibilities of our people
that they may hear the invitation to take wing
and fly on the airways of the Spirit.
We offer you the life of this place,
that it may bring light to many.
We offer our shared discoveries and new beginnings,
our healings and refreshment,
our invigoration and new life.

We offer you the seeds planted here
that they may grow and flourish as they should.
We offer you the elevation
of an incorrupt spirit in the corruption.

291 As we pour out this wine
we offer to you the wasted creativities,
the wanings, the waste,
the pain and sacrifices of ourselves
and of so many people, especially [names].
We offer you those in the community of the church
who feel they do not belong;
all who miss the vision of their true selves in you
and turn to material and worldly success;
those who are powerless in our society,
humiliated through being the underclass;
we offer you the homeless, refugees, illegal immigrants,
and the beggar at our gate.

292 Father, all love comes from you.
Fed by your Word and sacrament
may we leave to spread beauty and goodness
in the image and likeness of your Son;
through whom we make this prayer.

293 Blessed are you, King of all creation,
for this bread which Earth has given
and human hands have made.
It will become for us the Bread of Life.
Blessed are you, King of all creation,
for this wine, fruit of the vine,
work of human hands;
it will become our spiritual drink.

294 Lamb of God, Defenceless Victor,
take from us our sin.
Give to us the food of eternal life.

295 As we eat and drink,
help us to touch your utter, self-giving love.

296 Sweet Jesus flowing into us,
     giving us poise, giving us balance.
     Nectar of sweetness
     flowing into us and our neighbours,
     making us one.

297 This is the Saving Sacrifice
     which comes with tears downpouring.

298 Creator, you give us grain and grape.
     Saviour, you give us yourself
     as Bread of Life and Wine of Heaven.
     Spirit, through you,
     these gifts of Earth shall now become
     our eternal food and drink.
     Blessed be God for ever.

299 We bless you, Lord;
     you became human
     so that we might share in your divine life.
     These gifts of Earth
     become for us eternal nourishment from heaven.

Closing blessings

300 The God of life go with us,
     the Risen Christ beside us,
     the vibrant Spirit within us.

301 We go in the sign of the cross of Christ:
     the cross before us to keep us true,
     the cross behind us to shield us from ill,
     the cross above us to lead us through.

Saints' days and holy days (including Eucharist prayers)

1, 2 February, Festival of Light, St Brigid, Candlemas, Imbolc

302   May the life that came through Mary come to you.
May the light that shone through Brigid,
Mary of the Gael,
shine through you.
Its goodness preserve you,
its energy enliven you.
And the blessing of the ever-fruitful Three
be upon you and all that is yours.

303   Blessed are you, God of the planet Earth.
You have set our world
like a radiant jewel in the heavens
and filled it with activity,
beauty, suffering and hope.

304   Teach us to forgo vengeance at all times
and to reach out our hands in love to all.
May our churches become
like large, extended families.

11 February, Caedmon

305   O God, you called Caedmon
from the care of your creatures
to sing praise to the Guardian of all creation.
Give us grace to heed your call,
that our lives may become one
with the song of all creation,
through Jesus Christ our Lord.

14 February, St Valentine's Day
(Quinquagesima – love)

306 Thrice-holy God,
     come as the morning dew.
     Display to us your love
     which draws all lesser loves to you.

307 God of love,
     on this St Valentine's Day
     teach us the gift of true love –
     to lay our lives down for another
     without jealousy, design or deceit.
     You alone, the All-compassionate One can give us this.
     Give it to us today.

308 And now we give you thanks
     that you show your divine love
     in many-splendoured showers,
     and mirror in this sacrament
     the love that nothing in heaven or Earth can destroy.

23 February, St Polycarp

309 Lord, you come to us at the breaking of the day.
     Come to us, too, in the breaking of the bread.
     Lord, as Polycarp became one with you
     in his time of martyrdom,
     in this Eucharist may we become one with you
     in your self-giving to the end.

310 We thank you for Polycarp's rapport
     with John the loved apostle,
     and for all he passed on to the family of the Church.
     Rekindle in your Church this sense of being your family;
     rekindle relationships of love between Christians
     in the churches of the world,
     in the churches of this land,
     in the churches of this island.

We thank you for Polycarp's life
laid down in faithful work.
We pray for all who are now going to work.
Rekindle a joy and a faithfulness in work.
May the wealth and work of the world
be available to all and for the exploitation of none.
May employers, employees and shareholders
work together like fingers on a hand for the common good.

We thank you for Polycarp's faithfulness
and transformation in the painful death in old age.
We pray for those in pain,
those with arthritis,
those nearing the end of their earthly journey.

We thank you for Polycarp's faithfulness
to you as King over all earthly rulers.
We pray for rulers, especially [name].
We thank you for the crown.

2 March, St Chad, St Cedd

311 Holy God, holy and immortal,
strengthen us as we seek to walk with you
in the way of the cross,
that in this Eucharist we may die with you
and rise with you.

312 Strip from us, Lord, all pretence and pride,
all that is false and fickle.
Grant us tears within and heartfelt sorrow
as we confess our sins to you.

313 Lord Jesus, you have taught us
that what we do for the least of our sisters and brothers
we do for you.
Give us the will to serve others
as did you, who gave your all
and who now lives with us,
one God for ever.

Rogation

314 Creator, you caused the Earth to bring forth the Saviour.
Spirit, come now and renew the face of the Earth,
all that grows on it, all who live on it.

315 And now we give you thanks,
because Earth's life and fruitfulness flow from you
and all times and seasons reflect your laws.

316 We give you thanks for your ancient promise
that while the Earth endures,
seedtime and harvest, cold and heat,
summer and winter, day and night,
will never cease.
We thank you for light,
without which nothing would grow.
We thank you for water,
without which plants would wither.
We thank you for air,
without which all would die.
Light of light, Source of water,
Breath of life, you are here.

317 May the Creator, the Saviour and the Sustaining Spirit
bless the Earth and all that grows on it;
bless your soul and all that comes from it;
that you may bring forth fruit on Earth and in eternity.

1 May, Beltane: Midsummer

318 At the start of Beltane, season of warmth,
we acknowledge your presence
in the mysterious shaping of our lives.
We dedicate to you our intentions,
our emotions, our deeds and all that we touch.
We dedicate to you the Earth
on which we shall make our life,
the people we shall work with.

We dedicate to you all that we shall touch,
the materials of this Earth and all that breathes.

Christ be in the earth and each thing we touch.
Christ be in the work and each thing we do.
Christ be in the mind and each thing we pursue.
Let us kindle our souls
at the forge of nature's soul-smith.
A spark of life to us,
a spark of light to us,
a spark of love to us.
As we enter this season of creativity,
may we think your thoughts after you.
As we enter our beds of hope,
may we dream your dreams after you.
As we explore new realms of life,
may your life renew our being.

319 O Holy One, I could run through the fields
and gather flowers of a thousand colours –
and pour them out at your feet.
Their beauty and their brightness
shout for joy in your presence.
You created the flowers of the fields
and made each one far more lovely
than all the skill of humans could design.
Accept my joy
along with the joy of the fields of blossom.
Holy One,
as the wind blows through spring flowers
till they dance in the ecstasy of creation,
send your Spirit to blow through my being
till I, too, bloom and dance with the fullness of your life.

21–22 June

320 May flowers of a thousand colours
give praise to you today.
May beauty and brightness
shout praise to you from the streets.

You make each of us more lovely
than even the flowers can be.
On this day in the middle of summer,
may our lives be sunshine to you.

24 June, St John the Baptist, summer solstice

321   Lord, thank you for your Spirit
moving John in the womb of his mother.
We pray for unborn babies;
may they be valued, prayed over
and moved by your Spirit.
May each human life be cherished,
from conception to the grave.

322   On these long, bright days
may our lives be a long 'yes' to you,
filled with gratitude that your life,
like the sun,
pulses through leaves
and windows
and our very being.

323   Lord, thank you for sending John
to learn your ways in the silent deserts.
Teach us the silence of humility.
Teach us the silence of wisdom.
Teach us the silence of faith
and then send us out.

324   Where crooks exploit asylum seekers for money,
turn their hearts, O Lord.
Where governments exploit voters through fear or favour,
turn their hearts, O Lord.
Where hooligans exploit peaceable citizens for kicks,
turn their hearts, O Lord.
Where monopoly financiers exploit nature
for short-term gain,
turn their hearts, O Lord.

LITURGY, EUCHARIST AND SPECIAL SERVICES

28 July, St Samson and Wilberforce

325   Father of the poor,
      Champion of justice,
      Spirit of Truth,
      you led your people of this land out of darkness
      through the holy prayers and powerful signs of Samson
      and great men of God such as William Wilberforce.
      May we who walk in the light of your presence
      acclaim your Christ, rising victorious,
      as he banishes all darkness from our lives
      and from our land today.

326   Thrice-holy God, eternal Three-in-One,
      make your people holy, make your people one.
      Stir up in us the flame that burns out pride and power.
      Restore in us the love
      that brings the servant heart to flower.
      Thrice-holy God, come as the morning dew.
      Hold up in us your love, which draws all lesser loves to you.

327   Guard for us our eyes,
      Jesus, Son of Mary,
      lest seeing another's wealth make us covetous.
      Guard for us our ears
      lest they listen to slander.
      Guard for us our tongues
      that they spread not gossip.
      Guard for us our hands
      that they be not stretched out for quarrelling.
      Guard for us our feet
      lest, bent on profitless errands,
      they abandon rest.

328   Lord of the holy and risen ones,
      May we, like Aidan,
      love and understand the peoples of our land.
      May we, like Brigid,
      welcome folk in to the warmth of hospitality.
      May we, like Cuthbert, storm the gates of heaven.
      May we become steeped in the A to Z of saintly qualities.

31 July, Joseph of Arimathea, Ignatius Loyala, Lammas Eve

329 Lord, summer ripens.
Blessings are stored, gratitude is ours;
the honour is yours.
In this Eucharist may we give you,
as our homage,
the best of our lives.

330 We bless you, giver of light.
We bless, provider of warmth.
We bless you, disperser of darkness.
In the spirit of Ignatius, may we let your light shine in us.

We bless you, giver of water.
We bless you who sends the dew and rain.
We bless you who refreshes the parched soil.
In the spirit of Ignatius,
may we be immersed in your presence.

We bless you who gives us the breath of life.
We bless you who sustains our world.
We bless you, the Spirit within us.
In the spirit of Ignatius,
may we let your Spirit flow though us.

We bless you for the bread of this Eucharist.
You who put ear in corn
and skill and love in human hands
that make and hold the bread:
you are the Food from which all souls are fed.

331 We pray for
flour mills, combine harvesters
and individuals who harvest by hand;
heavy-goods vehicles
delivering the flour and bread to the shops;
shops who stock and sell these good things of the Earth;
kitchens and homes,
that they may be symbols of blessing.
May we sustain the conditions for a well-watered world.

332 Kindle
    the memory of love,
    the memory of discovery,
    the memory of physical joys,
    and bring to dawn our wholeness.

333 Joseph of Arimathea gave you, at your death,
    the very best of graves,
    and is the inspiration of those who build
    the first and best of churches.
    We give back the months that are past.
    We offer our best for the future
    to you who will preserve us,
    in peace, in supplies,
    in work and well-being of soul.

1 August, Lammas

334 We adore you who puts life in soil and seed
    and beckons to us through every stone and star.
    We adore you, Creator Father;
    we adore you, Carpenter Son;
    we adore you, Comforting Spirit;
    ever Three and ever One.

335 You who put ear in wheat and lamb,
    you who put heaven in bread and wine,
    send us out in your strength
    to bring heaven on Earth.

336 Lord in your mercy . . .
    may the grains be wholesome,
    and not be signs of the poisoning of soil and rivers.
    May the womb which bears the world's water
    not be violated by mindless human action.
    We sustain the conditions for a plenteous water supply,
    Lord, in your mercy. . .

6 August, Transfiguration

337 You warm our hearts at your table;
you quench our thirst with the wine of delight.
In you is the source of our life;
by your light we see light.

338 You revealed your ways through Moses
and your will through Elijah.
Forgive us for breaking your laws
and falling away from your will.
Reveal your presence,
enchant our hearts,
shine on our acquaintances.

339 Eternal Light, shine into our hearts.
Eternal Goodness, deliver us from evil.
Eternal Wisdom, scatter the darkness from our ignorance.
Bring us who have tasted of you
to live in your holy presence for ever.

25 August, St Ebbe

340 Shine on us, Lord,
like the sun that lights up day.
As day follows night,
chase away the dark and all shadow of sin.
May we wake eager to hear your Word.
As day follows night may we be bathed in your glory.

28 August, Augustine of Hippo

341 Watch over your weeping ones.
Give angels care of your sleeping ones.
Bless your dying ones.
Soothe your suffering ones.
Pity your afflicted ones.
Shield your joyous ones,
all for love's sake.

8 September, the Birth of the Blessed Virgin Mary

342 Father, the birth of the Virgin Mary's Son
was the dawn of our salvation.
May this celebration of her birthday
bring us strength from heaven
and bring us closer to lasting peace.

343 As we bless you for Mary,
who brought forth the Life of the world,
so we bless you for this bread,
which shall become for us the Bread of Life.
As we bless you for Mary,
whose suffering brought forth
the Sacrificial Life outpoured,
so we bless you for this wine,
which shall become our spiritual drink.

344 Lord, your table gives us life.
Give us the humble obedience of Mary
that we may respond to you this day
as willing servants
and bring heaven into this Earth.

345 Mary, you nurtured the precious life in your womb
with such tenderness.
Blessed Lord, help us to nurture your life
in ourselves and in others.
Mary, such dignity rests on the one you brought forth.
Blessed Lord, grant to us the dignity of humbling
and the beauty of service.
Mary, you were bonded in the spirit to the Eternal Trinity.
Only thus could you have been such a channel of grace.
Blessed Lord, bond us in this week of contemplation
to your eternal Self.
Son of Wonder, Son of Humanity,
teach us to wonder,
that we may come to reflect your nobility.

14 September, Holy Cross Day

346 Jesus, by your cross you have redeemed us;
come to us
in this holy sacrament of your death and resurrection,
and save and help us, we humbly ask you.

347 We are the race that helped make the wood
on which you were crucified,
and still we misuse your creation;
Lord, have mercy.
We are the race that helped make the nails
that pierced your body,
yet still we work for gain at others' expense;
Christ, have mercy.
We are the race that did nothing
to stop your betrayers,
yet still we are ruled by comfort or cowardice.
Lord, have mercy.

348 Jesus, they call you God's Expert Carpenter.
In your carpenter's shop you took wood
and made fine objects from it.
May I be your wood.
May you chisel me into something useful, or even beautiful.
Through wood and nails you even changed
the wooden cross beams on which you were crucified
into a Tree of Passion which bore eternal fruit.
In my adversities, too, let some Passion Fruit grow.

349 Lord, keep united in the cross
all who share this food and drink
of Christ's unending life.

350 Lord, your body was broken on the cross for us
as this bread is to be broken for us.
Therefore let us give thanks and say:
blessed be God for ever.
Lord, your blood was poured out on the cross for us
as this wine is to be poured into us.

Therefore let us give thanks and say:
blessed be God for ever.

351   Blessed are you, God of pain, God of mercy,
for your Son has surely borne our griefs
and carried our sorrows.
He was despised, he was rejected.
He was pierced for our sins
and bruised through no fault of his own.
We thank you that his punishing
has brought forth our pardon
and by his wounds we are made whole.

11 November, St Martin of Tours (Remembrance)

352   On this day of remembrance
we give thanks especially for St Martin of Tours.
Inspired by Martin,
who exchanged a bishop's throne for a cow stool,
we humbly kneel before your throne of grace.
We are hungry;
feed us, that we may become strong in you.

353   Peace between victor and vanquished.
Peace between us and all people.
Peace of Christ above all peace.

Special Services
Wedding

354   *Before the start of a wedding service*
Open our eyes to your presence.
Open our ears to your call.
Open our hearts to your love.

355   *After the entrance of the bride as she stands beside the groom*
Most powerful Spirit of God,
come down upon us and subdue us.

From heaven –
where the ordinary is made glorious
and glory seems but ordinary –
bathe us with the brilliance
of your light, like dew.

356 *Before the vows*

May the Father take you
in his fragrant clasp of love,
in every up and every down of your life.

357 The love and affection of God be with you.
The love and affection of the angels
be with you.
The love and affection of the saints in heaven
be with you.
The love and affection of your friends on Earth
be with you,
to guard you,
to cherish you,
to bring you to your eternal fulfilment.

358 *Joining hands after the vows*

May you be bound
with unbreakable bonds of love to one another.
May you be bound
with unbreakable bonds of love to your God.
May your love for each other
reflect the love of your Maker, Saviour and Guide:
the Three of Limitless Love.

359 *A bridal blessing after the vows*

May the Father take you in his fragrant clasp of love.
May the Virgin Mary's Son guide you
through the maze of life.
May the generous Spirit release forgiving love within you.
Hour by hour, by day and by night, in joy and in failure,
may each man and each woman who is a saint in heaven
urge you on to complete your course.

360 God's own presence with you stay,
Jesus to shield you in the fray,
Spirit to protect you from all ill,
Trinity there guiding you still.

On sea or land, in ebb or flow,
God be with you wherever you go;
in flow or ebb, on land or sea,
God's great might your protecting be.

361 May you share hopes and dreams,
but also walk through hard times hand in hand.
May your love for each other keep burning bright,
but if ever it flickers low may Jesus,
the Eternal Fire Kindler, light up the fire again.
In your old age, as now when you are younger,
may you be best friends,
and give each other room to be yourselves.

Renewal of wedding vows

362 When we have buried your insight beneath falsehoods,
when we have insulated ourselves
from being vulnerable to others,
when we have been closed to your renewing of our minds,
have mercy on us.
Break through our resistance.
Open our hearts to love.

363 Source of our being and goal of our longing,
give us wisdom to harvest our life
and find the wholeness of memory.
We bring to you abandoned areas of our lives.
Heal our wounds, keep bright the flame.
Kindle in us the memory of love and discovery.

364 Eternal Wisdom, firstborn of creation,
you emptied yourself of power
and became foolish for our sake.

You laboured with us on the cross
and became Wisdom's crown.
At this table we lay down our proud pretensions
and become one with you.
We pray for
the oppressed and powerless peoples of the world,
that in their powerlessness
they may discover Wisdom's Way.

365 Warm-winged Spirit, brooding over creation,
draw forth the divine beauty in every person on Earth:
in women who feel degraded
and in men who abuse their role;
in children who are orphaned
and in the disabled who are frail.

366 Wisdom, breathing through all creation,
you planted your likeness in us.
As a mother tenderly gathers her children
you embraced a people as your own.

367 Heavenly Father,
we offer you our praise and thanksgiving
for [number] years together;
for all the joys we have shared;
for our friends and family (especially our children [names]).
May they always know of our love for them,
and grant us wisdom in the years to come.

368 Forgive us
when we grumble about the married state;
when we complain we haven't enough money;
when we are quarrelsome
and won't admit we are wrong;
and when we find fault with each other.

369 O God,
we confess our ingratitude for your goodness
and our selfishness in using your gifts.
We ask you to forgive us and to use us to your glory.

370 Heavenly Father,
we offer you our souls and bodies,
our thoughts and words and deeds,
our love for one another,
our past and our future.
Unite our will in your will.
May we and our children
grow together in love and peace
all the days of our life,
through Jesus Christ our Lord.

371 The Lord renew his place in your lives,
give you grace to complete
the work in you he has begun.
The Lord bless you and watch over you
and be gracious to you;
the Lord look kindly on you
and give you peace now and always.

Baptism of believers

372 Into the life of the Father I immerse you,
that he may protect you from harm,
bring you peace and calm.
Into the boundless life of your Maker I immerse you.

Into the life of the Son I immerse you,
that he may save you from hell,
keep you washed and well.
Into the sinless life of your Saviour I immerse you.

Into the life of the Spirit I immerse you,
that he may light up your night,
give you power to do right.
Into the endless life of your Soul Friend I immerse you.

Into the life of the Three I immerse you,
that they may fill you with love,
lift you to heaven above.
Into the selfless love of the Trinity I immerse you.

Baptism and dedication of infants

373 May the cross of Christ
be always between you and the evil powers;
may the cross of Christ
be always between you and all ill will and mishap;
may the cross of Christ
be always between you and everything dark or shameful;
may the cross of Christ
be always between you
and all that hurts or harms your soul.

Infant blessing

374 *Three drops of warm water are poured on the baby's forehead,
one during each of the first three sentences*

A little drop of your Creator
on your forehead, precious one. Amen.

A little drop of your Saviour
on your forehead, precious one. Amen.

A little drop of your Guardian Spirit
on your forehead, precious one. Amen.

The little drop of the Three
to shield you from harm
to fill you with their virtue. Amen

375 God our Creator,
in giving us this child you have shown us your love.
We thank you from our hearts for the joy of this child,
for the wonder of this life,
for a safe delivery
and for the privilege of being parents.

376 Circle her/him, Lord, keep peace within.
Circle her/him, Lord, keep love within.
Circle her/him, Lord, keep trust within.
Circle her/him, Lord, keep truth within.
Circle her/him, Lord, keep good within.

Circle [her/him], Lord, keep harm without.
Circle [her/him], Lord, keep evil without.
Circle [her/him], Lord, keep strife without.
Circle [her/him], Lord, keep lies without.
Circle [her/him], Lord, keep hatred without.

377 *A prayer for parents*

Father of love,
accept the thanksgiving of these parents.
May their spirits, lifted to you now in humble gratitude,
always turn to you for help and strength.
Give them wisdom, tenderness and patience
to guide their child to know right from wrong.

378 *A prayer for parents who are married*

Father, may [name] and [name] be to each other
a strength in need, a comfort in sorrow,
a companion in joy.
Knit their wills together in your will,
that they may live together
in love, hope and peace
all of their days.

379 *A prayer for family, godparents and friends*

May you respect one another;
may the goodness of friendship grow in you;
may the love that covers a multitude of sins be upon you.
God's peace be with you, whatever you do;
God's light to guide you wherever you go;
God's goodness to fill you and help you to grow.

Blessings for homes and other buildings

380 *Front door*

May this house be built upon the Rock of Christ,
so that no onslaught can undermine it
and no ill wind can unsettle it.

May the guardian angel
welcome all who enter this place
and repel all that would harm it.
We invite Christ to be the Master of this household
and of everything in it.

381 *Kitchen*

We consecrate this kitchen to you.
May the deep peace of the Son of Mary
possess all who work amid the clatter of this place;
may all be done in a spirit of humble service,
may all be done as to You.
Bless the washing,
bring forth fullness in the cooking,
put your glory in the working.

382 *Dining room*

Bless this room.
May the eating be a celebration of God's goodness.
May the feasting be a fellowship with God's friends.
As you drink the sweet fruits of creation,
may you drink the sweetness of God's life
and be preserved from the poisons of envy.

383 *Children's rooms*

May the loving Father God
always be here with you
and make you feel safe.
May friendly Jesus
always be here with you
and make you feel happy.
May his kindly Spirit
always be here with you
to listen to you.
May you enjoy their company as you play.
May angels look after you when you sleep
and when you dream,
and help you to wake with a smile on your face.

LITURGY, EUCHARIST AND SPECIAL SERVICES

384 *Adult bedroom*

In the name of the eternal Father,
in the name of the loving Son,
in the name of the gentle Spirit,
the friendly Three in One:
bless and make holy this room,
and may angels guard all who sleep here.
That part of you that did not grow at morning,
may it grow at night.
That part that did not grow at night,
may it grow in the morning.

385 *Couple's bedroom*

God give you delight and tenderness
in your lying together.
God give you peace and forgiveness
in your sleeping together.
God give you solitude and space
to be yourselves for each other.

386 *Guest room*

Fill this room with a spirit of hospitality.
May every person who sleeps here
be enfolded in the loving arms of the Saviour.
Bless the work, the play or the study done here.
Make fruitful the reading, the writing, the planning.
May all that is done
reflect the peace and order of creation.

387 *Bathroom or toilets*

May all who bathe their bodies here
bathe them in the mild rays of the Sun of suns,
as Mary bathed Christ in the rich milk of Egypt.

The sweetness of Christ
be in your mouth as you clean your teeth;
the beauty of Christ
be upon your face as you comb your hair;
the love of Christ
flow over you as you wash your frame.

As you look in a mirror, may you see
the hands of Mary washing you,
the hands of angels cleansing you,
the hands of the saints straightening you,
the hands of Jesus restoring you.

388   *For the household*

We place into your hands
all people who will live together here.
May they know that everything here is yours,
and they belong here.
May they sense your love here.
May the presence of the Three Kindly Persons
free each to accept personal pain,
to grow through each stage of development,
to give space to others,
to express feelings,
to forgive from the heart,
to flower as a person.

389   *Back entrance; garden*

Dear Lord, may all that is here
reflect the harmony and wholeness
that you want for all your creation.

May the cat(s) purr with the pleasures of friendship;
may the dog(s) wag with the delights of meetings;
may [name of pet or 'they'] be happy and healthy;
may the wild creatures find nature here is friendly;
may the birds find food here and chirp with gladness.

If there is unease about the house's past

390   Almighty Father,
Victorious Saviour,
Holy Spirit,
you are stronger than the elements,
stronger than the shadows,
stronger than the fears,

stronger than human wills,
stronger than the spirits;
we enthrone you in this place
and lift you up with our praise.

391 In the name of the crucified and risen Christ,
we set this place free from the power of the past.
In the name of Christ,
we say to all powers that do not reverence him as Lord:
be gone from this place. Be gone.

Encircling the whole property

392 *The Caim is said by all:*
Circle this place by day and by night;
circle it in winter, circle it in summer.
Look down upon it with your smile;
lift it up with your strength.
Keep far from it all that harms;
keep all that's good within Christ's arms.

393 May this place be fragrant
with the presence of the Lord.
May this place overflow
with the gratitude of his people.
May this place echo
with the sounds of joy.
May clouds of God's peace
envelop this place.
God's peace be always here
and in those who dwell here.
Let us enjoy his presence now.
The lovely likeness of the Lord is in your face.

394 In the beginning, O God,
your Spirit swept over the chaos of the cosmos
like a wild wind,
and creation was born.

In the deep and troubled unsettled waters
of our lives and our lands today,
let there be new birthings of your almighty Spirit.

Spirit of the quiet Earth,
bring hope and love in us to birth.
Spirit, kindle fire that darts,
Spirit, waken song in hearts.
Spirit blowing through creation,
inspire good deeds for proclamation.
Spirit, whence our life derives,
restore your wholeness to our lives.
Spirit tearing down the walls,
be the voice that pricks and calls.

395   Flame of love, reach into our inmost heart.
Flame of truth, reach into our inmost mind.
Flame of seeing, reach into our inmost vision.

396   Flame of love, light us up.
Flame of beauty, light us up.
Flame of wisdom, light us up.
Flame of peace, light us up.

Dying, funerals and wakes

397   Go to your eternal home of welcome,
our loved companion.
Go into the sleep of Jesus,
the restoring sleep of Jesus,
the young sleep of Jesus.
Go into the kiss and the peace and glory of Jesus;
into the arms of the Jesus of blessings;
into the generous Christ with his hands around you;
drawing near to the Trinity,
freed from your pains,
pardoned from your sins,
Christ beside you
bringing peace to your mind.

398 May you who were baptised as
[deceased person's baptismal names]
now be immersed in the life of God.
Into the presence of the Creator we immerse you.
Into the presence of the Saviour we immerse you.
Into the presence of the Spirit we immerse you.

399 Lord of the Great Passage,
you hold a crown ready in your hand.
If I trust in my own will
I cannot receive it.
I trust in you alone
and I am eager to come to you.

After the funeral

400 Holy God, holy and mighty,
you alone are Creator,
you alone are Saviour of all,
you alone are immortal.

401 We are mortal,
formed from the earth, returning to the earth;
for you ordained
that we should come from dust and go to dust.
Yet through Christ you ordained also
that with our tears at the dark night of parting
should be mingled the Alleluias
of the glory that pierces the gloom from beyond.
So as we remember the shadows,
and as we linger with our precious memories
may we feel your presence.
May we be touched by your hope.
May we be changed by your glory.

402 We arise today
in the strength of the mighty Creator,
in the strength of the rising Saviour,
in the strength of the life-giving Spirit,
in the strength of the mighty Three
whose love is One.

We arise today
in the strength of the angels and archangels,
in the strength of the prophets and apostles,
in the strength of the martyrs and saints.

We arise today
in the strength of heaven and Earth,
in the strength of sun and moon,
in the strength of fire and wind.

We arise today
in the strength of Christ's birth and baptism,
in the strength of Christ's death and rising,
in the strength of Christ's judgement to come.

403 Strength-giver, may your fibre grow in us.
Fortifier, may your praises swell in us.
Indweller, may your presence dwell in us.

404 You led your people by a cloud;
lead us by your Spirit now.
You lit your people by a fire;
light us by your Spirit now.

405 O Spirit, be free in us.
Let us not bind you through fear
of where your disturbing power will lead.
Burst through these brittle shells;
shake us to the foundations;
strip us to the core
which is our essence and your love.
Echoes an anonymous prayer

Past abortions recalled

406 Dear God, I am sorry
that I have forgotten and ignored them.
I ask their forgiveness and yours.
It helps to know that no child is lost to you.

407　First, I wish to say
I am especially sorry
that the life of my [first, second, etc.] child
was taken through abortion.
I am grateful, Lord,
that you know all about the pressures
that caused me to take that decision.
Lord,
I am truly sorry for the taking of this life.
I ask forgiveness from you
and from the child who has died.
I acknowledge before you
that this was truly a child and was truly my own.
I place this child into your tender care.
I assure [him/her] of my love.

408　*A minister or friend*
We release [name of aborted person] into your hands.
May your blessing and your peace be upon [name].
Bring [her/him] to wholeness in your eternal kingdom.

409　*Parent*
Now, dear Jesus,
I wish to name before you the one who was born on [date].
In faith I name [her/him] [name].
I ask you to heal [name] of any shock or hurt
[he/she] has carried as a result of the way [he/she] died.

410　*Blessings on the parent by a soul friend or minister*
Lord Jesus,
in your name we break the power of the past
to have a hold over [name] now.
May the cross of Christ
come between you and your past.
The love of Jesus fill you,
a lamb of his choosing,
that you may rest in his arms
and walk free into the fruitful paths he has for you.

411 *A parent's prayer*

Dear Lord Jesus, kind and loving Friend,
you were always glad to be in the company of children.
You taught us that we must be like them
in the kingdom of heaven.
I now realise that I have more children
than at first it seemed.

The child who was lost through miscarriage
is mine and yours.
I give this child the name [name].
I pray that you will heal the scars of [name].
May [name] be enfolded in your love.
May [name] find healing.
Set [name] free from all shock or hurt
that hinders [her/his] journey
into wholeness in your kingdom,
so that [name] may live with you in light and joy for ever.
I look forward to that day when,
through faith in Jesus Christ,
we may be reunited in paradise.

412 *A cross, flower, plant or plaque may be placed in a place of remembrance. Three drops of water may be poured on that spot, using this prayer for a baby*

A little drop of your Creator, precious one.
A little drop of your Saviour, precious one.
A little drop of your Guardian Spirit, precious one,
to bless you with virtue and sweetness,
to keep you in eternal life.

Earth blessing

413 *Solstices and Moons*

As moon circles Earth
and ocean responds with rhythms of the tide,
so may we circle you
and reflect back your rhythms in our lives.

Summer solstice

414 The sun rises daily because you, O Lord, command it.
Its splendour will not last, created gods all perish.
Christ the true Sun nothing can destroy;
the Splendour of God, he shall reign for ever.

415 God of the long bright day
and of the martyr's long bright haul,
you who are eternally awake:
we offer you the energy and awareness of our days,
the flower of our humanity,
the creativity of our lives,
our potential and our all.
God of the rising sap and the sweeping blue,
may the bloom of cherries be on our lips
and the love of Jesus be filling us for everyone.

Winter solstice

416 Lord of the solstice, on this day of briefest light
help us to be at home with the treasures of the dark.
As the days have drawn in
help us to flow with the ebb tides of life.
At the turning of the year
help us to welcome the Dawn from on high.

417 At this time of briefest light,
may we bunker down with you,
grateful for memories, storing riches,
finding well-being in winter's patterns.

Healing

418 Source of Love,
God of Tender Beauty,
Bearer of our Pain,
you accept what we hardly dare name.
You know all,
even more than we can recall.

May we find no part of creation alien.
Embrace in your heart
what we have rejected in ourselves.
Your reflection is in our deepest core.
Flow through
every cranny of our being and our memory
like a pure, life-giving stream,
that we may daily grow more whole.

419 *Talking to the diseased organ*

To [name the affected organ]:
the God of gods, the Healer of healers, the Spirit of eternity,
the perfect Three of power:
restore you.

420 *To a stye*

Go back! Go back! Go back!
You thievish rascal of the stye!

421 *For the removal of a microbe in the body*

May God search them, may God remove them
from your blood, from your flesh, from your urine,
from your smooth, fragrant bones;
from your close veins, from your hard kidney,
from your pith, from your marrow, dear one,
from this day and every day
till the day you shall end your life.

422 *To a blind or affected eye while bathing or touching it*

Pour, King of life,
pour, Christ of peace,
pour, Spirit of cleansing.
You who created the orb
and placed the pupil in the eye,
search the mystery within the lid.
Befriend its sight, O God.
Make whole this day the eye;
restore this day the sight.

LITURGY, EUCHARIST AND SPECIAL SERVICES

423 *For any disease of the body*

May the strong Lord of life
destroy your disease of body
from the crown of your head
to the base of your heel –
with the power of the Christ of love
and the Creator of the seasons;
with the aid of the Holy Spirit
and the powers of wholeness together.

424 *For a swelling*

Peace come into this swelling,
the peace of the King of power.
Subsiding come to your swelling,
in the holy presence of the Father,
in the holy presence of the Son,
in the holy presence of the Spirit,
the holy presence of compassion.
Look, O Christ, on this swelling.
Since you are the King of power,
give rest to this person.
Bring the microbe out of [his/her] tumour.
Be whole.
Let your swelling now shrink.

425 *For any skin or blood disease*

May God heal you, my dear one.
I am now placing my hand on you
in the name of Father, Son and Spirit of virtue,
Three Persons who encompass you for ever.
Full healing come to your blood,
perfect healing to your soft flesh,
another healing to your smooth skin,
in the name of the powers of the Holy Three.

426 *For removal of a disease of the spirit*

As Christ removed the sleep
from the little child of the grave,
may he remove from you, dear one,
each frown, each envy, each malice.

427 *The healing rhythm of the Trinity*
    I commend you, [name],
    in the eye of God,
    in the love of Jesus,
    in the name of Spirit,
    in Trinity of power.

428 *When a person suffers from insecurity or a lack of identity*
    An eye was seeing you,
    a mouth has named you,
    a heart has thought of you,
    a mind has desired you:
    May Three Persons sanctify you,
    May Three Persons help you,
    the Father and the Son and the perfect Spirit.

429 *Healing with water*
    May this water be for your healing
    in the holy name of the Father,
    in the holy name of the Son,
    in the holy name of the Spirit,
    in the holy name of the Three,
    everlasting, kindly, wise.

Healing of places

430 Thank you for the life of this place,
    made holy by the prayers of the years.
    Circle it today to keep it holy.
    Kindle in the people who now live here
    a desire to develop holy lives.

431 We confess on behalf of [name place]
    these sins that mar its life: [list them in silence];
    these areas that have been neglected: [list them in silence];
    these unjust deeds that have been inflicted: [list them in silence];
    these integrities that have been violated: [list them in silence].

Show us what harm can be restored
and the place where we may begin.

432 We bring to you, Healer of our souls,
unvisited places that have no name for love;
abandoned places that lie untended;
stunted places that long to grow again;
resentful places that await forgiving touch;
fearful places that need you as a coach;
defeated places where fresh belief can come.

Daily rhythm

Waking/morning

433 We arise today in the fullness of our humanity.
We arise today in the glory of creation.
We arise today in the strength of the living God.
We arise today in gratitude.
We arise today in forgiveness.
We arise today in eagerness.

434 We arise today in the power of the great Father
who brings manhood and womanhood into being.
We arise today in the power of the great Son
who surmounts the things that shrink our being.
We arise today in the power of the great Spirit
who enables our humanness to grow.

435 Life-giving God, the world lies open before you
and you summon the day to dawn.
Open our being
and we shall show life.
Open our hearts
and we shall show love.
Open our mouths
and we shall show praise.

436 Creator of light,
at the rising of your sun
we rise to greet you,
meet you and reflect your light on Earth.

437 Make whole the leisure and activity of this day.
Restrain its hostile impulses,
fill its moments.

438 Come, Creator Spirit,
fresh as the morning dew.
Revive us and make us new.

439 We arise today
in joy of being alive,

in freedom of God's Spirit,
in eagerness of service.

440 We arise today
in the wisdom of the One
who brought to birth the giant plains,
the water and the first beings.
We arise today
in the brightness of the One
who created the blazing sun,
the shining stars and the twinkle in our eyes.
We arise today
in the mercy of the One
who gave us dreams
and memories and hearts.

441 We arise today
in the brilliance of the sun:
its fire to warm us,
its beams to light us,
its rays to cheer us.
We arise today
in the power of the Sun of suns:
the Sun of truth,
the Sun of life,
the Sun without end.

442 We arise today
in the Eternal Flow of Mercy
who was here when the land began to breathe,
when the first tribes began to roam,
and when the colonists came to settle.
We arise today
in the Eternal Flow of Wisdom
who is dimly perceived in the stones,
the stories and the studies of all our peoples.
We arise today
in the Eternal Flow of Life
who seeps through land and limb and love.

443 We arise today,
　　the sun to encircle us,
　　the Earth to uphold us,
　　the air to enfold us.
　　We arise today,
　　God's laws to uphold us,
　　God's gifts to equip us,
　　God's love to inspire us.

444 Awaken us to your glory,
　　stir us to adventure,
　　restore our seeing,
　　cure our deafness,
　　heal our hardness,
　　steer us towards our destiny.

445 We arise today in the goodness of creation.
　　We arise today in the verdure of the fertile ground.
　　We arise today in the promise of the rising seed.

446 God of life, you summon the day to dawn
　　and call us to create with you.
　　You are the Rock from which all Earth is fashioned.
　　You are the Food from which all souls are fed.
　　You are the Force from which all power lines travel.
　　You are the Source who is creation's head.

　　You are the Heart from which all hearts are beating.
　　You are the Mind from which come thoughts and dreams.
　　You are the Eye from which comes all our seeing.
　　You are the Gift from whom all mercy streams.

　　You are the Ache from which comes all our longing.
　　You are the Pain in which we bear our grief.
　　You are the Wind by which all souls go winging.
　　You are the One from whom flows all our life.

447 We arise today
　　in the simplicity of the empty soil,
　　in the strength of the fierce elements,
　　in the deep formation of winter.

Stripped of inessentials we stand, rooted in you.
In the anticipation of gathering strength,
you sustain our well-being.
In the humility of the bare earth,
we invite you to do your work in us.

448 We arise today
through the strength
of Christ's birth and baptism.
We arise today
through the strength
of Christ's crucifixion and burial.
We arise today
through the strength
of his resurrection and ascension.
We arise today
in the brightness of sun.
We arise today
in the splendour of fire.
We arise today
in the speed of lightning.
Echoes St Patrick's Breastplate

449 Lord, I don't feel alive, but I thank you for the gift of life.
I don't look forward to this day,
but I thank you for the gift of day.
You are.
I am.
We'll be.

450 Lord, do you really call us to be awake and aware?
Even on the morning after?
Even when I have a migraine?
Even when I can't face what's in store?
In that case, take me as I am
and do something about me, your problem child.
At least I am your child.
I put my hand in yours.

Gift me a lift.
Wipe the frown from my face.
Let's step out together.

451 We weave this day
silence of knowing,
clearness of seeing,
grace of speaking.
We weave this day
humility of listening,
depth of understanding,
joy of serving.
We weave this day
peace of being,
gift of loving,
power of meeting.

452 Be with us today
in our meetings,
in our temptations,
in our loneliness.
Be with us today
in the humdrum,
in the heat,
in the opportunities.

453 Glad Bringer of brightness,
day's blessing, rainbow's embrace,
teach our hearts to open as the buds open;
and to welcome in your grace.
Teach us to dance with the playful clouds
and to laugh with the sun's smile on our faces.
The Earth is yours; may it bring forth its produce.
The birds are yours; may they bring forth their songs.
Our work is yours; may it bring forth its yield.

454 Lord, we offer you all we are,
all we have, all we do,
and all whom we shall meet this day,
that you will be given the glory.

We offer you our homes and work,
our schools and leisure,
and everyone in our community today;
may all be done as if for you.
We offer you the broken and hungry.
May the wealth and work of the world
be available to all and for the exploitation of none.
May your presence be known to all.

455 Illumine our hearts, O Lord;
implant in us a desire for your truth.
May all that is false within us flee.

456 May we walk in the hope of your kingdom.
Fill us with your light and love.
Be with us all through this day,
Father, Son and Holy Spirit.

457 Risen Christ,
scatter the sin from our souls
as the mist scatters from the hills.
Be in what we do, inform what we say,
redeem who we are.

458 May we see the face of Christ
in everyone we meet.
May everyone we meet
see the face of Christ in us.

459 Holy Spirit, refine us,
that we may be just and true.
Sending Spirit, release us,
that we may touch lives for you.
Disturbing Spirit, recharge us,
wasted lives to renew.

460 On those whose day is drab,
come, Holy Spirit.
On those who harbour fear,
come, Holy Spirit.

On a parched land,
come, Holy Spirit.

461 Birther of the human race,
you summon the day to dawn
and call us to live in communion.

462 Thrice holy God,
eternal Three in One,
make your people holy,
make your people one.
Stir up in us the flame
that burns out pride and power.
Restore in us the trust
that brings the servant heart to flower.
Thrice holy God,
come as the morning dew.
Inflame in us your love
that draws all lesser loves to you.

463 Good morning, God.
My moans and groans I give now to you.
Today, may your glory be seen in me
as I become fully alive, warts and all.
Life of Being, flow through me now.

464 We believe, O God of all gods,
that you are the eternal God of life.
We believe, O God of all peoples,
that you are the eternal God of love.
We believe that you create Earth and seas and skies.
We believe that you create us in your image
and give us eternal worth.
We honour you with our whole being
and consecrate this day to you.

465 I arise today in the strength of the Birther.
I arise today in the compassion of the Saviour.
I arise today in the peace of the Spirit.

466 May we do this day on Earth
as the saints do in heaven.
May we live this day in your light
and walk in the hope of your kingdom.

467 O Son of God, change our hearts.
Your Spirit composes the songs of the birds
and the buzz of the bees.
Your creation is a million wondrous miracles,
beautiful to look upon,
We ask of you just one more miracle:
beautify our souls.

468 God bless the earth that is beneath us,
the sky that is above us,
the day that lies before us,
your image deep within us.

469 The sun rises daily
only because you command it.
Its splendour will not last;
created things all perish.
Christ the true Sun
nothing can destroy.
He shall reign for ever.

470 Great Spirit, whose breath is felt in the soft breeze,
we seek your strength at noon.
May we, and the peoples of the world,
work in dignity and walk in the beauty of the day.

471 Great Spirit, out of your love the universe was born.
You have put in place all that is needed for growth
and have trusted us to attend to it.
Forgive our delusion of self-sufficiency
and our harming of the environment.
Forgive our taking food for granted,
our dishonouring of the farmer.
Restore us and restore the land.

472 We give you thanks
because Earth's life and fruitfulness flow from you
and all times and seasons reflect your laws.
We give you thanks
because you created the world in love,
you redeemed the world through love,
you maintain the world by your love.
Help us to give our love to you.

473 God, bless to us our bodies.
God, bless to us our souls.
God, bless to us our living.
God, bless to us our goals.

474 Lord, a thousand voices shout at us this day:
sound bites and slogans, images and screens,
conversations and traffic, newspapers and Internet.
Help us to filter out and turn away all that is not of you,
and to spot and hold to all that is of you.

475 Wind of Heaven,
blow away dross and deceits;
refresh our battered souls,
brace us for what is to come.

476 Creator God,
the raw materials are yours,
the energy is yours,
the skills are yours,
those we work with are yours.
Work is your gift.
Into your hands we place
our materials,
our energies,
our skills,
our colleagues.
You are our reward.
Rising from death, today Christ greets his people.
Rising with all creation, we greet him as our King.

477 Glory to you, Christ our King,
radiant with light,
the Sun who shines on all the world.
Earth exalt!
Heaven rejoice!
Morning and night, give thanks and praise!

478 When in decrepitude I awake,
turn my eyes to the Presence.
When in gloom I arise,
make me thankful that day follows night.

479 O loving Christ, hanged on a tree
yet risen in the morning,
scatter the sin from our souls
as the mist from the hills.
Echoes a prayer from Iona Abbey

480 Gratitude for the sun: blinding, pulsing light
through trunks of trees, through mists, through walls,
warming caves and corridors
– he who wakes us –
in our minds so be it.
Echoes a Mohawk prayer

481 Life of Jesus, Sun of suns,
filling every part of us,
life be in our speech,
sense in what we say,
the bloom of cherries on our lips
till you come back again.
Love of Jesus, Sun of suns,
filling every heart for us,
give us love in what we do,
filling us for everyone.
Traversing sea and road and field,
rays of Jesus be our shield.
Echoes an early Celtic prayer

482 May this be a day of resurrection and refreshment
for families and single people,
for traders and communities.
May our homes be places of hospitality and hope,
that we may know your risen presence
as we share ourselves and enjoy the company of others.
May our churches worship in a way
that brings honour to you;
joy to the people, and healing to the land.

483 We welcome the light that burns in the rising sun.
We welcome the light that dawns through the Son of God.
We welcome the light that gleams
through the growing earth.
We welcome the light that shines through saints and signs.
We welcome the light you kindle in our souls.

484 We rise up clothed in the strength of Christ.
We shall not be imprisoned, we shall not be harmed.
We shall not be downtrodden, we shall not be left alone.
We shall not be tainted, we shall not be overwhelmed.
We go clothed in Christ's white garments.
We go freed to weave Christ's patterns.
We go loved to serve Christ's weak ones.

485 Thank you for the gift of sleep.
Thank you for the gift of a new day.
All that we are we offer to you.
All that we do we offer to you.
All who we'll meet today
we offer now to you.
We arise today
in joy of being alive,
in freedom of wind,
in peace of readiness.

486 On your world, Lord,
your love descend today.
On all who work, Lord,
your love descend today.

Where there is strife, Lord,
your love descend today.
Where there is neglect, Lord,
your love descend today.
On your world, Lord,
your love descend today.

487 Our Father in heaven,
your kingdom come,
your will be done
on Earth, as in heaven.
In our pleasures,
your kingdom come.
In our leaders,
your kingdom come.
In our gatherings,
your kingdom come.
On the roads,
your kingdom come.
On the networks,
your kingdom come.
In each thing we do this day,
your kingdom come.

488 Thank you for bringing us
to the beginning of this week.
Keep us from falling into sin.

Midday

489 Holy Spirit,
come as a gentle breeze
that cools in the heat of the day.
Come as the calming presence
that restores stillness to our being.
Rest like dew on the peoples of the world
and on all whom we meet this day.
Rest like dew on our tired souls
and on all that we do this day.

490 As the press of work pauses at noon,
     may God's rest be upon us.
     As the sun rides high at noon,
     may the Sun of Righteousness shine upon us.
     As the rain refreshes the stained, stale streets,
     may the Spirit bring rain upon our dry ground.

491 *For busy people*
     We come into the presence of the creating Father.
     We come into the presence of the workaday Son.
     We come into the presence of the renewing Spirit.
     We come into the presence of the Three in One.

492 Lead us from death to life,
     from falsehood to truth.
     Lead us from despair to hope,
     from fear to trust.
     Lead us from hate to love,
     from war to peace.
     Deep peace of the Son of peace,
     fill our hearts, our workplace, our world.
     Echoes the Universal Prayer for Peace

493 Bless us now, Lord, in the middle of the day.
     Be with us and all who are dear to us.
     Keep us in the beautiful attitudes,
     joyful, simple and gentle.

494 May the Three of Limitless Love
     be in the eye of each one we shall meet,
     and pour upon us more and more generously
     hour by hour.

495 You give us well-being in the midst of the day:
     a day of renewal,
     a day of growth,
     a day of sharing food.

496 Great Spirit, whose breath is felt in the soft breeze
and whose life surges through socket and screen,
we seek your strength in the middle of the day.
May we, and the peoples of the world,
work in dignity and walk in the beauty of the day.

497 O God, you called all life into being;
your presence is around us now;
your Spirit enlivens all who work.
May your kingdom come on Earth.
Impart to us wisdom to understand your ways,
to manage well the tasks of this day.
Make us co-creators with you,
that when day fades
we may come to you without shame.

498 Good God, be with us in every experience of life.
When we neglect you,
remind us of your presence.
When we are frightened,
give us courage.
When we are tempted,
give us the power to resist.
When we are anxious and worried,
give us peace.
When we are weary in service,
renew our tired frame.

499 In the whirling wheels of the world
you are with us.
When the day takes its toll
you are with us.
In the clamour of strife
you are with us.
When the world turns sour
you are with us.

500 Make us aware, dear God, of
the eye that beholds us,
the hand that holds us,
the heart that loves us,
the presence that enfolds us.

501 Circle us, O God,
for the rest of the day.
Keep harm without,
keep good within.

502 May the Eternal Glory shine upon us.
May the Son of Mary stay beside us.
May the life-giving Spirit be a canopy over us.
May the eternal Three be ever with us.

503 Perfect Comforter! Wonderful Refreshment!
You make peace to dwell in our soul.
In our labour you offer rest;
in temptation, strength.
From heaven shine forth with your glorious light.

504 God of justice, God of peace,
in the heat of the day
we take refuge in you.

505 God is great.
In the middle of the day
we will remember you.
We will please you with our work.
We will please you with our words.
We will please you with our willingness
to love our neighbour.
We kneel and adore you.

506 God of community,
Spirit of energy and change,
pour on us without reserve or distinction,
that we may have strength
to plant your justice on Earth.

507 Lord Jesus, at this hour you hung on the cross,
stretching out your arms in love to all.
May the peoples of the world
be drawn to your uplifted love,
especially those with whom we shall work this day.
Give us the will to share our bread with the hungry,
to give shelter to those who feel rejected
and to reach out to those in need.

508 We pray for those whose tasks are backbreaking,
whose bodies are mutilated or whose spirits are crushed.

509 Lord Jesus,
in the midst of mockery and madness,
you found peace
to remain in your Father's will.
In the middle of our fretful day,
give us peace
to remain in our Father's will.

510 O Being of life!
O Being of peace!
O Being of time!
Be with us in the middle of the day.
O Being of truth!
O Being of sight!
O Being of wisdom!
Be with us in the middle of the day.

511 In God is our strength;
God alone is sufficient.

512 Guardian, be over the restless people,
a covering of truth and peace.

513 Renew us, O Risen Christ,
in the midst of the day.
In doubt bring faith,
in disillusion bring hope,

in cold indifference bring tender mercy,
in shoddy expediency bring untarnished ideals,
in the staleness of routine bring stirrings of life.

Evening

514   Let the light fade and the work be done.
      Let the flowers and the laptops close.
      Let the sun go down and the world become still
      and let the Son of God draw near.

515   Spirit of the Risen Christ,
      as lamps light up the evening,
      shine into our hearts and kindle in us
      the fire of your love.

516   We offer to you, Lord, the troubles of this day;
      we lay down our burdens at your feet.
      Forgive us our sins, give us your peace,
      and help us to receive your Word.

517   We give you thanks that you are always present,
      in all things, each day and each night.
      We give you thanks for your gifts of creation, life
      and friendship.
      We give you thanks for the blessings of this day.

518   May the Light of lights come to our dark hearts;
      may the Spirit's wisdom come to us from our Saviour:
      the wisdom of the humble heart and the listening ear,
      the wisdom of the attentive mind and the tender speech,
      the wisdom of all wisdom, Christ the wellspring of life.

519   Into your hands, O Lord,
      we place our families, our neighbours,
      our brothers and sisters in Christ,
      and all whom we have met today:
      enfold them in your will.

EVENING

Into your hands, O Lord,
we place all who are victims of prejudice,
oppression or neglect;
the unwanted, the frail.
May everyone be cherished,
from conception to the grave.

Into your hands, O Lord,
we place all who are restless,
sick, or prey to the powers of evil.
Watch over them and watch over us this night.

Into your hands, O Lord,
we place these members of our community.

520 We bless you, O God, and forget not all your benefits.
We bless you for your creation
which is alive with your glory.
You nod and beckon to us through every stone and star.
As the sun sets in the west, may we settle down with you.

521 The Creator who brought order out of chaos,
give peace to us.
The Saviour who calmed the raging sea,
give peace to us.
The Spirit who broods upon the deeps,
give peace to us.

522 Lord, you were tested by the evil one;
break in us the hold of power and pride.
You knew deep tears and weaknesses;
help us to be vulnerable for you.
You followed to the end the way of the cross;
help us to be faithful to you to the end of our days.

523 God of the call,
as we give thanks for the saints,
we pray for those who feel thwarted in their vocations.
May they do on Earth as the saints do in heaven.

God from whom all truth and justice flow,
we pray for the rule of law to prevail.
May we do on Earth as the saints do in heaven.
God of resurrection,
in their worship,
may our churches bring honour to you,
joy to the people and healing to the land.
May they do on Earth as the saints do in heaven.

524 Lord, we offer you this day's troubles.
Give us
strength to bear them,
wisdom to handle them,
compassion for those who brought them,
peace as to their outcome.

525 Thank you for your love for us, strong and nurturing;
we give back our lives to you.
Thank you for our minds and bodies;
we give back our lives to you.
Thank you for the past day;
we give back our lives to you.
After creation God rested;
we give back our lives to you.

Night

526 The day slips away:
may we be held in your clasp.
The night draws near:
may we draw near to you.
Blest be the evening tryst with you.

527 Sleep in peace.
Sleep soundly.
Sleep in love.
Weaver of dreams,
weave well in us as we sleep.

NIGHT

528 Wisdom,
come in to the storehouse of our memories,
be present though the silent hours
and bring us safely to your glorious light.

529 May heaven's peacekeepers
encircle us all with their outstretched arms
to protect us from the hostile powers,
to put balm into our dreams,
to give us contented, sweet repose.

530 At the drawing in of the day,
may your contemplations bring you peace.
May the soft mists of God's presence
wrap you in their gentle folds.
May the light of God's presence lengthen you.
May the might of God's presence strengthen you.
May the warmth of God's presence restore you.
May all that God has sowed in your life flower and ripen.
May God's harvest in your life be fruitful and abundant.
Echoes Blessings from Rock Community Church, Dunbarton, Scotland, 2000

531 We lie down in peace, knowing our sins are forgiven;
we lie down in peace, knowing death has no fear.
We lie down in peace, knowing no powers can harm us;
we lie down in peace, knowing Jesus is near.

532 O Christ, Son of the living God,
may your holy angels guard our sleep.
May they watch over us as we rest
and hover around our beds.
Let them reveal to us in our dreams
visions of your glorious truth.
May no fears or worries delay
our willing, prompt repose.

533 As the sun sets in the west,
    may we settle down with you, O God.
    Into your hands we place our failings and irritations.
    In your presence we give thanks for the blessings of this day.
    We will lie down at one with you,
    that we may rise up ready to do your will.

534 We lie down this night with God,
    and God will lie down with us;
    we lie down this night with Christ,
    and Christ will lie down with us;
    we lie down this night with the Spirit,
    and the Spirit will lie down with us;
    God and Christ and the Spirit,
    lying down with us.

535 The almighty and merciful Three circle us,
    that awake we may watch with Christ,
    and asleep we may rest in peace.

536 We place our souls and bodies
    under your guarding this night, O God,
    O Father of help to frail pilgrims,
    Protector of heaven and Earth.

    We place our souls and bodies
    under your guiding this night, O Christ,
    O Son of the tears and the woundings,
    may your cross this night be our shield.

    We place our souls and bodies
    under your glowing this night, O Spirit,
    O gentle Companion and Soul Friend,
    our hearts' eternal warmth.

537 You are our Saviour and Lord;
    in our stumbling be our shield;
    in our tiredness be our rest;
    in our darkness be our light.

538 Lord Jesus Christ, who at this hour lay in the tomb
and so hallowed the grave to be a bed of hope,
may we lie down in hope and rise up with you.

We will no longer fear death,
for by your death you have destroyed death.

We will not lie down in anger,
for love has triumphed over hate.

We will not sleep as those without hope,
for by your rising you bring hope and life eternal.

539 Guardian, Source of Order,
protect us through the hours of dark.
Take the restless maelstrom of our waking life
and, as once you did with the cosmos,
create order out of chaos.
And then be pleased with us,
as you were pleased with your creation,
for we are your creation too.

540 This night, O Victor over death,
raise us from the death of denial;
raise us from the death of fear;
raise us from the death of despair.

This night, O Victor over death,
wake us to the eternal 'Yes';
wake us to the rays of hope;
wake us to the light of dawn.

541 Renew us this night, Lord,
in body and soul,
that waking or sleeping
we may know your presence with us.

542 You fell asleep in mortal flesh, O God,
but on the third day you rose again.
Now you watch over us as we sleep,
you restore our souls and preserve our lives.
In love of you we will take our rest.

543 Great God,
   as you brought Christ
   safely through the night of sin and death
   to his rising at dawn,
   so bring us through this night
   that we may offer you our prayers at dawn
   and walk in light eternal.

544 Blest be all creation
   and all that has life.
   Blest be the Earth:
   may it uplift our bed tonight.
   Blest be the fire:
   may it glow in us tonight.
   Blest be the water:
   may it bathe our being tonight.
   Blest be the air:
   may it make our night breath sweet.

545 Protect us through the hours of this night,
   be they silent or stormy,
   that we who are wearied
   by the changes and chances of a restless world
   may rest upon you eternally.

546 God to enfold you,
   Christ to uphold you,
   Spirit to inflame you,
   this night and always.

547 Father, Mother of us all,
   your name be hallowed this night.
   Earth mover, pain bearer, giver of life,
   in joy we lie down to sleep.

548 When we are still we can sense you, our Maker;
   we can feel your hand upon us.
   All that has been made
   stirs within us creation's song of praise.
   Now we give you thanks for work completed;
   we give you thanks for rest of night.

549 You created the world out of love.
     Now we return to you in love.

550 The peace of the Spirit be ours this night,
     the peace of the Son be ours this night,
     the peace of the Father be ours this night,
     the peace of all peace be ours this night,
     each morning and evening of our lives.

551 May fears of day recede,
     may treasures of night draw near.

552 Great Spirit, who broods over the sleeping world,
     as we sleep this night,
     restore the garment of our self-respect
     and remake us in your beauty.
     Renew in us as we sleep
     the stillness of our being,
     the soundness of our bodies,
     and bring to dawn our wholeness.

553 On your world, Lord,
     your love descend this night.
     On your Church, Lord,
     your love descend this night.
     On all who work, Lord,
     your love descend this night.
     Where there is strife, Lord,
     your love descend this night.
     Where there is neglect, Lord,
     your love descend this night.
     On all who sleep, Lord,
     your love descend this night.

554 We thank you for your presence through the day
     and for friends who have helped us on our way.
     As shadows fall and the wheels of the world grow still,
     forgive us for our failures in love.

555 Kindle in our hearts, O God,
the flame of that love which never ceases,
that it may burn in us this night
till we shine for ever in your presence.

556 Support us, Lord,
through life's troubled day,
until the shadows lengthen
and evening comes,
the fever of life is over
and our work is done.
Then, Lord, in your mercy,
give us a holy rest
and peace at the last.
After a prayer of Cardinal Newman

557 God with us lying down,
God with us rising up;
Christ with us sleeping,
Christ with us waking;
Spirit with us now,
Spirit with us evermore.

558 Shadows darken this day,
the day Christ was laid in a grave.
The darkness shall not engulf us,
for with you the darkness is light.

559 Lord, by your cross and precious death,
save us from the powers of evil.
Save us from another's harm;
save us from our selfish failings.
Come this night and give us calm.

560 Give us sorrow for our sins against
human dignity and hospitality.
Give us sorrow for the sins of this day,
that when our bodies become but ashes
we may live with you for ever.

561 O Christ, who at this evening hour rested in the tomb
and made it become a bed of hope,
visit this house tonight
that we may pass through the death of sleep
and rise from our beds in hope of life eternal.

562 In our tiredness be our rest;
in our stumbling be our shield.
Into our place of darkness,
into our place of strife,
into our fears and worries,
come with eternal life.

563 Risen Christ,
you have entered into darkness, despair and death.
Rising in glory,
you accompany all who have to enter into these.
You give us the cup of life.
You quench our every thirst.
You turn hearts of stone into flesh.
You clothe the peacemakers in raiment of light.
Live in us now
and bring us to our resurrection without end.

564 Risen Christ,
you burned in the hearts of two walkers
who made room in their conversation for you.
Burn in us as we converse.
You revealed yourself to them
as they welcomed you into their home.
Reveal yourself to us
as we make you welcome in our homes.
You fell asleep in mortal flesh, O Lord and Leader,
but on the third day you rose again.
Now you watch over us as we sleep.
You restore our souls and preserve our lives.
In love of you we will take our rest.

565 Nature's breath and eyes are clearest blue;
O purest God, gaze on us this night.
The blackbird's call is wild and free,
rejoicing at the new abundance of food;
may our spirits become free this night,
rejoicing in your abundance.

566 We wait in the darkness expectantly, longingly.
Only in the darkness may we see
the splendour of the universe and the glowing stars.
It was in the darkness that the wise three
saw the star that led them to the Christ-child.
In the darkness of sleep dreams rise up.
In the darkness, God gave dreams
to Joseph and the wise three.
With you, Creator God, there is treasure in the darkness.

567 Now we give you thanks for work completed.
Now we lie down in peace.

568 Lighten our darkness at the end of the day.
Defend us from perils, our fears allay.
Lighten our burdens, bring joy to our rest
and grant, on our waking, we give you our best.

569 Guardian of the planets,
kindler of the stars,
we pass into the darkness
encompassed by you.

570 Peace be upon our breath.
Peace be upon our eyes.
Peace be upon our sleep.

571 Spirit of Truth, look down
upon a world in thrall to lies and illusions.
Work in the darkness
to bring all things into light.

572 In the name of the God of wholeness,
in the name of Compassion's Son,
in the name of the healing Spirit,
tonight may we be one.

573 Healing Christ,
you walk the world with those who suffer
in broken places of the world.
We come to you with our wounds and theirs.
Encircle those for whom we pray.
Enter their bodies, minds and spirits.
And heal them of all that harms.

574 Still is the earth;
make still our bodies.
Still is the night;
make still our minds.
Still are the spheres;
make still our souls.

575 We wrap our souls and our bodies from fears
under your guarding, O Christ.
O Christ of the tears,
of the wounds, of the piercings,
may your cross this night be our eternal shield;
your cross between us and all enemies without;
your cross between us and all enemies within;
your cross our sure way from Earth to heaven.

576 As it was in the stillness of the morning,
so may it be in the silence of the night.
As it was in the hidden vitality of the womb,
so may it be in the hidden life of our sleep.

577 We know that night is not dark with you, O Lord;
but a great deal of us is not yet one with you.
In the night, the things we fear come to the surface.
The unacknowledged parts of our personalities
poke through the shadows to haunt us.

It helps us to know that the blackness will lift
as surely as the dawn follows night.
But before that there is work to do.
Night has a purpose of its own.
Our task is to acknowledge the shadows
and bring them to you who are the Morning Star.
You are the author of light and dark.
The morning star would be nothing to us
without its prelude, the night.
So thank you, Lord, for the night.

578 May we rest this night
in the stillness of your being.

579 Creator Spirit,
wellspring of life and love,
as we sleep,
renew the springs of our life,
refresh our weak frame,
restore love into our soul.

580 O Radiant Dawn, splendour of eternal light,
come and shine on us
that we may sleep in the warmth of your radiance.
O Emmanuel, God with us,
we will lie down with you
and you will lie down with us.
And the dawn shall come,
and so will your appearing,
and we shall know as we are known.
And in pleasure you will receive us.
Call forth this night bearers of your presence.
Call forth this night believers in your truth,

581 You created the world out of love.
Now we return to you in love.
Let us rest in God this night
and awake in newness of life.
When we are still we can sense you, our Maker.

We can feel your hand upon us.
All that has been made
stirs within us creation's song of praise.
Now we give you thanks for work completed.
We give you thanks for rest of night.

582 Blest be God the giver of light.
Blest be God the provider of warmth.
Blest be God the dispeller of darkness.
Blest be God the giver of sleep.

583 Call forth this night bearers of your presence,
that we may we rest in the undying flame of your love
and wake to the light of your dawning.

584 Come, Guardian of heaven and Earth,
and cover us with night.
Spread your grace over us as you promised you would.
Your promises are more than all the stars in the sky.
Night comes with the cold.
Night comes with the breath of death.
Night comes, the end comes, you come.
Your mercy is deeper than the night.
Echoes a prayer from Ghana

585 Have mercy this night on a surfeited world
which, through grasping, can't be grasped by you.
Have mercy this night on the weak and broken,
on the hungry, the homeless and souls without hope.

586 We give thanks for the gift of sleep,
but also for the gift of struggle.
Awake, may we watch with you;
asleep, may we rest in peace.

587 Great God, as the haze rises from mountaintops,
raise our souls from the granite of death
before we go to sleep.

588 As we lay down our clothes,
may we lay down our struggles
before we go to our sleep.

589 Lift from us our anguish;
lift from us our malice;
lift from us our empty pride
before we go to our sleep.

590 Great God, give us light;
Great God, give us grace;
Great God, give us joy
before we go to our sleep.

591 O Trinity of Love,
you have been with us at the world's beginning:
be with us till the world's end.
You have been with us at our life's shaping:
be with us at our life's end.
You have been with us at the sun's rising:
be with us till the day's end.

592 Eternal Creator of the weeks and years,
as this week draws to a close, draw close to us
and we will draw close to you.
Eternal Creator of the days and nights,
as darkness deepens, draw near to us
and we will draw near to you.

593 *A boozer's night prayer*
I'm not in a fit state to pray, Lord.
I'm somewhere in between
a big high and a big low.
I've been showing off.
I've drunk too much.
I've taken a few things I shouldn't have.
But it's not all bad;
I've had fun and you like fun.

I'm confused.
Do I have to choose between being all good
and being all bad?
I'm nearly out now.
Yet deep down I want you.
I've got a hangover,
but I don't want you and me
to be for ever hung up on each other.
I'd prefer not to sleep with my back turned to you.
But everything's too complicated to sort out now.
Sorry, Lord.

Now repeat between ten and one hundred times
Lord, have mercy on me.

If you're not asleep by now, you will be before you've finished saying what comes next.
Repeat between ten and one hundred times
I will lie down with God
and God will lie down with me.

Children's prayers

594   Jesus, you helped your dad in a woodwork shop.
      You made nice things out of wood.
      We are like wood in your hands.
      Sometimes we are hard.
      Please make us into nice people.

595   Dear Jesus,
      some people don't notice us and we feel left out.
      You were not like that –
      you noticed people and put yourself in their shoes.
      Help us to notice people and put ourselves in their shoes.
      Help us to feel for them and be friends.

596   Good morning, God.
      How are you?
      I am OK, but sometimes I get upset.
      Help me to do things your way.

597 Dear God, when we wake up,
may we feel the sun is shining on us
because you are smiling down on us.
Chase away bad, dark thoughts.
Make us smile.

598 *Midday*
Stop!
It's the middle of the day.
We get too full of ourselves.
Please, God,
calm us down.

599 *Evening*
Mr Sun, you settle down.
God made you, God made us.
Mr God,
help us to think before we speak
and settle down with you.

600 Dear God,
if you came to church
we would feel happy.
We might
clap
or laugh
or cry
or dance
or paint
or sing
or show you our playthings
or just sit quietly.
Help us make church like that anyway,
ready for you to turn up any time.

601 Teach us, dear God, to
know you better,
explore your world,
learn from mistakes,

understand others,
use our talents,
remember important things,
and grow like Jesus.

602 Dear Jesus,
there is a good voice
and a bad voice inside us.
Help us to listen to the good voice
and throw out the bad voice.

603 Teach us to dance like clouds that play.
Teach us to laugh like sun that glistens.
Teach us to flow like streams that sing.
Teach us to fly like birds that chirp.
Teach us to dream like rainbows that gleam.
Teach us to have fun with you.

604 Jesus,
bless our eyes – so we notice others.
Bless our hearts – so we love others.
Bless our hands – so we help others.
Where there is hate, let us bring love.
Where there are quarrels, let us bring peace.
Where there is darkness, let us bring light.
Where there is sadness, let us bring joy.

605 God bless the air.
Help us not to spoil it.
God bless the sea.
Help us not to poison it.
God bless the earth.
Help us not to trample it.
God bless the planet.
Help us not to ruin it.
God bless here.
Help us look after it.

606 When we eat our food,
    may we think of the earth that gives it.
    When we have rides in a car,
    may we think of the oil that moves it.
    When we buy something in a shop,
    may we think of the people who made it.
    When we go to sleep,
    may we think of you who creates us.

607 Dear Jesus,
    the Church is your world family.
    You have given treasures
    to different parts of this family
    and we don't know what they are.
    Help us, in our church,
    to find different treasures like
    the Bible,
    the Holy Spirit,
    friends,
    stillness,
    communion,
    beautiful art,
    the saints,
    the poor,
    celebrations,
    prayer,
    and other things
    we have not yet thought of.

608 Our Father in heaven,
    your kingdom come, your will be done
    on Earth as it is in heaven.
    Your kingdom come
    because we are honest and do not cheat;
    because we are fair and do not steal;
    because we listen and do not laugh at others;
    because we are friends and do not gossip;
    because we love and do not hate;
    because we share and do not grab.

609 Dear God,
   help us make a church without walls;
   help us to pray all over the place;
   help us to have parties wherever there's space;
   help us to visit, play and tell stories
   to new and old friends.
   Dear God, who is present to all,
   put your love in our hearts and draw others to you.

School

610 Lord, circle this school and keep these good things within:
   eagerness to learn,
   flowering of talents,
   a sense of wonder,
   enjoyment of sport,
   experience of beauty,
   warmth of friendship,
   appreciation of arts,
   respect for all,
   service of others,
   teamwork between children and adults,
   care for the planet,
   reverence for life,
   fitness of body, mind and spirit.

   Lord, circle this school and keep these bad things without:
   low self-esteem,
   confusion,
   prejudice,
   pride,
   bullying,
   cheating,
   stealing,
   fear of appraisal,
   malicious gossip,
   absenteeism,
   'couldn't care less' attitudes.
   Lord, circle this school,
   for you are the source of all that is good and true.

611 *For a person joining a school*
   May smiling faces welcome you.
   May helping hands welcome you.
   May kind teachers welcome you.
   May fears fly away,
   temper go away,
   fibs stay away.
   May you make new friends,
   learn new things,
   grow strong limbs.
   May God make you thoughtful,
   Jesus make you happy,
   Spirit make you friendly.

612 *Leaving school*
   Dear God,
   we've come to the end of our school years
   with mixed feelings.
   As we look back and as we look to what is coming,
   we see all sorts of shapes and colours in flow and flux.
   God of shapes and colours, bless these to us
   and be in the flow and flux.
   As we look back and as we look to what is coming,
   we see all sorts of empty gaps.
   God of the gaps, fill these for us
   and be in the flow and flux.
   As we look back, bless us with forgiveness
   and the knowledge that nothing need be wasted with you.
   As we look forward, help us find what work is right for us.
   Bless our questioning and finding out.
   Will we get jobs?
   Bless our work and all the talents you have put within us;
   may they grow wherever we shall be.
   Be a vision to guide us, a voice to lead us,
   a Saviour to forgive us, a hand to hold us,
   a friend to teach us for ever.

Saints and other companions

*With so many witnesses in a great cloud all around us, we too,
then, should . . . keep running in the race which lies ahead
(Hebrews 12:1)*

613 We arise today
   in the glorious company of the holy and risen ones,
   in the prayers of the fathers and mothers,
   in the truths of apostles.
   We arise today
   in the visions of prophets,
   in the victory of martyrs,
   in the vigils of hermits.
   We arise today
   in the innocence of virgins,
   in the courage of heroes,
   in the friendship of those in love with the King of life.

614 We thank you that in your saints of yesterday and today
   we see the many-splendoured facets of human life
   flowing in its fullness.
   We thank you for those who give their all
   in the service of others;
   for those who overcome heroic odds with nobility of spirit;
   for those who are gracious in defeat
   and magnanimous in triumph;
   for those who show us truly how to love.

615 Kindle in us the adventure of obedience,
   the single eye,
   the humble and generous heart
   which marked your saints.

Abraham

616 God of the call, who led Abraham into the unknown
   in order to bless all nations and teach them
   the dignity of difference,
   bless Abraham's children
   – Jews, Christians and Muslims –
   and the whole world family of which we are part.

Adomnan

617 Faithful God,
who through Adomnan's writings
called to mind your hand in your people's journey,
and through his actions reached out
to establish justice for women and children,
stir us again with memory of your mighty deeds
and to acts of justice and mercy.

Aelred

618 Holy and loving God,
who revealed fresh facets of your grace
in the radiant friendship of your servant Aelred,
renew in us the gift of friendship,
so that in loving one another
we may more deeply reflect on Earth
the eternal love of the Trinity.

Aidan

619 God of Aidan of the gentle touch,
give us the gift of gentleness.
God of Aidan of the generous heart,
give us the gift of generosity.
God of Aidan of the ceaseless prayer,
give us the gift of prayer.
God of Aidan of the burning faith,
give us the gift of faith.
God of Aidan of simple habits,
give us the gift of simplicity.
God of Aidan of the friendly greeting,
give us the gift of meeting.

620 Lord Jesus, simplicity and a deep love for people
shone out of your apostle Aidan.
Grant that, like him, we may be gentle in our loving
and bold in our speaking,
that we might inspire others to learn your ways
and so pass on the fire of faith.

621 God of Providence,
oil blessed by saintly Aidan
brought calm to the raging seas.
You call us, also, to pour oil on troubled waters.
Pour generously upon those in turmoil now.
We bring to you the troubles in our places of work.
Calm us, and help us rest in you.
We bring to you the troubles in our households.
Calm us, and help us rest in you.
We bring to you the troubles in our church.
Calm us, and help us rest in you.
We bring to you the troubles of the world.
Calm us, and help us rest in you.

Alban

622 At midsummer, creation says yes.
Forgive us for saying no.
At midsummer, Alban gave his life for another.
Forgive us for holding back.
At midsummer, the world reflects your light.
Forgive us for hiding from you.

Ambrose

623 God of fair play,
who called Ambrose from a governor's throne
to be a shepherd and champion of the people,
replenish the Church with the spirit of sound learning
and the beauty of holiness,
that she may appoint teachers like Ambrose
to guide Christian people into the fullness of the Faith.

Anne and Joachim, grandparents of Jesus

624 God of Covenant,
who in the deep counsels of your wisdom
entrusted to Anne and Joachim

the preparation of the Blessed Virgin
for her most holy calling.
As we ponder the wonder of your hand on this family,
may we be drawn to trust completely
in your redeeming plans,
and in everything place ourselves in your keeping.

Antony

625   O Christ, who called your disciples
to be perfect as your Father is perfect,
thank you that Antony left all
to become an Athlete of Christ in the deserts of Egypt
and inspired a multitude to follow in his steps.
Help us to keep you always before our eyes
and to run with you as our prize.

Augustine

626   God of Beauty, so ancient yet so fresh,
who turned Augustine from the ugliness of sin
to the beauty of holiness,
change our restless hearts
until they find their rest in you.

Baldred

627   Rock of ages, who called Baldred
to a wild place where he held fast to you
and let his prayers become a shield to mainland people,
give us courage to journey with you
into the wild, unvisited parts of our lives,
and there let our prayers protect the land.

Barnabas

628 God of compassion,
who graced Barnabas with gifts of encouragement,
inspire us by his example
to be generous in our judgements
and to encourage others to holy callings
in the power of your Spirit.

Bede

629 God of our forebears, rock of their lives,
may we, like Bede, trace your hand in history,
study your noble works,
and persevere in well-doing until, with him,
we join our ascended Lord.

Bega

630 Gentle God, in Bega we glimpse the beauty of friendship
rising from the ashes of abuse.
Help us to create such stillness in our inner being
that we become aware of your gracious movements
in ourselves and others.

Benedict

631 God of good order,
enable us, after the example of Benedict,
to live as one family
in the stability of obedience to you
and respect for one another.

Benedict Biscop

632 Majestic God, whose servant Benedict Biscop
sought to reflect your greatness
in the liturgies and arts of the Church.
Save us from cramped and penny-pinching attitudes.
May we leave a legacy of beauty
that will long afterwards draw people to you.

Beuno

633 Builder of planets and of paradise,
may we, inspired by your servant Beuno,
spread the Faith, restore people to life
and bring many talents into the service of your Church.

Boisil

634 Living God, we thank you for your gifts
of teaching and prophecy in your servant Boisil.
Increase in us sensitivity to your voice,
that the spirit of authentic prophecy
may flourish in our time.

Billfrith

635 God our Eternal Treasure,
you give glorious minerals to your creation
and glorious skills to your people.
We bless you for the craft of Billfrith,
honed in prayerful practice.
Raise up skilled craftspeople
who will use creation's gifts and their own
for your glory.

Birinus

636 Baptising God,
who impelled Birinus across the sea
to bring your Word to a pagan people,
immerse us in your love,
and bring many into the company of those who believe.

Branwalader

637 God of the seas and fisherfolk,
with unwavering faith
Branwalader allowed you to sweep him to diverse shores,
where many were swept along by you.
Keep us moving,
with our eyes on the horizons you open up to us,
that we may be swept along in the greatness of your plans.

Brendan

638 God of the oceans,
thank you for Brendan's adventures for Christ on sea
and land,
and his drawing together of families and friends
into communities of love.
Kindle in us a spirit of endless adventure
and a love that forges fresh bonds of community.

Brigid

639 May our homes, like Brigid's,
be places of hospitality and holiness,
with the cross of our Saviour at their heart.
The cross in our cupboards and caravans;
the cross in our boats and box rooms;
the cross in the neglected areas of our lives.

640 Mary's Son, our friend, come and bless our kitchens.
May we have fullness through you.
Mary's Son, our friend, come and bless the soil.
May we have fullness through you.
Mary's Son, our friend, come and bless our work.
May we have fullness through you.
Echoes a prayer attributed to Brigid

641 May the fruits God gave Brigid lie on us.
May the delights God gave Brigid lie on us.
May the healings God gave Brigid lie on us.
May the virtues God gave Brigid lie on us.
And on our loved ones too.

Cadfan of Bardsey

642 Lord, human extremity is your opportunity.
As Cadfan turned personal upheaval
into bold new church planting,
teach us not to be cowed by disappointments
but to turn them into springboards
for the advancement of your kingdom.

Caedmon

643 As in the night vision Caedmon's soul sang out,
so may the music of our souls be released.
Release, O Craftsperson of the universe:
the music of speech,
the music of thought,
the music of seeing.
Release, O Guardian of the human race:
the music of craft,
the music of laughter,
the music of healing.

Canice (Kenneth)

644 We thank you for Canice,
friend of Columba, planter of churches,
holy hermit and scribe and converser with animals.
May we learn from his strong faith
to refer all things to you,
and to love with missionary purpose.

SAINTS AND OTHER COMPANIONS

Cassian

645   Holy God, source of friendship,
still centre of the universe,
teach us, like Cassian and the holy souls of the desert,
to pray from our hearts by day and night
until our souls are bathed in light from on high.

Cedd

646   Great-hearted God, we thank you for Cedd,
who was neither corroded by cynicism
nor cluttered by ecclesial bureaucracy,
but was straightforward, prayerful, confident.
Inspired by his fearless friendship,
his teaching and translating skills,
may we learn to serve you
for the wider good of Church and society.

Chad

647   Faithful God,
from Christ's first fruits of the English people
you called Chad to holy learning and high service
as a missionary monk and bishop.
May we learn from his humility and loving discipline
to pattern the ways of Christ in our time.

Ciaran

648   O Saviour of the human race,
O true physician of every disease,
O heart-pitier and assister of all misery,
O fount of true purity and true knowledge,
forgive.
O star-like sun,
O guiding light.
O home of the planets,

O fiery-maned and marvellous one,
forgive.
O holy scholar of holy strength,
O overflowing, loving, silent one,
O generous and thunderous giver of gifts,
O rock-like warrior of a hundred hosts,
forgive.
Attributed to Ciaran

Columba

649 Purity, wisdom and prophecy:
grant these gifts, O Trinity.
The lamp of the body is purity,
and those who have it their God shall see.
Your wisdom bestow as a light for the mind,
that we may grow compassionate, kind.
The gift of the soul is prophecy;
enlarge our vision that we may see.
Echoes Columba's prayer for three gifts

650 Mighty God, Columba's voice echoed across the Isles;
may the voice of your servants
sound clear above the clamour of our times.
Columba established communities of love and learning;
restore community and truth to our places of learning.
Columba extolled hard physical labour;
bless with dignity all who work with their hands today.
Columba sang of his joy in creation;
restore joy in creation to our distracted people.
Columba took action against injustice;
strengthen us to stand for fairness in our society.
Columba's departing to the heavenly country was glorious;
grant us a good and glorious end.

Columbanus

651 Give us, Lord, the love that does not fail;
renew in us the flame that burns for ever.
As we continually gaze on you, the Perpetual Light,
may we shine before you,
scattering this world's darkness, giving light to others.
Echoes Columbanus

652 You who are our Perpetual Light,
kindle the flames in our hearts,
that they may continually blaze,
always receiving light from you,
always giving light to others,
scattering the darkness of the world.
Echoes Columbanus

Comgall

653 As Comgall's monks transformed
their monastery at Bangor into a Valley of Angels,
so may we, with your help,
transmit your presence and your praises across the land,
and turn round the values of the world.

Cornish saints from Ireland

654 Baptising God,
who impelled your saints to cross the sea from Ireland
to plant the Faith in Cornwall,
we thank you for Birinus and Buryan,
Indract and Ive,
Elwyn and so many more.
Inspire us by their example,
immerse us in your love,
that we, too,
may leave behind our comforts
and bring others into the company
of those who believe.

Crispin and Crispinian

655 Carpenter Christ,
who learned your craft through long years of toil,
but toiled even more for the souls of humankind,
as we thank you for the resourcefulness
of these your shoemaker missionaries,
help us to put our resources at your disposal,
to do a good job, and with them,
to inherit an eternal reward.

Cuthbert

656 Tender Father,
who called Cuthbert from tending sheep
to be a shepherd of the people,
help us, inspired by his example,
to heal the sick, guard unity,
storm heaven's gates
and bring those who are lost home to your fold.

657 Holy God of Cuthbert,
bright star of the North,
may we become, like him,
peacemakers and hospitality-givers,
open to change and partnership,
Spirit-led in solitude and costly service.
We invite you, as he did,
to enter deeply into our lives and into our very bones.

Cyril and Methodius

658 Wide-winged Spirit,
you gave Cyril and Methodius tongues
to enlighten the Slavs with the gospel.
Make us one with you through the gospel
until East and West acknowledge
one Lord, one Faith, one Baptism,
one Body of Christ on Earth as in heaven.

David

659 Faithful God,
David worked with unflagging zeal.
Forgive us for our flickering flame.
David witnessed with unfaltering faith.
Forgive us for our faltering steps.
David served with unstinting generosity.
Forgive us for our fickle friendship.

660 Most merciful God, thank you for David:
for his love, flowing out through his tears;
for his faith, flowing out through his prayers;
for his work, continued by his peers.
Kindle the flame in us through the years.

661 As it began to be in the time of David,
so may it be again for us.
Everywhere may voices be raised to heaven in prayer.
Everywhere may virtues be restored
to the heart of the Church.
Everywhere may supplies be shared with the needy.

662 In the little things we do,
be present, Lord.
In the little things we speak,
be present, Lord.
In the little moments we fill,
be present, Lord.
In our working and our going,
be present, Lord.
Echoes David's dying words: 'Be faithful in the little things'

663 Great Spirit, as fish live in water, may we live in you.
Bathe us in your cleansing waters,
soak us in your healing streams.
Drench us in your powerful downfalls,
steel us in your mighty seas.
Cool us in your bracing rivers,
calm us by your quiet pools.

664 Lord, inspired by David and the Watermen,
help us to
live in you as fish live in water,
move in you as birds fly in air,
run for you as deer run on land,
blaze for you as flames burn in fire.
May the fire of faith blaze afresh in Wales;
may the fire of faith blaze afresh in us.

665 Great God, who called your servant David
to be an apostle and father in God to the people of Wales,
grant that, inspired by the fire of his faith
and the flexibility of his approach,
we too may see divine fruit in our land.

Denys

666 Father of peoples,
as we thank you for the simple courage of Denys
in planting the Faith at the heart of a nation,
strip from us what distracts us
from going to the heart of your will.

Drithelm

667 Eternal God, who drew aside heaven's curtain
for your servant Drithelm
and led him into a life of continual prayer and praise,
reveal to us the choices that make for life or death
and open to us the riches of eternal life.

668 Champion, save us from being fair-weather Christians.
When we get cold feet,
remind us of the example of people such as Drithelm.
May the praises of God be in our mouths,
whatever we feel like,
today and every day.

Eadfrith

669 Divine Artist, you endow us with gifts and call us to serve.
Anoint us by your Spirit that we, like your servant Eadfrith,
whose inspired fingers moved the bird's feather
over the stretched, brown skin of calf,
may make good use of our gifts
and be worthy of our calling.

Eanswyth

670 Eternal Spouse, who ever woos your people,
as we give you thanks
for the first brides of Christ among the English,
we pray that in every land
there may be no lack of people
who respond with all their being to your advances.

Edith

671 Gracious God of faithful Edith,
as we cherish her example,
reveal to us the royalty of service,
open our hearts to the poor,
and give us perpetual devotion
to the suffering heart of Christ.

Enda

672 Mentor and Seeker of souls,
who used Enda to ground Irish Christians
in the learning and fellowship of Christ,
equip your people today in sound learning,
wise counsel and bold experiments in faith.

Enoch

673 God who walks with your people
and communed with Enoch,
teach us by his example to walk in intimacy with you,
fleeing from everything that clouds our relationship,
until even death is but a gentle passing over
into your nearer presence.

Fechin

674 Fount of Life,
as Fechin struck rocks and drew water from them,
may we strike the rocks of human resistance
until we draw from them waters of salvation
and drink deeply of you.

Fiacre

675 Earth Maker, by whose life we are born and sustained:
as we thank you for the careful tending
of gardener saints such as Fiacre,
help us to tend this planet, your garden,
to the best of our ability.

Finbarr

676 God of the journey,
may we learn from Finbarr to give away
what is ours with joyful abandon,
to place our hand in yours,
and to let you lead us to our place of resurrection.

Francis

677 Teach us, O Christ,
according to the counsel of Francis,
to come into your presence as to a king,
to free ourselves from false attachments,
to seek your voice in the silence
and to dwell on the beauty of the virtues.

Fursey

678 God of the journey –
whose holy scholar Fursey,
impelled by the visions you entrusted to him,
gave his life as a pilgrim for love of you –
spare us your anger
and help us to heed and speed your Word.

Gall

679 Fisher of souls, we thank you that Gall,
like the Big Fisherman Peter,
was true to himself and true to you.
Help us to be so too.

George

680 God of heroic love,
who gave George valour
to witness to his risen Lord even to death,
arm us, who are heirs of all the victories of faith,
to slay the dragons of falsehood, greed, and prejudice.
Raise up among us prophets of speech and pen
to reveal to us the human condition,
to recall us to ways of truth
and to point us to our destiny.

Germanus

681 God our Champion,
who enabled Germanus
to give bold leadership in turbulent times
and to overcome evil with good,
build up our fibre,
that we may be more than conquerors
through Christ who gave himself for us.

Gideon

682 All-powerful One, we seem so powerless and puny,
yet if you could so mightily use Gideon,
born of humble stock,
pared down to a tiny force,
perhaps you can use us, too.
So help us God.

Gregory

683 Servant King,
who called Gregory to pattern your ways in the city
to assist the conversion of the English people,
and to be servant of the servants of God,
may we ever desire to live out your laws,
reach out to others
and serve your people.

Gregory of Tours

684 God of turbulent cities,
as we thank you for Gregory's steady, God-guided hand
on the affairs of Tours,
we pray for our cities today,
and ask that incorruptible leaders
of wise counsel and spiritual energy
may emerge.

Guthlac

685   Holy and Immortal God,
      who called Guthlac to be a soldier in the spiritual war,
      may his example spur us so to discipline our bodies
      that we become effective spiritual soldiers
      and complete our course in triumph.

Haggai

686   Mighty Provider,
      you remind us through Haggai
      that all the silver and gold in the world is yours.
      Forgive us for being so mean.
      Help us to use generously what we have
      to make a better world.

Herbert of Derwentwater

687   Divine Friend,
      who called Herbert to a life of contemplation
      and a life-long soul-friendship with Cuthbert,
      teach us to contemplate your presence in creation,
      to know the joys of soul friendship
      and to reach our day of resurrection.

Hilda

688   You made Hilda to shine like a jewel in the land.
      Help us, like her, to encourage others to their callings,
      to reconcile those who are divided
      and to praise you with our whole being.

689   Father, as Hilda shone like a jewel in her mother's womb,
      may we know that each of us is special
      and can shine for you.
      Jesus, as the birds saluted Hilda at Whitby,
      may we salute those who honour you.

Spirit, as Hilda drew out the songs
that were locked in shy Caedmon's heart,
may we draw out the talents that lie buried in others' lives.

690 God, our vision,
in our mother's womb
you formed us for your glory.
As your servant Hilda
shone like a jewel in the Church,
so we now delight to claim
the virtues and gifts
you delight to shower upon us.

691 Wisdom on High, help us to learn from the likes of Hilda:
to be reliable,
to grow in prudence,
to study, work and pray hard, but not too hard;
to treat every person with courtesy
and none with contempt;
to maintain resolute faith,
balanced judgement, and outgoing friendships.

692 Sacred Three, as we thank you for the life of Hilda,
a jewel in your Church who lit up a dark land,
release the hidden treasures in the lives of women
and in the lives of all your people today,
that we, too, may come to shine for you.

Hildegaard

693 God of vision,
whose servant Hildegaard
was caught up in the marvels of your heavenly courts
and brought colour to your Church through music and art,
open our eyes to glimpse your glory
and our lips to praise you with songs that are ever fresh.

Hybald

694 Holy God, holy and mighty,
who graced Hybald's travels
with stories of the victories of faith,
bless his land of Lincolnshire,
and make sacred the landscapes where we live and die.

Illtyd

695 All-wise God,
who raised up Illtyd to make many Britons wise, holy
and fruitful,
prosper the work of our hands, heads and hearts
that the virtues of hard work, holy living and wise learning
may flourish in our time.

Indract

696 God of Life,
who turned Christ's tree of death into a tree of life
and who changed the tragedy of Indract's death
into a victory sign for the people,
change our despair into hope,
and help us to turn every difficulty into an opportunity.

Irenaeus

697 Great Creator,
whose glory is seen in human life coming fully alive,
help us to live fully human lives for you,
in the power of Jesus Christ,
truly human, truly divine.

Isaac

698 God of covenant,
unending in your commitment to us,
out of your call came Isaac.
Keep us faithful to the lines of your plan.
May we neither deviate nor deceive but,
encouraged by Isaac's example,
trust you in all things.

Isaac of Nineveh

699 God of the compassionate heart,
who enflamed Isaac with a gentle love for all,
teach us to be weaned
from the addictive compulsions of our age,
until heaven enters our hearts
and becomes our delight beyond compare.

Ishmael

700 God of a hundred names,
for love of Ishmael and his people through the ages,
you have committed yourself to developing their greatness.
Forgive us for our jealous divisions,
and help us to honour one another
and seek the common good.

Ismael

701 Discipler of souls,
thank you for the great blessing
brought to us by families such as Ismael's,
who bent themselves to holy learning
and gave themselves to fostering the Faith in others.
Inspire us by their example
to learn all we can and build all we can.

SAINTS AND OTHER COMPANIONS

Isaiah

702 Holy God,
whose glory fills the Earth,
and who foresees the rise and fall of peoples,
we thank you for the unique inklings
you gave Isaiah of the coming of your Son.
May it lead us to welcome him with wonder and awe.

Jacob

703 God of covenant,
teach us to struggle with you
until we, with Jacob, can say,
'You are here, Lord, in this place;
you protect us wherever we go.'

James, brother of Jesus

704 O Christ, who chose as a brother
a man cautious of change, faithful to tradition,
yet obedient to a fresh revelation,
powerful in intercession and faithful to death,
we rejoice that you invite people of many temperaments,
races and viewpoints
to become part of your family.
Help us to treat them as our brothers and sisters, too.

Jesse

705 God of the generations,
thank you for Jesse's big faith and solid parenting.
Help us to be rooted and grounded in Christ,
and thus to be linked with Jesse's timeless faith.

John Chrysostom

706 God whose speech is glorious,
and who warmed the minds of many
through the golden tongue of John,
may your Spirit put into our mouths words
that open the unsearchable riches of Christ to others.

John of Beverley

707 Lover of the poor,
whose likeness shows most specially
in those with handicap of body,
we bless you for the tender faith of John.
Inspired by this lovable saint,
may we become more humane towards others.

John of the Cross

708 Lover of souls,
who always beckons us,
even through the dark night of the soul,
teach us, through the example
of your dear son John of the Cross,
that no suffering or misfortune is so great
that we cannot remain your spouse.

John the Forerunner

709 God of prophecy,
give us something of the spirit of John the Baptist:
his moral courage,
his contentment with simplicity,
his refusal to be fettered by this world,
his reaching out to the people,
his perseverance to the end.

710 Holy God, holy and mighty,
     who brought the holy John to birth in a barren womb,
     you can bring a new thing to birth in a barren land.
     Thank you for making John a front-runner
     who prepared a way for you.
     Help us to prepare a way for you.
     Where there is falsehood,
     help us prepare a way for you.
     Where there is violence,
     help us prepare a way for you.
     Where there is misuse of others,
     help us prepare a way for you.
     Where there is meanness,
     help us prepare a way for you.

John the loved disciple

711 Grant to us, O Lord,
     that tender love, that deathless vision,
     that flowing life that marked John the loved disciple;
     until the Logos, the Lamb and we,
     your little loved ones,
     flow together as one.

Joseph

712 God our Provider,
     who through Joseph led a nation
     to store food supplies during years of plenty
     to disperse to the needy during years of hardship,
     help our consumer society to learn this lesson,
     and have mercy on our world.

Joseph and the shepherds

713 Father,
you appointed Joseph
to be guardian of Jesus and husband to Mary.
Give to fathers, guardians and mothers
grace to make holy homes.
Give to those who work
in the fields of farm and commerce
an awareness of your presence among us.

Kevin

714 Give us courage to journey, like Kevin,
into the wild places,
for you who created each wild thing
created us.
Teach us, as you taught Kevin,
that if we journey with you
to the place of our greatest fear,
it can become the place of our greatest strength.

Machalus

715 God of a thousand places,
we thank you for Machalus,
a jewel in the crown of your Church.
Help us to be true and glorious like gold,
because we learn the way of penance
and are willing to be purified in your fires.

Maedoc

716 Guardian and Friend,
as we thank you for the numerous people
Maedoc befriended and turned into your friends,
release in us the spirit of friendship
and draw many folk into the circle of your love.

Malo

717 Rugged and real was your servant Malo, Lord,
a man of faith, though not without faults.
You are a real God
and on Earth you were tempted as we are.
Help us to be real for your sake
and for the sake of the world.

Martha, Mary and Lazarus

718 Tender Saviour,
who enjoyed the cosiness and company
of the Bethany household,
may the goodness of friendship
grow in our households:
friendship without guile,
friendship without malice,
friendship without striving.

Martin

719 Great God,
who called Martin from the armies of this world
to be a soldier of Christ
and to establish colonies of heaven,
inspire us to follow his example of humble service,
armed only with the sword of the Spirit.

720 Great God, thank you for Martin –
soldier, servant and soul-winner.
Inspire us by his example
to live lives of discipline and compassion
and to have an eye for building others up.

Mary Magdalene

721 O God our Desire,
you formed us in our mother's wombs
and call us by our names.
In the compassion of your suffering presence
may we know, as Mary Magdalene knew,
that you can make our violated bodies vessels of love.
In the strangeness of human attraction,
we put our trust in you,
knowing that we may live with you for ever.

Mary, mother of Jesus

722 Permeating Spirit,
in the darkness of the womb you brought Life,
and lit up Mary with joy.
Graceful her form, winsome her voice,
gentle her speech, stately her mien,
warm the look of her eye,
while her lovely white breast
heaves on her bosom
like the black-headed seagull
on the gently heaving wave.
Echoes Carmina Gadelica

723 Glory be to you
for the anointing of joy that you gave
to Mother Mary.
Glory be to you
for this queen among the angels
causing such delight in heaven,
such Life on Earth.

Matthew

724 God of insight,
who called Matthew
from the selfish pursuit of gain
to live and write
so that many would gain eternal riches,
free us from the possessive love of money,
that we may reveal
the treasures of your kingdom to others.

Modan

725 Sweet Saviour,
who made Modan a delight,
even to those who needed discipline,
help us to do our work with joy,
to say our piece with sweetness,
and to give pleasure by our wholeheartedness.

Mungo (Kentigern)

726 Thank you for Mungo's mother
who cherished a child born of rape.
Thank you for the robin restored
through Mungo's boyhood prayers.
Thank you for Mungo who spread the Faith
among peoples of cruel unbelief.
Thank you for Glasgow
which began as Mungo's dear little family.

Mellangell

727 Alive to you through her calling of prayer,
Melangell blessed the land of Pennant.
She made it into a sanctuary
and you have hallowed it ever since.

Teach us to cherish your creatures
and hallow the place where we live.
Draw us into that place
where we are safe at last in your heart's core.
Echoes a prayer of a Pennant Melangell pilgrim

Nathan

728 Pilgrim God,
who through the prophet Nathan
rebuked a king's misdoing
and reminded your people
that you always seek to lead them on,
restore honesty to our public life.
May our position never be a pretext
for resisting your Spirit.

Nectan

729 Holy God,
who led your servant Nectan
to plant the Faith of Christ in virgin Cornish land
and to reach out to others in the victorious Spirit of Christ,
may the Tree of Death become the healing Tree of Life
in barren and violent places today.

Neot

730 Spacious God, though Neot was small in stature,
you made him great by your boundless grace.
In our littleness, enlarge our wisdom;
in our need, give us provision;
in difficult times, may praise fill our days.

Nicholas

731 Parent of orphans,
Guardian of the young,
who through Nicholas rescued girls in danger,
make us aware of children's hidden cries for help;
inspire us to give our young people a good start in life,
and revive in us the true spirit of Santa Claus.

Ninian

732 We pray for modern Ninians
who will establish communities of light in slum places;
sanctuaries of prayer in unvisited places;
links of faith and love with the wider Christian world,
our spiritual home.

733 In Ninian there was nothing of fear; all was love.
Forgive us for the places in our lives
where fear has driven out love.
In Ninian truth and holiness shone out.
Forgive us for the places in our lives
which are false or frozen.
Help us to take authority in your name
over every confused or unsavoury situation.

Oswald

734 High King of heaven,
whose servant Oswald
was the first to model Christlike rule
among the English people,
redeem our land from the curse of disobedience
and bring it into the wholeness
of your just and gentle rule.

Pachomius

735 God of order born of love,
who through Pachomius
drew people to live in colonies of heaven
as bees live in hives:
come into our disordered world
and build colonies of heaven
suited to our time.

Patrick

736 Like Patrick, Father,
give us winsomeness
to woo a rising generation for you.
Saviour, give us boldness
to confront the seats of evil for you.
Spirit, give us imagination
to communicate the Truth for you.
Trinity, give us grace
to turn adversity into advance for you.
True and only God, give us holiness
to conquer the corroding invasion of worldly charms.

737 Father, you affirmed your Son at his baptism
before he entered a time of testing.
Father, you affirmed your servant Patrick
in the midst of his time of trial.
Father, affirm us in our time of need.
May we rest in the assurance
that we are each the apple of your eye.

Petroc

738 Gentle Christ of Bodmin Moor,
who kept Petroc's monks and friends of fur,
Great Protector, strong to save,
whose arm can bind the restless wave,
hear our cry, O Trinity,
for those at risk on land and sea.

Piran

739 As we thank you for Piran's faith communities in Cornwall
and for his 'animal monastery' on Bodmin Moor, we pray:
deep harmony of the forest be ours;
childlike love for God's creatures be ours;
growing trust in God's providence be ours.

Ruth

740 God of all peoples,
in the life of Ruth you show us
how through faith people of all races and creeds
can become part of your family.
May we cherish every human life
and embrace folk of every race
as brothers and sisters of the Infant King.

Samson

741 We bless you, Lord,
that Samson's birth, schooling and calling
were the fruit of prophecy.
We thank you, Lord, that his prayer,
his heroic acts of witness,
his courtesy and wonderful love towards all
won pagans to the Faith and patterned
a new way of being the Church.
As we contemplate his life,
give us a holy renewal.

Sebastian

742 Holy God, strong and patient,
resolute against wrong,
make us firmer in our faith,
inspire us by the martyrdom and the story of Sebastian,
and put fibre into our being.

Sebbi

743 All-advancing God, help us, after setback,
like Sebbi to think and pray on the grand scale,
and to reach out prayerfully.

Seraphim

744 Eternal Fire,
who lit up the cold stable at Bethlehem
through the birth of your Son,
and enflamed the snows of Russia
through your servant Seraphim,
pour upon the weakness of our nature
the transforming fire of your presence.

Stephen

745 The dying martyr Stephen knelt down
and cried, 'Lord Jesus, receive my spirit.'
Jesus, my Helper,
my Encircler, receive my spirit.
Jesus, only begotten Son
and Lamb of God the Father, receive my spirit.
Jesus, Son of David,
my Strength Everlasting, receive my spirit.
You who gave the wine-blood of your body
to buy me from the grave, receive my spirit.
My Christ, my Shield,
my Encircler, receive my spirit.
In my standing, in my stumbling,
in my ending, receive my spirit.

Sunniva and her companions

746 Blest are those women who crossed the sea
and made holy a hard place.
May pilgrims to Selje be inspired
by their story to take risks for you.

Teresa of Avila

747 Spouse of Heaven,
     who called Teresa to holy daring,
     may we walk this royal road through joy and pain
     until we know that in all things you are sufficient.

Theodore

748 God of Unity,
     who alone can create order that is life-giving,
     may we learn from your faithful servant Theodore
     to work for the common good,
     to encourage holy learning
     and to be faithful stewards
     of what you have handed on to us.

Tuda

749 Overarching God,
     we thank you for the authenticity of Tuda's faith
     lived out in a changing framework at Lindisfarne.
     Keep us in the beautiful attitudes:
     simple, prayerful and generous.

Tudwal

750 Mighty God,
     you sheltered Tudwal and his people
     during their flight to Brittany
     as once you sheltered the holy family
     during their flight to Egypt.
     Shelter us in the unsettling transitions of our lives.

Wenceslas

751 All-forgiving God, thank you for Wenceslas,
clear of purpose, full of courage and compassion.
We pray for those in leadership today, that,
hostage to neither fear nor favour,
they may model forgiveness in politics
and tread a path for the world to follow.

All saints

752 With Christ, to whom the spirits were subject,
we claim the victory of the Lord.
With the desert Christians from whom the demons fled,
we claim the victory of the Lord.
With hermits who made wild places safe with love,
we claim the victory of the Lord.
With martyrs who vaulted over death,
we claim the victory of the Lord.
With prayer warriors who overthrew hell's great might,
we claim the victory of the Lord.
With Patrick who freed his land of serpent powers,
we claim the victory of the Lord.
With Columba who rebuked the powers of dark,
we claim the victory of the Lord.
With Brigid who turned strongholds into havens of peace,
we claim the victory of the Lord;
With Cuthbert, healer and conqueror of the dark places,
we claim the victory of the Lord.
We place into your hands
the places that will be little used
in the season of dark and cold.
God of the waiting ones,
as the saints do in heaven
may we do on Earth:
in using our gifts,
in caring for others,
in holy dying.

753 We give thanks for your saints
 who shine in radiant brightness.
 May the saints and the angels light up our night
 and urge us on to heavenly virtues:
 the virtues of peace and love,
 devotion to you and justice to all,
 wise friendship and a constant life,
 faithful work and constant praise.

754 Eternal Friend, as we thank you
 for your cloud of witnesses who shine so brightly
 and who beckon to us so eagerly,
 help us to grow strong and holy like them,
 that we may live more fully and boldly for you
 and keep our eyes on the eternal kingdom.

755 Great Spirit,
 encouraged by your cloud of witnesses,
 give us an increased anointing.
 Help us to take your Word deep into our souls,
 to live it out, bravely, freely, creatively;
 to be cheerful when we want to complain,
 to be patient when we want to flare up,
 to push on when we want to stand still,
 to keep silent when we want to prattle,
 and to love when we want to harden our hearts.

God with us

Awareness of the Presence

756 God of signs and wonders,
you teach us through your prophets
that these come only
through the continual washing of the eyes.
Wash our eyes, and take our ears;
teach us to listen,
not to the surface babble of a sick society,
but to the deep, pure truth that comes from you.

757 We come into the presence of the sending Father.
We come into the presence of the pilgrim Son.
We come into the presence of the blowing Spirit,
into the presence of the Three in One.

758 All-aware One,
quieten our fevered minds,
subdue our overheated souls,
rest our stressed bodies.
In quietness and confidence be our strength.

759 Help me to listen
to the fragile feelings,
not to the clashing fury;
to the still centre,
not to the noisy clamour;
to the deep symphonies,
not to the surface discord.

760 When the ride is bumpy and the world passes us by,
you are God with us.
When we are edged aside and doors are shut in our faces,
you are God with us.
When others are out to get us
and our homes are not secure,
you are God with us.
When our lives are but a flicker in the encroaching dark,
you are God with us.
The God of life be our champion and leader.

We shall not be left in the hand of the wicked;
we shall not be bent in the court of the false;
we shall rise victorious above them
as rise victorious the crests of the waves.

761 Great Creator of the deep red moon and falling stars;
Great Saviour of the miraculous birth
and rising from death;
Great Spirit of the seers and sacred words:
come into our minds,
come into our mouths
until we become your presence and sign.

762 O Yahweh,
I Am, Being.
In you is my being.
Eternal Source.
Fount of Life.
In you is my life.
You are with us.
We are with you.

763 God be in our day and in our sleeping.
God be in our work and in our resting.
God be in our gain and in our losing.
God be in our growth and in our fading.
God be in our life and in our departing.

764 God of the thunder,
God of the sap,
God of the future,
God of the map,
God of the silence,
God of the gap,
God of our happenings,
God in our lap.

765 May you be honoured in our hearts,
in our homes, in our homeland.
May you be honoured in the workplace,
in the war zones, in the world.
May your will be done in our places of need,
in their place of need.
May your economy, your civilisation,
come on Earth as it is in heaven.

766 Fill this moment, Lord.
Open our eyes to your presence;
open our ears to your call;
open our hearts to your glory;
now, in us, in all.

767 God of gods, establish your presence among us.
God of gods, may your fire purge the wastelands.
May your people advance from one virtue to another
and may the kingdoms of this world
become the kingdom of our God.

768 Christ, born of the loveliest Mary,
you are with us in our birth.
Christ, brought up as a carpenter,
you are with us in our work.
Christ, friend of seeker and outcast,
you are with us in our friendships.
Christ, noble in suffering and death,
you are with us in our trials.
Christ, eternal Son of God,
you are with us evermore.

769 Jesus –
truly God, truly human,
truly infinite, truly frail.
Your greatness holds the universe.
Your lovely countenance attracts our hearts.
Your goodness beckons all that is good in us.
Your wisdom searches us.

Your truth sheds light on our darkness.
Your generosity enriches our poverty.
Your friendship consoles the unwanted.
Your strength turns away all evils.
Your justice deters wrongdoing.
Your power conquers hell.
Your love-enflamed heart kindles our cold hearts.
Your miraculous hand fills us with all blessings.
Your sweet and holy name rejoices all who love you.
Your mercy brings forgiveness.
Have mercy on us.
Give us eternal life,
for your glory fills eternity;
your glory fills the universe.

770 We bind to ourselves today
the nurturing Parent,
the befriending Christ,
the blowing Spirit.

771 God in our rising and lying down;
God in our dressing and undressing;
God in our cleaning and cooking;
God in our locking and unlocking;
God in our greeting and speaking;
God in our counting and viewing;
God in the little things;
God in this thing;
God in that thing;
God in all things.

772 The Three who are over our head,
the Three who provide our bread,
be with us wherever we tread.

773 Jesus, Master Carpenter of Nazareth,
who through wood and nails won our full salvation,
wield well your tools in this your workshop,
that we who come to you rough-hewn
may here be fashioned into a truer beauty by your hand.

774 God who has made us to live in rhythm,
   help us to find the rhythm you desire for each of us.
   Help us to live in it,
   to thrive on it
   and to grow through it,
   until we reflect your rhythms on earth as they are in heaven.

775 Silently the Earth yields her fruits.
   Silently we lie as in earth.
   Do your work in us,
   slowly, soundlessly.
   This is the mystery of Being.
   This is your Presence in us.

776 From today and always, may we
   look upon each person we meet
   with the eyes of Christ,
   speak to each person we meet
   with the words of Christ,
   and go wherever we are led
   with the peace of Christ.

777 Help us, Great Spirit, to
   live in you as fish live in water,
   soar with you as birds fly in air,
   run for you as deer run in woods,
   flow with you as water flows in streams,
   blaze for you as twigs burn in fire.

778 Help us to sense your presence among us, O Christ,
   in the gentle touch,
   in the listening ear,
   in the patient toil,
   in the concern for the poor,
   in the challenging of wrong,
   in the brokenness of life.

779 You are here, Lord, in this place.
   May your cross free it.
   May your love woo it.

May your prayers hallow it.
May your peace still it.
May your life renew it.

780 Jesus, Pattern of goodness,
be our Pattern today.
Jesus, Hope of the weak,
be our Hope today.
Jesus, Fulfiller of our longings,
be our Fulfiller today.
Jesus, Bridge between Earth and heaven,
be our Bridge today.

781 You who shaped the coastlines
and put healing sounds into the earth,
may our hearts flow into you
as small springs flow into the big sea.

782 Day by day, dear God,
teach us from your Word and your world;
lead us on our pilgrimage of life;
help us to live in your rhythms;
spur us to overcoming prayer;
strip from us all that clutters;
cherish through us your creation;
heal through us what is broken;
blow us to places beyond our comfort zones;
inspire us to foster unity;
reach out through us with your justice, truth and love,
that we may flame and struggle for you for ever.

783 Lord, give us that love which does not fail people;
make our lives like an open fire
that you are always kindling,
which nothing can quench.
O Saviour most sweet,
may we receive perpetual light from you,
so that the world's darkness may be driven from us.
O eternal Priest, may we see you,
observe you, desire you, and love you alone
as you shine in your eternal temple.

784 Thank you, Father, for your free gift of fire,
because it is through fire
that you draw near to us every day;
it is with fire that you constantly bless us.
Our Father, bless this fire today.

785 God direct our hours,
protect our belongings,
still our hearts.

786 Risen Christ, give us your resurrection eyes
to see eternity in a grain of sand
and God in a gang of troublemakers;
to see fresh flowerings in worn-out places
and fresh life in burned-out believers.
Risen Christ, come to make all things new.

787 Peace and blessing from the Spirit
and from the Three who are ever One.

788 Eternal Light, shine into our hearts.
Eternal Goodness, deliver us from evil.
Eternal Power, strengthen us.
Eternal Wisdom, scatter the darkness of our ignorance.
Eternal Pity, have mercy on us.
With our whole being we shall seek your face
until we are brought to your holy presence.
After Alcuin

789 Christ be within us,
Christ be beside us,
Christ in the stranger,
Christ in the friend,
Christ in our speaking,
Christ in our thinking,
Christ in our working,
Christ at our end.

790 We make the sign of the Cross of Christ [make sign].
Our Christ, our Shield, our Saviour,
each day, each night, in light, in dark,
our Treasure, our dear One,
our eternal home.

791 We come to you, God of surprises,
alert and watchful.
Awaken in us awareness of our origins in you
and the needs of the world,
that droplets of eternity may fall from us on this Earth.
Make us sensitive to the motions of your Spirit –
in our souls, in the faces of others,
and in the meetings we did not expect.

Make us prepared, like a samurai warrior,
for the next move.
May we move with you, attentive and supple,
alert to opportunities and pitfalls.
Make us aware of your presence
in each waking moment.
Keep us ready,
even in the depths of night and the evening of life,
that we may relish the coming privilege
of sitting at table with you and being served by you.

792 Lord Jesus,
take my gaze away from the false persona of myself
as the person who is right.
Lord Jesus,
take my gaze away from my false projections of others
as the persons who are wrong.
Gently turn my gaze to you.
You see into the place of hurt and weakness in me
and there allow love to be revealed.
And let me see your beauty in the face of another.

793 Silent, surrendered, at your feet,
we bow before your presence.
Open to your every word
we linger, longing, waiting.

794 We are sorry that we have not given time to be present:
to turn off the screen and have fun with those in our home,
to grow our own vegetables and savour the earth and its yield,
to keep a day of rest and value human community,
to sleep and spare others the battering of a mindless life.

795 In silence I become aware of you, O God.
In the silence I adore you.
In the silence my sins stand out and are washed away.
In the silence my problems fall into their rightful place.
In the silence I become a grateful person,
and in the silence, O God, we become one.

796 Keeper of eternity,
help me keep you ever before me.
Help me keep the example of your saints
ever before me.
Help me keep sufficient sense of proportion
to relax when needed,
to savour the blessings of hospitality
with ever-grateful poise.

797 I see to the fridge in the presence
of the angel of the loveliest delights.
I see to the washer in the presence
of Mary of the pure-white demeanour.
I see to the garage in the presence
of Joseph of the fine workmanship.
I see to the office in the presence
of the Creator of order.
I see to the people I shall meet in the presence
of the all-friendly Christ.
I see to the things that will batter my mind
in the presence of the all-calming Dove.

798 We bring to you the child that craves affection.
We bring to you the child that fears to trust.
We bring to you the child that shrinks at conflict.
We bring to you our assets going to rust.

Compassion

799 All-compassionate One,
pour out your compassion through us,
that we may be instruments to set others free:
those who walk through life with their feet in fetters,
clobbered with unjust burdens,
captives in prisons of body or spirit.

800 Dearest Christ, you have given love,
given it exquisitely.
In your tiredness
you washed your friends' tired feet.
In your generosity
you gave bread to your betrayer.
In your all-seeing provision
you bequeathed a sacrament of nourishment for our souls
that makes you constantly present to us.
In your prayers
you ever place your people
in the Divine heart.
Out of love for you,
we too will offer
a many-splendoured love to the world.

801 Spirit, kindle in our hearts
a flame of love
to our foes,
to our friends,
to all.

802 Take our hands, dear Christ,
that your compassion
may flow through them out to others.
With these hands give tender touch
to those who are forgotten.
With these hands give warmth
to those left in the cold.
With these hands shield your messengers
from ills that would attack them.

With these hands dispel darkness from the old.
With these hands heal lost and suffering people.
Take our hands, dear Christ,
that your compassion
may flow through them out to others.

803 Lord Jesus Christ,
Light of the World,
by your cross
you have overcome all darkness that oppresses.
Come and shine on us,
that we may grow and live together in your love
that makes us one with all humanity.

804 Great God who mothers us all,
gather the sufferings of all
into the communion of the crucified Christ.
Shield and deliver them
and look on them with your merciful gaze.

805 Merciful One,
may your compassion flow through our hands.
May they offer tender touch
to people who are deprived of touch or tenderness.
May they offer human warmth
to people who are cold or dispirited.
May they offer practical care
to people who are weary and overworked.

806 O Christ, you had compassion on the crowds;
you drew people to yourself;
you repelled none who came in need.
Grant us hearts like yours,
hearts that go out in genuine greeting
and humble welcome,
until, in the fellowship of sharing,
souls are drawn to you.

807 O God,
   you have prepared for those who love you
   such good things as pass our understanding.
   Pour into our hearts such love towards you
   that we love every person and every thing
   with your heart of compassion.

Love for all

808 God of outpouring mercy,
   pour into us your love of the whole human family.
   Move our hearts with compassion to cry mercy
   for a world lost in illusion, greed and war.
   Deliver us from praying our own agenda,
   that we may seek your best for all.
   Renew us in your Spirit
   with the passion to intercede.

809 Father, Mother God,
   we are your children.
   Meet our need to be needed.
   Help us so to love ourselves and others
   that we can say 'Yes' out of love and 'No' out of love
   and trust that you will bless the outcome.

Work

810 Your glory be seen in work that is done from the heart.
   Your glory be seen in work that meets true needs.
   Your glory be seen
   in communication that ennobles the spirit.
   Your glory be seen in beauty of form and friendship.

811 Divine Benefactor, whose desire is that work
   be a character-forming gift,
   help us to welcome and engage in work,
   whether it be the routine duties of life or paid employment.

When work becomes a perversion of your gift,
we pray that it may be redeemed,
that every business may put humane values above greed.
Help us to stand against pressures to overwork,
which robs you, others and ourselves
of the time that belongs to each.

812 Be in the humdrum,
be in the highs.
Be in the setbacks,
be in the skies.
Be in the interruptions,
be in the cries.
Be in the people,
be in the eyes.

813 Christ be in the work and each thing we do.
Christ be in our hands and each thing we touch.
Christ be in our minds and each thing we think.
We pray for those who are jaded by the pressures of work:
put colour into their lives.
We pray for workplaces where conditions are grim:
put colour into these places.
We pray for ourselves in the heat and burden of the day:
put colour into our being.

814 Help me to put my best into my work,
to think of things I can be grateful for,
to strive to improve working conditions
for my colleagues and myself,
and for those who have no workplace protection,
considering it an honour to develop,
by means of labour, some of the gifts
God has given me.

815 Bless all work done today
that enables the human family
to be clothed, fed and housed,

to travel and learn,
to communicate and exchange wisely,
to craft and celebrate,
in everything reflecting your glory.

816 Worker Christ, as we enter our workplace,
may we bring your presence with us.
Grace us to speak your peace and perfect order
into its atmosphere.
Remind us to acknowledge your authority
over all that will be thought, decided
and accomplished within it.
Give us a fresh supply of truth and beauty
on which to draw as we work.
Echoes a prayer of Julia McGuinness

817 Bless to us, O God,
everything our eyes shall see.
Bless to us, O God,
everything our hands shall do.
Bless to us, O God,
everything our brains shall think.
Bless to us, O God,
each person we shall work with.
Bless to us, O God,
the place and the equipment.
Bless to us, O God,
the people we shall serve through our work.

818 Be in the interruptions and the setbacks.
Be in the eye of the person who is difficult.
Be in the eye of the person who is a delight.

819 May our work be faithful.
May our work be honest.
May our work be blessed.
May our work bless others.
May our work bless you.

820 Lord Jesus, as we think of your teaching
that we should use our talents,
we give you what talents we have,
even if we think they are not much.
We have time to give
helping hands and listening ears.
Give us wisdom and flare to use these
to the full for the building up of your ways on Earth.

821 Lord Jesus,
you taught that your apostles would be given
great responsibilities in the next life.
Remind us that we neither come to a standstill
nor are we snuffed out when we leave this body,
and that how we use our opportunities on Earth
affects how you will use us in heaven.
So motivate us to work hard
with all that you give our hands and hearts to do.

822 May I do my rounds today under the shield of the angels.
May I mix the ingredients of our meals
in the presence of Mary of the Nazareth kitchen.
May I plan my business dealings
with the Gatekeeper who keeps out what is false.
May I use my hands with the Cross often in my fingers.
May I exercise my body
with thankfulness pulsing in my mind.
May I rest my head on my pillow
with the Three lying beside me.

823 Your glory be seen
in work that is done from the heart.
Your glory be seen
in work that meets true needs.
Your glory be seen
in communication that ennobles the spirit.
Your glory be seen
in beauty of form and friendship.

824   Each of us has some work to do.
We do our work as to you, Lord.
We think our thoughts as to you.
We clean our rooms as to you, Lord.
We send messages as to you.
We shop and eat as to you, Lord.
We care for others as to you.

825   Come and put a glory in our work today.
Come and put a shine on the noontime fray.
May the Glory come now from the heavens high,
the Glory come to us; the Glory come nigh.

826   *Office*

Bless this little space
that so many people come through.
May the papers be kept in order.
May unnecessary things come to their end.
May each telephone call
be met with a welcoming voice.
When something breaks down,
may we rise up.
Bless the people who come into this space.

827   *New job/position*

God's blessing be upon you in this new office.
May you be
not too conceited, or you will lose the bonds of trust;
not too naive, or you will be deceived;
not too diffident, or you will fail to convince;
not too talkative, or you will not be heard;
not too silent, or you will not be heeded;
not too hard, or you will be broken;
not too feeble, or you will be disregarded.

Redundancy

828 Bless to us, O God,
    this loss, that we may grow through grieving;
    this worry, that we may learn through trusting;
    this space, that we may develop through creating;
    this grim time,
    that we may become gracious through bearing.

829 God bless to you this loss,
    that you may know the eternal boss.
    God bless you in being poor,
    that providence will open its door.
    God bless to you this 'grave',
    and help you rise from it brave.

830 *Joining up – armed forces*
    May you have
    truth in your hearts,
    strength in your arms,
    consistency in your tongues,
    nobility in your deeds,
    mercy in your being.

Healing: physical and spiritual

831 May the Divine Father
    make us instruments of healing.
    May the Complete Christ
    take from us all that frustrates healing.
    May the Holy Spirit
    give us power for healing.

832 We invite you, generous Healer,
    into abandoned and wasted areas of our lives.
    Visit these places with compassion.
    Shine kindly and forgiving rays
    of understanding upon them,
    until the beauty that is within us comes forth,
    and our spirits sing again.

833 May we be lit by the glory of God,
     filled with the health of God,
     always tender and true.

834 Great Spirit who broods over the world,
     restore the garment of our self-respect
     and remake us in your beauty.
     Renew in us
     the stillness of our being,
     the soundness of our bodies,
     and bring to dawn our wholeness.

835 Lord, help me to understand my own story,
     to fear nothing except fear itself,
     and to live at peace
     with myself, the creatures and the world.

836 May failures be forgiven,
     wounds be healed,
     confusions be resolved,
     ignorance be dispelled,
     relationships be treasured.

837 God, Source of our Being,
     we acknowledge that we are fragmented.
     Our communities are suffering.
     Give us courage to look at the wound
     at the heart of everything:
     the wound we run away from,
     the wound we hardly dare name.

838 In each hidden thought our minds start to weave,
     be our canvas and our weaver.
     In each wounded memory to which we cleave
     be our counsel and our healer.

839 We confess that we wound one another.
     Our world is disordered.
     Accompany us on a journey towards wholeness.

840 Spirit of the living God, present with us now,
     circle these we have named.
     Enter their bodies, minds and spirits,
     and heal them of all that harms.

841 May illness depart from our eyes.
     May weakness depart from our eyes.
     May soreness depart from our eyes.
     May hardness depart from our eyes.
     May sourness depart from our eyes.
     May lewdness depart from our eyes,
     in the name of the all-seeing Healer.

842 Give us faith that heeds your call to heal.
     Give us eyes that see your healing rays.
     Give us speech that transmits your healing words.
     Give us hands that bring your healing touch.
     Give us grace to give to you the glory.

843 Before your Cross, O Christ,
     we recollect one story of wounding.
     We ask for your mercy
     upon this wounded person and people.
     We ask your forgiveness for our people.
     We ask for the healing of the wound
     and the birth of our common humanity.

844 Life-giver, Pain-bearer, Being of Love,
     you hold in your heart our names
     and the hurts we cannot bear to speak of.
     You journey with us through pain
     until you reconcile
     all that we have rejected in ourselves,
     and no part of your creation is alien to us.

845 We come to God as we are,
     with our hurts and our hungers.
     We come to the One whose love restores us.
     We encircle ourselves and others.

Heal our ailments.
Renew our weary frames.
Make us whole.

846 Help us, O Healing One,
to stop dwelling on what others achieve that we don't.
As we look on the pattern in the palm of each hand,
we thank you that each is uniquely personal.
May we grow in confidence, love and creativity
according to the designs you have for us.
We forgive the ones who make us feel inferior.
Meet their needs; help them find their best course.
Heal and have mercy on us all.

847 Jesus, you healed a mother of her sickness:
heal those who have caught an infection.
Jesus, you restored the troubled to their right mind:
restore those whose minds are fragmented.
Jesus, you raised the dead:
raise up those who have been struck down.

848 Forgive our nations for bingeing on borrowed money
that our children will have to repay.
Cure our debt addiction.
Have mercy upon us as we reap what we sow,
that we may show mercy to one another.

849 Jesus, when we are weak,
remind us that your strength
can reach others through our weakness.
Open our eyes
to notice what you notice.
Open our mouths
to speak one healing, life-giving word.

Hospitals

850 God of wholeness,
may our hospitals not be centres of disease
but centres of healing.
May they not treat cases but help people.
May nurses and doctors,
cleaners and chaplains,
administrators and ambulance drivers
increase their compassion.
May many grow well,
others die well,
and staff work well.
Through Christ the Great Physician.

Grace of God

851 Guide us, our great Mentor,
through the ups and downs of life.
Strengthen us to leave behind what hinders our calling,
and to keep moving towards ever-greater reality.

852 O Being of truth,
O Being of sight,
O Being of wisdom,
give us judgement in our choices.

O Being of life,
O Being of peace,
O Being of time,
be with us now.

We quieten our souls under the stillness of sky.
Peace be upon our breath.
Peace be upon our eyes.
Peace be upon our hearts.

853 Great Spirit, help us to relax into your plan for us.
Unfold it for us as the acorn unfolds into the oak.

HEALING: PHYSICAL AND SPIRITUAL

854 Ever-shielding Father,
ever-loving Son,
life-giving Holy Spirit,
ever Three in One:
rain grace on us and heal us
and we shall lie down in peace.
Rain grace on us and heal us
and we shall lie down in peace.

855 God, fill your people with your Spirit
and give us skill, ability and understanding
of every kind of artistic work.

856 Glorious Three,
shine upon our tired and drooping hearts.
Complete the work to which you have called us.
Pour lovingly and generously upon us hour by hour.

857 Zeal of God, fill our being.
Truth of God, light our way.
Peace of God, redeem our past.
Love of God, come in to stay.

Seeking God's help

Learning with God: weaknesses

858 Lord, in our hour of need, come to us.
In our weakness, give us strength.
In our actions, give us courage.
In our words, give us grace.

859 Lord, when we are insulted,
help us to refrain from hitting back;
throw away resentment
and offer a challenge of tough love.
When our rights are overridden
or our privileges are taken for granted,

help us to refrain from enforcing them with malice
or selfishly clutching at them,
but to inspire, through acts of generosity,
the other person to change.

When a bureaucrat requires us
to carry out some uncongenial task,
help us to refrain from the sour face,
catty remark or grudging body language;
rather, help us to be cheerful, friendly,
and to soften up the bureaucrat
by doing a little bit extra.

Enjoying life

860 As nature laughs in spring,
restore laughter to our lives.
When we become complaining and sour-faced,
put something funny into our minds.
Help us not to take ourselves too seriously
and to enjoy the world with you.

861 Make us eager to align our wills with yours.
Give us joy in our hearts, keep us serving.
May we grow in intimacy with you
until every one of our acts
is a glad response to your promptings.

862 *Qualities to aspire to*
Lord, make us true like arrows.
Make us dependable like rock.
Make us deep like anchors.
Make us incorruptible like salt.

863 *Our dealings with others*
Father, free us to enjoy and not possess another;
and free each to be oneself.
Grant us the purity within which friendship thrives.
Restore the joy of communion to us.

Serving the Lord

864 As we gaze into your light,
may the obedience of angels be ours;
may the joy of saints be ours;
may the humility of Mary be ours;
may the suffering of the cross be ours;
may the freeing of the bound spirits be ours;
may the glory of eternity be ours.

865 Divine Light encompassing us,
penetrate our souls, our minds and our bodies.
Cleansing, healing soul-light,
shine out into our business dealings;
shine out into all dealings;
shine out into the architecture of life.

Faith and trust

866 Lord, we have not much faith,
and we can't help it.
But help us to use the little faith we have,
so that it grows day by day.
May we daily increase in trust and in valour.

867 Give to us thoughts greater than our own thoughts,
prayers deeper than our own prayers.
Give to us the arts of prayer –
prayers that rise like incense,
and thoughts that penetrate to the Throne.

Discipleship

868 Teach us, dear God,
to be lifelong disciples;
to think your thoughts after you,
to develop a sense of wonder,
to trace your hand in history,
to understand the times;

to distinguish the true from the false,
to relate the part to the whole,
to see and serve the greatness in others.

869　We give you worship with our whole life.
We give you praise with our whole tongue.
We give you service with our whole body.
We give you love with our whole heart.
We give you honour with our whole desire.
We give you our best thoughts, our deeds, our words,
our wills, our understanding, our relationships,
our intellects, our journeys, our ends.

Echoes a prayer from Carmina Gadelica

870　Lord, make our lives an open book
that good people may read.
Take from us the judging heart
and the spirit that bangs doors shut.
Weed out falseness.
Help us accept our weakness.
May our light shine.

871　Help us, God of the whole created world, to:
buy wisely,
use energy carefully,
travel prayerfully,
eat mindfully,
exchange thoughtfully.

872　Help us, Lord,
to respond to fresh initiatives of your Spirit
in a way that honours other Christians
and builds up the Body of Christ.

873　May we be mindful in our speaking and in our eating.
May we be peaceful in our sleeping and in our rising.
May we be noble in our acting and in our dying.

874 Thank you for those who have made covenant with you.
Inspired by their example,
may we pledge ourselves to be faithful
in both achievement and adversity,
to be constant in disappointment,
to reach out in love even when others fail us;
to encourage the talents of those who lack confidence,
to be graceful in our speech and unceasing in our praise.

875 Lord, with joy we pledge our love of you.
We are no longer our own but yours.
Put us to what you will;
place us with whom you will;
let us be put to work for you or put aside for you;
let us be full, let us be empty;
let us have all things, let us have nothing.
We freely and, with all our heart,
give you all things for you to use.
May we walk together with you
into the community, that nothing can perish.

876 O our Lord,
make our coming in true and honest
and our going out true and honest.
And from your presence,
grant us your enabling power.
For you are the Creator of all.
You are the One and the only,
the all-competent.

Truth

877 Kindle our imaginations.
Rivet our attention with graphic truth.
Restock our memories with noble themes.

878 You are the refined molten forge of the human race.
Purge us of all that is false and unreal;
forge our characters until we are true:
true to ourselves, to others, to you.

879 God, eternally True,
save us from complicity in the lie,
the refusal to speak out,
the acquiescence in misrepresentation.
Steel us to speak out to expose what is wrong,
to vanquish lies,
in the strength of the One
who was put to death by a lie
but remained undefeated.

Contentment

880 Earth-maker God,
as the hand is made for holding and the eyes for seeing,
you have fashioned us for joy.
Grant us your vision that we may find it everywhere –
in the sunlit faces of our world,
in the wild flower's beauty, in the lark's melody,
in a child's smile, in a mother's love,
in the face of a steadfast man.

881 Our society is ever restless,
always craving one more thing to do,
seeking happiness through more and more possessions.
Teach us to be at peace with what we have;
to embrace what we have given and received;
to know that enough is enough,
until our strivings cease
and we rest content in you alone.

882 God of destiny,
who through dreams
brought Joseph from poverty to plenty,
weave your dreams into our lives,
and make us content with your will,
in bad times and in good.

Appreciation and awareness

883   Make us attentive to the lap of the waves.
Make us attentive to the movements of the sky.
Make us attentive to the grasses that grow.
Make us attentive to the soul's every sigh.
Make us aware of the landscape that passes.
Make us aware of new scapes coming in.
Make us aware of your precious heartbeats.
Make us aware of the world within.

884   God of creation,
make us aware of your presence
in every cell of creation
and in every cell of our being.

885   In the flavour of a fruit,
in the flowing of a stream,
in the feeling of a sunset,
may we know that you are good.

886   When all was prepared,
you formed human beings from the soil.
You breathed your life into them.
May we never forget
that we are mortal creatures;
from earth we come, to earth we go.

887   May the media develop
a passion to understand the world
and interpret its many facets of reality
to its peoples.
Give us sight to see
when people are in distress.

888   God of creation,
your Spirit brooded over the chaos
and brought a universe to birth.
You rejoiced at each day of creation,
delighting in its goodness before the hosts of heaven.

You breathed your life into all creatures
and your Spirit into us,
and so made a marriage of heaven and Earth in us.
May we treasure our kinship with all creation,
which finds its liberation with ours in Jesus Christ.

889 You who put beam in moon and sun,
you who put fish in stream and sea,
you who put food in ear and herd,
send your blessing up to us.
Bring forth the warmth, the tears, the laughter
from our repressed and frozen ground;
bring forth loving, healing, forgiving
to our fretting, festering wound.

890 Craftsperson of the heavens,
you have stretched out above us
a canopy of stars which are signs
of hope renewed in darkest times.
Brightener of the night,
open to us the treasures of darkness:
its deepest wisdom and its healing power

891 There is no plant in the ground
but it is full of your virtue,
O King of the virtues.
May these plants bring your blessing to us.
There is no life in the earth
but it proclaims your goodness,
O King of goodness.
May these plants bring your goodness to us.

892 May we be real like the elements.
May we be true like the fire.
May we be free like the wind.
May the love that is within us flow like water.
And may we not forget the fifth element, the flowers.
Dear God, give us fragrance in our relationships.

893 Great Creator of the glowing moon and falling stars;
great Saviour of the miraculous birth and rising from death;
great Spirit of the seers and sacred words:
come into our minds,
come into our dreams,
come into our mouths,
until we become your presence and sign.

894 The elements bear your Creator's stamp –
the air that enables all things to breathe,
the fire that allows us to cook.
These proclaim your presence and so shall we:
in bikes and buses,
cartwheels and calligraphy,
clothes and cakes,
climbing and clapping,
coins and credit cards,
cars and caravans,
drums and dance,
football and food,
fashion and films,
ice cream and ice skating,
paint and pigment,
postcards and posters,
rising and running,
trains and planes,
swimming and skateboarding,
wine and whisky.

895 Divine Fashioner of Forms,
we trace your footprints in coral reefs and choral music,
in ancient fossils and modern festivals,
in mountain torrents and satellite towers,
in ocean waves and wireless transmissions.
All things work together for good.
How wonderful are your works.

896 Lord, you are our island; in your bosom we rest.
You are the calm of the sea; in that peace we stay.
You are the deep waves of the shining ocean;
with their eternal sound we sing.

You are the song of the birds; in that tune is our joy.
You are the smooth white sand of the shore;
in you is no gloom.
You are the breaking of the waves on the rock;
your praise is echoed in the swell.
You are the Lord of our lives; in you we dwell.
Echoes a prayer attributed to St Columba

897 Bathe us in your cleansing rivers.
Soak us in your healing waters.
Drench us in your powerful downfalls.
Cool us in your bracing baths.
Refresh us in your sparkling streams.
Master us in your mighty seas.
Calm us by your quiet pools.

898 Great Spirit,
you nod and beckon to us through every stone and star.
Your life surges towards us in every greening leaf.
We hear you in the quiet pools and storm-tossed waves.
We are touched by your beauty in bird-wing and blossom.
We come to you.

899 Uncreated Beauty,
who graces everything that has been created,
as the hand is made for holding and the eyes for seeing,
grant that we may behold your beauty
in the lovers' embrace,
in a mother's love, in the face of a steadfast man,
and in the twilight of the gloaming;
until the beauty that is within us
comes forth and sings to you.

900 May those who are bereft of loved ones
after an act of terror walk out their loss
and find a healing process.
May each one who died be replaced
by one who makes a new way of life.
As Nehemiah rebuilt the ruined city walls,
may we rebuild what is broken, God being our helper.

901 Earth, teach us stillness.
Earth, teach us humility.
May we allow ourselves to be
softened by rain,
dug deep by Providence,
planted with Wisdom's seeds,
replenished by rest
and made into a hospitable bed for others.

Authenticity

902 Lord help me
never to pretend
to know more than I do know,
always to be ready to speak out of my experience –
up to my experience
but not to speak beyond it.

903 Make us true,
for there are those who trust us.
Make us right with you –
all else is treachery.
Life-saving –
hold that in our heads;
peace-making please,
wherever we tread.
Your Word to sharpen us
and give a cutting edge.
Faith and prayer,
these to you we pledge.

904 God with us.
Be in my waking and working,
be in my cleaning and counting.
God with us.
Be in my talking and texting,
be in my shopping and sharing.
God in the little things;
God in this thing;
God in that thing;
God in all things.

905 Take from me, O God:
pride and prejudice,
hardness and hypocrisy,
selfishness and self-sufficiency,
that I may be vulnerable, like you.

906 Lord, I crave the approval of others
and I don't like standing out in a crowd.
Yet you want me to be true and honest.
Give me grace to pray for and stand by
people who are mocked because of their faith.

907 Give me the ambition
to use everything I have for the highest purposes,
to abuse no person,
to misuse no powers,
to harness skills to service,
and to bring great things to flower.

908 Servant King,
be king of my hearth and king of my heart;
be king of my hands and king of my head;
be king of my shoes and king of my style.

909 Lord, may these graces flower as never before:
the grace of authenticity and trust,
the grace of forgiving love and laughter,
the maturity of pity for those who manipulate.

910 Help me to be true to myself and true to you.
Help me to be true to others and true to the call.
Help me to be true to Earth and true to heaven.

Led by God

911 Christ who stilled the storm,
still the turmoil within.
Christ who overcame ill,
overcome the evil without.

912 Holy Three,
help us to live at the still centre
of the world's whirring wheels,
where everything is led by you.

913 Three of Limitless Love, may I fall into your lap.
I strain to be accepted by people whose approval I desire.
I fear lest I go astray or be left adrift on the ocean,
alone in a little boat named 'Ego'.
You are always there, inviting me to come in from the cold.
But I do not know how to.
I am conditioned to be stuck where I am.
Jesus, reach into my soul and place me
on the lap of the Three of Limitless Love.

914 Help us to follow you
in strength of Trinity, living
by Scripture's guidance,
in soul friends' confidence,
in life's rhythms,
in overcoming prayer,
in simplicity of life,
in stewardship of creation,
in the healing of the world,
in the stream of God's Spirit,
in solidarity with others,
in sharing with all.
After the vows of the Community of Aidan and Hilda

915 Lead us from that which binds to that which frees;
lead us from that which cramps to that which creates;
lead us from that which lies to that which speaks truth;
lead us from that which blights to that which ennobles;
lead us from that which hides to that which celebrates;
lead us from that which fades to that which endures.

916 Eternal Guide,
you led our forebears by cloud and fire;
lead us through the days and years.
You led your saints by sign and sail;
lead us now through whisper and wind.

917 We give you thanks, Kindly Light,
that you led our forebears in the Faith
through a cloud by day and a fire by night
and that you ever lead your people on.
We give you thanks that you have led us to this place.
Pour forth your kindness on your people,
Creator, Saviour, and radiant Spirit.

918 Lead us from wasting time to making good use of time.
Lead us from showing off to showing love.
Lead us from being unreal to being real.

919 Lead us from that which is partial
to that which makes whole.
Lead us from that which is false
to that which is real.
Lead us from that which is self-centred
to that which is good.
Lead us from that which fades
to that which endures.

920 Mighty Anchor in our storms,
brightest Light in our darkness,
lead us from despair to hope,
contempt to praise,
falsehood to truth,
hatred to love,
violence to peace.

Peace

921 So much of the media is sound and fury signifying nothing.
Teach it to signify something.
So much of the Internet is much ado about nothing.
Teach us to make much of what is eternally important.

922 May our nation find your will as her destiny,
and have God-guided representatives at home and abroad.
May she find peace within herself
and become a peacemaker in the international family.

923 Source of Peace,
war is the price we pay
for the selfishness of nations.
Help us to wage endless war against selfishness.
Peace is the fruit of constant endeavour for the good.
Help us to struggle without ceasing
for good to triumph over evil.

924 All-seeing Restrainer,
bless the peacemakers
and encourage those
who are engaged in conflict resolution.
May more people emulate you
and reach out to those who are different or defiant.

925 In the middle of bustle, give us stillness.
In the middle of tinsel, fill us with awe.
In the middle of tension, infuse us with peace.

926 Christ, the peace of things above
and the rest of those below,
establish in your peace the five continents,
and especially your universal Church.
Destroy wars and the causes of war
and disperse those who delight in terror.

927 Mighty Restorer, who brings back all,
with you we pray to the four corners of the world:
Al-Salem, Shalom, Peace, Harmony –
with our neighbours, with our environment,
with ourselves and with God.

928 Help us, Lord,
to guard our words,
to overcome hostility with love,
to make peace
in love of the King of Life.

May we look upon everyone
with the eyes of the Risen Christ:
shoppers and beggars,
politicians and Jihadists,
friends, critics
and the next person we meet.

929   We swear by peace and love to stand,
heart to heart and hand in hand.
Mark, O Spirit, and hear us now,
confirming this our sacred vow.

930   May the Sun of suns shine upon us,
bringing peace and poise.
May the healing rays come through us
until we frolic like the lambs.

Holy Spirit/spiritual gifts

931   Gracious God,
may your glory be seen in the stature of waiting.
May your glory be seen in the grace of unknowing.
May your glory be seen in the dignity of humbling.

932   Spirit of God, be wild and free in us.
Batter our proud and stubborn wills.
Blow us where you choose.
Break us down if you must.
Refashion us as you will.
Move us powerfully away
from the games we play
to try to tame you.
Lead us into the wild places,
the places of dream or scream,
the long, dark tunnels
or the wide, sunny vistas,
to speak to lions,
to move mountains,
to bear tragedy,
to mirror you.

933 Kindling Spirit, come,
inflame our waiting hearts.
Anointing Spirit, come,
distribute among us your gifts:
wisdom, understanding and strength,
knowledge, reverence and insight.
Come like fire and kindle love in our hearts.
Come like wind and breathe life into our frames.
Come like water and flow through our souls.
Come like the earth: sustain and nourish our beings.

934 You who became poor to make many rich,
on your last days on Earth
you promised to leave us the Holy Spirit.
As we meet and eat,
may your Spirit come like blood into our veins
so that we will be driven entirely by your will.
Blow over the wealthy people so that they will be humble.
Blow over the poor people
so that they will receive their true worth.
Echoes a prayer from Ghana

935 Spirit of God, as fresh as the dawn,
freshen our weary brow.
Come like the dew in the early morn,
settle upon us now.
Come like a wind,
brace us and blow.
Come in the heat of day.
Come like a dove,
peaceful and calm,
touch us now with your love.

936 Comforting Spirit,
come to all who pass through trial
and to those we love.

937 May the fire of the Spirit
kindle in us a great blaze,
consuming all that is of us,
leaving only that which is from God.

938 Give us the eye of the eagle that
gazes into your face,
traces the movements of your hand,
penetrates the depths of your heart,
scans the reaches of your mind
and glimpses the horizons of your Spirit.

939 Give us your firelight, Holy Spirit,
as we go down into the things stored in our memories,
dreams and hurts.
Journey with us beyond these
to the seed of our nature you planted in us
at our beginning.
May we become that seed, which is our true self,
and may it grow and produce much fruit.

940 Anointing Spirit,
distribute among us your gifts:
wisdom, understanding and strength,
knowledge, reverence and insight.

941 Holy Spirit, you have anointed your servants
from the Day of Pentecost until now.
Anoint us as you will for the callings you will.
Here we wait, alert and open,
praying that you will come to us.

942 *Come, Holy Spirit*

Come, Holy Spirit, our souls inspire
and lighten with eternal fire.
Implant in us your grace from above;
enter our minds and hearts with love.

O come, anointing Spirit of peace,
wellspring of life and gentleness.
Past ages called you the Paraclete;
with sevenfold gifts you make us complete.

You are the Power of God's right hand,
promise of God to Church and land.
Life-giving words to us impart;
illumine and transform our heart.

Into our souls your love now pour.
Refresh our weak frame with strength and power.
Give grace and courage to endure.
Cast far away our deadly foe.

Grant us your peace through every day
with you as Guide upon the way.
Evil no more our souls shall harm.
We shall know as we are known.

Teach us the Trinity to know,
Father, Son and Spirit, too:
the Three in One and One in Three,
now and ever, eternally.
Adapted by Ray Simpson from Veni Creator Spiritus, ascribed to Rabanus Maurus, a ninth-century Solitary in Gaul

943 Divine Artist,
you uniquely shape our characters,
endow us with gifts
and pattern our lives.
May your inspired fingers work upon us,
that we may become your works of art.

944 In your presence
we affirm that every organ,
action and function of our bodies
is animated by your living Spirit.
By day and by night,
may your Life flowing through us
renew every cell of our bodies
after your indwelling image.

945 Make us rich in your eyes, dear God.
Help us to take freely of the treasures of heaven.
Clothe us in the virtues whose attractions increase.
Feed us with food that never goes bad.
Adorn us with beauty that never fades.
Free us to stride through the courts of mammon,
uncluttered by its enticements,
content with you.

946 Divine Artist,
     the world is your canvas,
     and we your prime exhibits.
     Bring to flower the artist
     you have planted within us,
     and transform art to become
     a panorama of healing.

947 Call forth life within us,
     Father of life.
     Bless the swarming sperm
     that teem with life so manifold.
     Spirit of life,
     bless the welcoming egg
     that patiently waits to conceive.
     Saviour of Life,
     change the barren water of this womb
     into a wine-like ferment of life.
     Call forth life within us.

948 Bless to us, O God, the anguish that is ours.
     Change the stagnant void in our hearts
     into a life-giving stream,
     that we may become pregnant with fresh creativities,
     love pouring forth abundantly from us,
     mothering and fathering an orphaned world,
     bringing to flower
     the seeds you have planted in us,
     faith and joy outpouring.

949 Great Spirit, water the world.
     Revive our dryness,
     soak our soreness,
     refresh our tiredness,
     wash our filthiness,
     bathe our woundedness,
     immerse us in your love.

950 Come like fire and warm our hearts.
Come like wind and refresh our frames.
Come like water and revive our souls.
Come like the earth and nourish our being.

Renewal and recreation

951 Holy God, holy and mighty,
who brought to birth an heir
in Sarah's barren womb:
bring a new thing to birth in our barren places.
Holy God, holy and mighty,
we would have faith to move mountains
but our faith is weak, like a little seed.
Encouraged by Abraham's example,
we give this seed to you, Lord.
Take it, water it and multiply it,
that there may be much fruit.

952 Immerse us in your pure water
and your gift of your tender heart.
Immerse us in your healing water
and your gift of wisdom.
Immerse us in your renewing waters
and your gift of reverence.

953 We love you, Lord, and we lift our voices
to honour you and to rejoice.
As thirsty deer go down to the pool,
so our thirsty souls are refreshed in you.
By day you guide us along the way;
at night you guard and with us stay.

954 You are the well of heaven.
When we visit wells of the earth,
the way to you is opened.
Touch us. Refresh us. Heal us.
Flow over us and make us whole.

955 Dear Son of Mary,
     you took flesh to redeem us;
     change our hearts.
     Dear Son of God,
     you came to us with sacrificial love;
     change our hearts.

956 May we, like Agatha Christie's Miss Marple,
     determine that nothing is settled until it's settled right.
     When something is settled right,
     may we be magnanimous,
     and rejoice to see friendship renewed,
     endeavour reawakened, or love blossom.

957 Risen Christ, bring newness of life
     into our stale routines,
     into our wearied spirits,
     into our tarnished relationships.

958 Light-bringer,
     we have buried your insight beneath falsehoods.
     We have insulated ourselves
     from being vulnerable to others.
     We have been closed
     to your renewing of our minds.
     Break through our resistance.
     Free us from the past.
     Open our hearts to love.

959 Help me conquer anger by gentleness,
     greed by generosity,
     apathy by fervour.

960 You are the Vine.
     We are the branches.
     Everything we need in life
     we find in you, our Source.
     What has died, we'll pass it by.
     When you prune, we will let go.
     Live in us, Lord,
     and we will live in you.

961   Source of Creativity,
        teach us
        to dance with the playful clouds
        and to laugh with the glinting sun.
        Teach us
        to flow like the sparkling streams
        and to soar like the high-winged birds.
        Teach us
        to dream of rainbow and mountain
        and to attempt what we see.
        Teach us
        to restock memory's treasure-house
        and to give it all away.

962   Christ of the gentle heart,
        we place ourselves under your yoke.
        We plan our diaries by your priorities.
        We direct our feet along your way.
        Help us to
        see clearly,
        act courageously
        and move on calmly
        day by day.

963   God make us fit for purpose,
        alive in heart and limb.
        God stretch our creaking bodies
        till they tingle and feel trim.

        Put fibre in our being,
        take flabbiness away.
        Strengthen what is weak,
        keep binge and bulge at bay.

        May each body be a temple
        of your Spirit who is true;
        a picture frame on Earth
        of eternity on view.

964 We place our souls and bodies
under your shaping, O God.
Shape their times of rest.
Shape their times of zest.
Change the fretting moth
that eats away their peace
into sweet rest in you.

965 Lord, we leave behind with you
affections, habits and attitudes which are
no part of a whole life.
This one thing we do:
we look to you, to the fellowship of your sufferings,
to the power of your resurrection
and to the goal of the whole created universe
becoming one with you.
So help us God.

966 Grant us grace to
eat well,
think well
and move well,
until our bodies, minds and souls
are truly temples of your Holy Spirit.

967 The glory of God in our working;
the glory of God in our thinking;
the glory of God in our speaking;
the glory of God in our eating;
the glory of God in our hearing;
the glory of God in our meeting.
Today's step,
we step away from fret,
we step towards rest.

968 Lord, show us how to pray like this
over our work
and teach us not to count our chickens
until they are hatched.

969 Lord, today may the needs of our bodies
and the needs of our minds,
the practical needs of work
and the social needs
each be given their rightful place
and be kept in balance.
May the needs for rest and fun,
study and sleep,
household order and justifiable work
all be answered.

970 God who is One,
you create us in diversity.
God who is Three,
you draw us into unity.
We give you thanks
for the little trinities
that reflect your nature
to us in community.

We pray for places
where community has been destroyed.
May the love of the Three
give birth to new community.
May the life of the Three
give birth to new creativity.
May the oneness of the Three
give birth to a new unity.

971 God of rest,
come as dew
that rests on our tired frames.
Come as breeze
that cools in the heat of the day.
Come as the calming presence
that restores stillness to our being.
Come as Sabbath rest
and renew our being.

972 We of this day are children of confusion:
restore the vision of God to us.
The noise of the city
deafens us to the still, small voice:
restore the hearing of God to us.
The pace of modern living deadens us:
restore the alertness of God to us.
Reveal to us in our dreams
visions of your glorious truth.

973 Search out in us, O God,
the seeds of disunity:
wilfulness, insecurity and ignorance.
Transform them
into service, trust and awareness,
that unity in a common cause
may be born.

974 Power of powers,
a household divided against itself cannot last.
Bring the proud walls tumbling down,
and from the rubble let there grow up
lovely little plants
of truth, goodness and love.

975 Save us from the arrogance of self-sufficiency.
Open our eyes to see what you see.
Strip naivety from us.
Help us to face up to evil.
Deliver us from evil.
For yours is the power and the glory for ever.

976 We arise today in a Mighty Power:
the power of the One who is Three,
the Creator, the Christ and the Spirit.
In their name, we say:
lies – perish;
confusion – depart;
demons – flee;
people – bow before your God.

977 Almighty God of the invincible force field,
repel these alien invaders.
Disarm these hidden persuaders.
Evaporate these false imaginations,
and fill with your loving fragrance
the places they vacate.

978 We arise today
with the legions of God around us,
with God's sounds to distract ill-doers,
with God's winds to impel good-doers.
We arise today
in dependence on the Father,
in the daring of the Son,
in the direction of the Spirit.

979 Great and awesome God,
ever faithful to those who love you,
we have done wrong and turned against your ways.
We have not listened to those who spoke your truth.
Because you are just,
you have brought disaster upon us.
Yet now, drive this from us,
listen to our heart cries, forgive us our sins,
for deeper than all our disobedience
is the fact that we belong to you,
and so does our sacred place.
Rebuild it, Lord, as your place.
Echoes Daniel 9

980 As Cuthbert stormed the gates of heaven,
we knock on your door, Lord, and ask for bread,
not for ourselves but for your desperate ones.
We storm your gates, Lord, and plead for mercy,
not for ourselves but for your feuding ones.
We persist through the hours,
not for ourselves but for your sheep for whom you died.

Simple lifestyle

981 Remove the clutter from our lives, Lord,
and give us the grace of Blessed Simplicity.
Remove the divided affections from our lives, Lord,
and give us the grace of undivided love for all.
Remove the dominating spirit from our lives, Lord,
and give us the grace of seeking the good in the other.

982 Divine Saviour, your birth in the stable at Bethlehem
reveals the simplicity of the Father's love.
Help us, like you, to fling away burdensome accessories
and live in simplicity and joy.

983 Holy God,
help us to live at the still centre
of the world's whirring wheels,
where everything is led by you,
where all is one and we are at peace.

984 Lord of Earth and heaven,
the food we eat is earth, water and air,
coming to us through pleasing plants or creatures.
When we eat, help us to keep these in mind
and to keep it simple.

Justice

985 Help us to live simply, that others may simply live.
Free us from false attachments,
that we may be
true to ourselves,
true to others
and true to you.

986 All-merciful One,
you hold the poor closely to your heart:
forgive those of us who have enough
for closing our hearts to the poor.

Forgive those of us who have nothing
for closing our hearts to the rich.
Show us how all people and all places
can receive their worth;
in the name of the One
who had nowhere to lay his head.

987   In the strength of the Warrior of God
I oppose all that pollutes.
In the eye of the Face of God
I expose all that deceives.
In the energy of the Servant of God
I bind up all that is broken.

988   Delayer, if you were not patient,
our selfishness would cause the planet to implode;
give us one more chance to change over to your ways.
You who are the First,
spur us to put you first and to know that
in you is our beginning and our end.
You who are the Last, teach us that we perish but you abide;
help us to acquire treasure that never fades.

989   May each land find its well-being in your will.
Give us that dynamic which calls out and combines
the moral and spiritual responsibility of individuals
for their immediate sphere of action.
We pray for an uprising of people
who give leadership free from the bondage of fear,
sorry for the blindness of the past,
rising above ambition,
flexible to the direction of your Spirit,
reaching out with generous hearts
to neighbouring peoples.

990   We draw aside in the midst of the day.
We weep for the hungry and poor,
the children mistreated, those broken by force,
and the maimed who can't finish their course.
We plead for your justice to fill all the lands
as the waters cover the sands.

> We pray against cruelty, hatred and pain,
> against pride and greed for gain.
> We pray for the homeless and victims of war,
> the strangers to love at the door.
> We plead for your justice to fill all the lands
> as the waters cover the sands.
>
> *After a prayer by Andrew Dick*

991 Christ of the loving heart,
may we look upon everyone with a smile
that reflects a ray of the True and Universal Sun,
the smile of acceptance and understanding.
May we be builders of a world that is free from prejudice,
where everyone, however wayward,
is seen as a child of Love.

992 Your kingdom come, your will be done
on Earth as it is in heaven.
Your kingdom come here
in honesty at work and home,
in fair treatment and fair trade,
in respect for human life,
in friendship between people
of different races and religions,
in freedom from hate, fear and greed,
in generosity and goodness,
in mercy that knows no end.

993 God of Providence,
show us how to become a people of well-being.
May we not, through vainglory,
tamper with what is good in the work we inherit;
nor, through handing down unnecessary regulations,
disrespect those who have to carry them out.
Embolden us to bless regulations that enable
and to remove those that disable.
We pray this in the name
of the One who trusts us,
Jesus Christ our Lord.

994 Give your counsel to our government.
Grant us honest financiers,
whole health workers, wise educators.
Raise up those who have fallen,
support the weak, give vision to our writers
and refresh your Church.

995 We pray for those
whose tasks are backbreaking,
whose bodies are mutilated
or whose spirits are crushed.
Give us the will
to share our bread with the hungry,
to give shelter to those who feel rejected
and to reach out to those in need.

996 Holy Spirit, free us to be just and true.
Sending Spirit, empower us to touch lives for you.
Disturbing Spirit, stir us, wasted lives to renew.

997 Where people long for an end to injustice,
shine into their hearts.
Where people long for conflict to cease,
shine into their hearts.
Where people long to right
inhuman working conditions,
shine into their hearts.
Where people long to restore
the scarred places of Earth,
shine into their hearts.
Where people long for dignity
in human relationships,
shine into their hearts.

Mission and witness

998 Let there be
respect for the Earth,
peace for its people,

love in our lives,
delight in the good,
forgiveness for past wrongs
and a new start.

999 Unfold to us
the meaning of your commission –
may we not be blind
to what you seek to accomplish.
Kindle in us the spirit of an apostle,
the willingness to pass on
what you have imparted to us.
Reveal to us what it means
to reach all the world;
whether near or far,
may every bit of the world we touch
be immersed in you.

1000 Thank you, Jesus, for your love for us;
for hurts you have healed
and faults you have changed;
for the thoughts you have inspired
and callings you have given.
May we share these joys as naturally
as we share the joys of a lovely day.

1001 We give ourselves to you, Lord,
our wills we hand to you.
We yield to those who heed you, Lord.
Now free our hearts to sing.

1002 Bend our wills to the holy yoke of obedience, O Lord.
Make us faithful in the little things.
May every necessary chore become an act of worship.
And grant that some fruit may fall upon us.

1003 O Christ, you laid your life down for us.
May each thing we do this day
be a laying down of our lives.

1004 Divine Restorer, aid us
   in setting our affairs in the simple beauty of creation.
   May our belongings, activities and relationships
   be ordered in a way that liberates the spirit.
   May our clothes and furniture reflect
   God-given features of our personalities.
   May we set before you
   our income, savings and possessions,
   conscious that we are your stewards,
   not possessors of these things,
   and make them available as you require of us.

1005 Great Creator, we are made in your likeness
   and you call us to be co-creators with you.
   Water the seeds of creativity you have planted in us;
   let not fear, over-busyness or low self-image
   hold us back from letting these come to flower.
   May we, in a second-hand and sterile society,
   be signs of your creative life.

1006 Thank you for the countless numbers
   who have been made more whole through prayer.
   Thank you for those who can now see, or write,
   or believe in themselves for the first time.
   Thank you for people of hate and violence
   who now spread love and forgiveness.
   Thank you for communities of hope
   in an otherwise hopeless place.

1007 Make us
   patient in our observing,
   sensitive in our listening,
   generous in our befriending
   and compelling in our speaking,
   that we may open new frontiers for you.

1008 Heroic Love,
   help us in our vulnerability
   not to retreat, close up or pretend,

       but to think clearly, act decisively,
       confront lovingly,
       and go wherever you send.

1009 Child of Heaven, Defenceless Love,
       in order to come to us
       you had to travel far from your eternal home.
       Give us your childlike spirit.
       Help us to move out of our places of comfort
       to the little child, to the straying sheep;
       to have an eye for those who are overlooked;
       to learn from those who,
       though least in this world's eyes,
       teach us to trust.
       Teach us
       to notice the little things,
       to serve you in the least of your children
       and in the prayer of the humble heart.

1010 Eternal Mind, thank you for the minds
       that make sense of the world.
       Eternal Beauty, thank you for the beauty
       that puts soul into the world.
       Eternal Life, thank you for the lives
       that point beyond themselves.

1011 Help us to tell our story:
       the wonder of each birth,
       the paths that led to glory
       or that brought us down to earth.

       Help us trace the times of light
       when you were by our side;
       through Scripture, prayer or insight,
       when we sang and when we cried.

       Help us to share our story,
       dear Lord, who for us died;
       whose death became the victory
       in which we now abide.

1012 Impart to us imagination
to find the places in people
where we may connect.
Give us the grace of self-acceptance,
that we may accept a gift from another.
Grace us with love that empowers us
to share of ourselves.

1013 When a person sails by with eyes all glazed,
may our eyes give them rays of love.
When a person passes, cold or hard,
may our hearts melt them with welcoming warmth.

1014 Break in us the drive to manipulate others;
embolden us to clear out the clutter;
inspire us to give all, in trust that you will provide.

1015 Great God of mercy,
your world is becoming a wasteland;
calm us to prepare a way for you.
May we discover and live
ways that are life-giving:
ways of integrity, respect,
and awareness of your presence in all.

1016 Word of God, rays from you
light people of many beliefs.
May these rays lead us
to the places where we may sit and eat
and be one with those who are different from us,
until you emerge in their clothes,
revealing a new facet
of your never-ending glory.

1017 Triune God, Forgiving One,
we pray for those
who do not yet know you as Father.
As we take a fatherly or motherly interest
in one another's faith journey,
and share nurturing experiences,
reveal yourself to us all.

1018 Fire of God,
    may the flame of the fire warm our hearts.
    May the sparks among the stubble
    dance in our hearts.
    May the glow of the fire shine in our hearts.
    May the crackle of the fire
    set us all ablaze for the
    Three of Uncreated Love.
    Echoes a prayer of Sister Dorothy Stella of OHP Whitby

1019 Great God who mothers us all,
    develop among us those who will
    cradle the wee ones
    and free the older ones
    to leave childish attachments
    and face the world with love;
    kindle the desire for holy living;
    teach us to drink deeply
    from the wells of wisdom;
    nurture a nation and shape it for God.

1020 Lord, when we cry out to you,
    you bring us comfort and rest.
    Be with us in all areas of our lives
    so we may labour with an easy heart.

1021 Divine Father,
    help us to affirm the good in others.
    Divine Friend,
    help us to reach out warmly to others.
    Divine Spirit,
    help us to connect well with others
    across the shores that separate.

1022 Break the ties that bind us to our past;
    free us to go wherever you direct.
    Bless the tiredness
    that blinds us to your presence;
    grace us with
    the scents of the company of heaven.

Burden us with the evils
that would ravage your children;
spur us to struggle until the tide is turned.

1023 May your tender love burn inside us
and impel us on the road to seek for Christ
in the stranger's face
or, sensing his absence,
introduce his presence.

1024 We raise our hands
and bless the hungry and the poor.
We lay these hands
to tend the hurting and the sore.
We stretch out these hands
to welcome the stranger at the door.

1025 God of the Call,
Make me willing to do anything
and go anywhere for you.
All that I am, all that I do,
all that I'll ever be, I offer now to you.

1026 Almighty God,
you gave to your servant Hilda
gifts of vision and energy,
order and common sense,
insight and devotion.
Inspired by her example,
may we walk as one family
in the paths of love and obedience,
and attain the reward of the poor in spirit,
through Jesus Christ our Lord.

Growing, exploring, listening, discerning

1027 Free me, Immense Spirit
from a lifetime's crippling habits,
from a closed and cabined mind,

      from a cowering, timid spirit,
      from blinkered, haughty habits,
      to be who I am, clothed and in my right mind.

1028 Restore to us, O God,
      your rhythms that we have lost:
      the rhythm of rising and sleeping;
      the rhythm of rest and work;
      the rhythm of breathing and walking;
      the rhythm of quiet and speech;
      the rhythm of loving and losing;
      the rhythm of light and dark.

1029 Help us, Lord,
      to trade with the gifts you have given us
      and to bend our minds to holy learning,
      that we may escape the fretting moth
      of littleness of mind that would wear out our souls.
      Brace our wills to actions
      that they may not be the spoils of weak desires.
      Train our hearts and lips
      to song which gives courage to the soul.
      Being buffeted by trials, may we learn to laugh.
      Being reproved, may we give thanks.
      Having failed, may we determine to succeed.
      Echoes the anonymous 'Homily of St Hilda'

1030 God our Wisdom,
      who set Hilda as a mother in the Church,
      may we now delight to claim her gifts of wisdom:
      the wisdom of silence and the wisdom of speech;
      the wisdom of observation and the wisdom of revealing;
      the wisdom of memory and the wisdom of work;
      the wisdom of deeds and the wisdom of being.

1031 God of Monday and of Sunday,
      you have created a world
      of limited natural resources,
      and you have created humans
      of limited duration and energy.

May we accept that we are mortal.
May we stop trying to be God.
May we live in a balance of input and output.

1032 Teach us to leave behind
the things that tie our spirits down
and to learn again to be your pilgrim people:
through fasting from the frenzied feeding of false desires.
Through study of your Word,
meditation
and acts of service,
restore the clearness of our seeing
and free us to share your generous love
with all.

1033 Bring to flower in your children
the seeds that dormant lie.
In those who have none to encourage them,
bring the seeds of confidence to flower.
In those who are trapped by their circumstances,
bring the seeds of possibility to flower.
In those who find it difficult to learn,
bring the seeds of understanding to flower.
In those at the bottom of the social pile,
bring the seeds of empowerment to flower.

1034 You who are Heroic Love,
alive in every leaf and lane,
beckon us through star and stone
to stride across our petty ways
in pursuit of the Endless Adventure.

1035 God of Order and Beauty,
help us to clothe our bodies and our homes
with beauty appropriate to the season.
Give to us a sense of balance and of order,
with room for spontaneity.
Show us what bubbles and what brings calm,
what brings energy and what brings charm.

1036 You whose Heroic Love comes in a thousand ways,
may we be the clay that laughs in the hands of the potter,
sails borne by the wind,
trees earthed in the soil,
dancers in tune with the rhythm.

1037 May each thing we do be without regret.
May each minute we spend be used for the best.
May each thought we have be without waste.
May each moment we're in be in God's time.

1038 Lord, you know each of us by name,
more intimately than anyone else.
Help us to notice,
from among the countless thoughts
that cross our minds,
the thoughts that come as gifts
from someone who knows us from the inside.
In other words, help us to recognise your voice.

1039 Divine Dream-weaver,
may your holy angels guard our sleep.
May they watch over us as we rest,
and hover around our beds.
Let them reveal to us in our dreams,
visions of your glorious truth.

1040 May you be like an oak tree of wisdom
with roots deep in the soil of holy reflection.
May your reach be high,
wide and hospitable to all.
May you be strong to withstand gales,
may your life be long
and may you birth many oaklings.

1041 Word of God,
out of the silence of eternity
you ceaselessly speak to your children.

Teach us to listen,
not to the discordant babble of a sick society,
but to the treasures of truth
in the deeps of silence.

1042 Carpenter Christ, give us common sense
and save us from a life of nonsense.
Help us to discern where circumstances
herald rather than hinder your unfolding purpose.
Speak through nature, prick our consciences,
and make us aware of what we are on this Earth for.
Then, Lord, prompt us to take the next step.

1043 Holy God, who speaks words of life,
make us ready writers.
Speak through our confusion.
Help us to write honestly and simply,
and to name and carry out your priorities for today.
Grace us to catch your soothing tones,
your quiet intimations,
your stirrings in our souls
and your bold commands.

1044 Thank you that you are a God who speaks.
Grace us to accept that we are hard of hearing.
Help us to attune our ears to your promptings
at the crossroads of each day
and in the movements of our souls.

1045 Stretch our hearts, Lord,
and broaden our minds.
Open our eyes, Lord,
that we may find
fresh horizons,
a holy grail,
a noble challenge,
a height to scale,
and the theme of our sleep.

Be the shape in the gloom
and the piercing of darkness.
All-seeing God,
may our vision be yours.

1046 Creator of love,
make us aware that you are present
in every cell of creation
and in every cell of our being.
May we hear you
in the movements of the sky
and in the soul's every sigh.
May we hear you
in the passing of a fly
and in a poor creature's cry.
When our pets race and dart,
may we catch the beatings of your heart.

1047 Show us, Lord,
that for which the time has come,
be it small or great.
Show us what lies in this moment.
Show us what you are bringing to a head,
or bringing to an end, or bringing to birth.
And we will obey.

1048 Father, Mother,
free us from unthinking, jaundiced ways
of looking at others.
Sensitise our hearts
to detect the uppermost need of the moment.
Sharpen us to reach out
and not flinch at the reactions
of those who will feel insecure.
So help us God.

1049 All-seeing God, be our vision.
Be the light in our eyes
and the bright beam before us.
Be the thought in our heads.

1050 Speak, Lord,
    in stillness or storm,
    in circumstance or sign,
    in Scripture or word,
    in conscience or heart,
    in encounter or art.
    Stir up the gift in us.

1051 God of the prophet Moses,
    man of meekness,
    may we not use the gifts of the Spirit
    unless they bear the fruits of the Spirit.
    May we not say things
    that bolster our self-esteem
    unless we first esteem the other
    more highly than ourselves.
    May we not speak a word we have been given
    unless we are willing for it
    to be weighed by others.
    May we not speak at all out of season.

1052 Great Creator of the gleaming moon
    and falling stars;
    Great Saviour of the miraculous birth
    and rising from death;
    Great Spirit of the seers
    and sacred words,
    come into our minds,
    come into our mouths,
    until we become your message and sign.

1053 God of wisdom, give us good judgement.
    Help us to distinguish
    that which confuses from that which brings light;
    that which brings peace from that which brings strife;
    that which brings reality from that which cloaks it;
    that which builds love from that which feeds distrust.

1054 God, our Vision,
   impelled by the visions you entrust to us,
   may we break through
   the brittle shell of our unbelief
   and move, untrammelled,
   towards the heavenly horizons.

1055 Stop us, dear God,
   from rushing in where angels fear to tread.
   Rebuke our headstrong ways.
   Deflect us from foolhardy paths.
   Alert us to meet a crisis that requires us to be prepared.

1056 Help us to grow today
   in understanding and sensitivity,
   in patience and prayerfulness.

1057 Good God,
   from you flows all goodness, all light.
   Help us to discern goodness wherever it surfaces
   and to make common cause with it,
   for you are the Father of light.

1058 Universal God, you have a plan
   for every person
   and for every situation in the world.
   But we are so dim.
   We are so deaf.
   Help us to become God-guided instruments
   and always to be in just the place you wish us to be.

1059 Teach me when to be silent and when to speak,
   when to listen and when to leave,
   when to praise and when to refrain,
   when to laugh and when to weigh,
   when to tell and when to wait.

1060 High King of the universe,
   we offer you our possessions.
   Make them all your own.

We offer you our mindsets
and we place them at your feet.
May we be filled with your Presence
as incense fills a holy place.
We offer you the shadows of our lives,
the things that are crushed,
our little deaths and our final death.
May these be like the straw in the out-stable.
May something beautiful for you
be born in all this straw.

1061 Thank you, Lord,
that even if we are difficult or blinkered people,
you can put holy desires into our hearts
and divine intimations before our eyes,
so that we come through obstacles
to our eternal resurrection.

1062 Lord, grant me the strength to do without things.
Grant me the wisdom to see the 'within' of things.
Grant me the knowledge to take the measure of evil spirits.
Grant me understanding to know you who alone are true.

1063 Infinite One of the wise heart,
Saving One of the clear sight,
Knowing One of the hidden deeps,
may I learn from you as an eager pupil,
may I learn from life as a humble child,
may I learn from night, may I learn from day,
may I learn from soul friends, may I learn from stillness.

1064 All-seeing God,
who has given to us the holy Scriptures,
help us so to value them,
to read, mark, learn and inwardly digest them,
that we may grow in wisdom
and in understanding of your ways,
now and for eternity.

1065 Eternal Word of God,
   whose Spirit moves prophets, recordists and readers,
   give us discernment of spirits
   and help us understand every part of Scripture
   in the light of the True Way.

1066 Lord, you remember us
   and know our every thought.
   Help us to remember you
   and know your words to us.

1067 Risen Christ, as we read this passage,
   may we be aware that you are here with us.
   Eternal truth flows through the words we read.
   You know the particular word
   that we most need now.
   We open ourselves to you.
   Please speak to us.

1068 Make us sensitive, Lord,
   to your tones, your style, your feelings
   as we recall your work in Bible times.
   Re-envision us.
   Recharge us.
   May we touch the earth that you touched.
   May you touch the earth
   upon which we stand today.

1069 Make us attentive to your clear commands.
   Make us attentive to the sighing of your world.
   Make us attentive to your whispering tones.
   Make us attentive to your slightest wish.

1070 Eternal Truth,
   grant us humility to know how little we know.
   Give us clarity to know what is best for us to learn.
   Show us a good way to this.
   Form us in the art of asking useful questions.
   Help us grow, like Jesus, in understanding.

1071 Christ of fearless love,
   take us to our point of greatest weakness
   and let us find you there.
   May your strength
   be made complete in our frailty.

1072 Holy, True and Real One,
   help us to be true, help us to be real.
   Help us to know our own mind.
   Help us to know what we must say 'Yes' to
   and what we must say 'No' to.
   May our lives be like a blank sheet of paper.

1073 God of Wisdom, teach us to
   use our minds well,
   study with a humble heart,
   relate the parts to the whole,
   explore things with wonder,
   listen to those who know more than we do
   and learn from our mistakes.

1074 All-knowing God, make fruitful our learning.
   May we acquire information
   that forms us for a good purpose
   and does not distract us from it.
   May we link up what we learn today
   with what we already know,
   and so become more whole.
   May we offer to you in love what we learn,
   so that it shows in our words, our silences,
   and our actions.

1075 Help us to know and accept our limits.
   Help us to mind the gaps –
   to honour you by keeping margins,
   to receive as well as to give,
   to be a sign of renewal,
   for Christ's sake.

1076 Open our eyes to the poisons of our time,
    that we may avoid them.
    Alert us to the angry horses of our time,
    that we may calm them.
    Prepare us for the prowling lions of our time,
    that we may bring them to nothing.

1077 Help us pluck out by the roots
    Adam's sinful greed in Eden
    that proved so deadly to the world.
    Help us to touch the tree of the cross
    that pours out immortality on the world,
    that we may flow
    with the new river from Paradise
    by which all things are made alive.

1078 Divine Source of Truth, Beauty and Goodness,
    our minds are like a field.
    In this field, please grow many good things,
    many beautiful things,
    and many true things with deep roots.
    Teach us also how to weed and sift and sort,
    how to water and prune wisely.

1079 Lord, help us to think things through,
    to sense the season, and to relate what we do
    to the signs of the times.
    Help us to act and speak appropriately.

1080 We pray for the cleansing of our perceptions,
    that we may hear,
    that we may see,
    that we may understand with our hearts
    and that we may be healed.

1081 Examine us, O God, and know our thoughts.
    Reveal to us the cause of any divided or angry thoughts.
    We place failures and frustrations into your hands.
    We give thanks to you for our blessings.
    Take what we have learned, and work in us as we sleep,
    that tomorrow we may be more effective as human beings.

1082 Bend our minds to holy learning.
Give us
wisdom to know the nub of things,
memory to recall the important things
and clarity to express what we learn.
May your truth reshape us
and may we always walk humbly in the light.

1083 O God, Eternal Love, Courage and Wisdom,
may the love in our hearts be growing,
may the courage in our guts be galvanised,
may the wisdom of our days be garnered.

1084 Help us to breathe in step with you.
Help us to know the time.
Help us to go with the flow.

1085 Teach us, dear God, to
know your ways,
explore your world,
learn from mistakes,
understand people,
manage our time and talents,
weave meaning out of memory,
gain insight from inspired people,
grow into the stature of Christ.

1086 Lord, unlock the treasures of wisdom to us,
but first give us hearts for humble learning.

1087 Train us
to trade with the gifts you have granted us,
to teach with the knowledge you have grown in us,
to touch the lives you have given us.

1088 Toughen me, Lord.
Give me a heart of love
but a backbone of steel.

1089 Faithful God, teach me that defeat, if given to you,
is your opportunity for a new advance.
Help me to remain faithful in every setback today.

1090 O Mighty One, may I put no one on a pedestal.
Help me to honour my parents
but never to put them in the place
that only you should have.

1091 Holy God, holy and mighty,
strip from me all that is false and out of place.
Strengthen my roots in you.
Bring me to that place
where I desire you alone.

Guidance for the journey

1092 Jesus, we will follow you.
We are willing to leave behind
whatever gets in the way.
We leave behind the 'nets' that, though good,
are the enemy of the best.
We leave behind the tangles
that are not for us to unravel.
We leave in your hands
those who are dear to us
but who can thrive without us.
Jesus, you may lead us up or down hill.
You may lead us to the unknown
or to the familiar.
Wherever you lead, we will follow.

1093 Jesus, may we journey with you,
firm in the faith,
loyal to your teaching,
obedient to your Father's will,
encompassed by the Spirit
along the way that leads to life.

1094 Father, you call us
    to listen to your Son and follow him.
    Forgive us for fossilising good experiences.
    Help us, rather,
    to use them as launching pads,
    from which we may go into
    places of discontent,
    willing to give even our lives for you,
    reassured that,
    whatever trials we pass through,
    we shall rise with you in glory.

1095 Leaving what is past,
    we journey in your light.
    Seeking what is just,
    we journey in your truth.
    Forgiving those who have harmed us,
    we journey in your love.
    The eternal Creator keep us,
    the beloved Companion beside us,
    the Spirit's smile upon us.

1096 As fish live in water, may we live in you.
    As birds soar high and carefree,
    may we soar with you.
    As deer run straight and graceful,
    may we run with you.
    As water flows so freely,
    may we flow with you.

1097 Guide us, good and great Redeemer,
    pilgrims through this barren land.
    We are weak, but you are mighty.
    Hold us with your powerful hand.
    When we reach the river's crossing,
    lead us to the other side.
    Hold us in your heart for ever.
    Always we'll with you abide.
    Echoes the hymn by William Williams, 'Guide Me O Thou great Redeemer'

The Soul Friend

1098 Christ of the Journey,
    you allowed yourself to travel alone when necessary,
    but you invited treasured friends
    to share much of the journey with you:
    sacred moments and frightening ordeals;
    humdrum tasks, tiring days, draining duties.
    Share our journey.
    Bring us to companions on the way who are
    true friends of our souls.

1099 Father, you give us many gifts
    that we may share them
    in the work of building up your people.
    Help us to receive deeply
    and to give ourselves generously,
    that in the work to which you call us
    we may know the wonder of your presence
    in another human life.

1100 May the Creator who fathers,
    the Christ who succours
    and the Spirit who counsels
    bring divine blessings to birth in us.
    May they grant us gifts of
    friendship and discretion,
    integrity and understanding,
    faithfulness and spiritual strength,
    and the ability to be ourselves
    in the presence of the other.

1101 Gentle God, reveal to us
    the beauty of sensitive friendship.
    Help us to create such stillness in our inner beings
    that we become aware
    of your gracious movements
    in the souls of others.

1102 Faithful God,
thank you for the glorious company
of steadfast believers
and the friendship
of spiritual mothers and fathers.
Establish our resolve.
Keep us steadfast, faithful and true,
that we may climb every mountain
and overcome every obstacle.

1103 Thank you for the gift of a good soul friend:
a companion on a long journey,
a fire to a cold hearth,
an anchor to a blown ship,
a pruning knife to an overgrown plant,
a window onto a new world,
gentle rain on new seeds.
Thank you for the gift of a soul friend.

1104 I pray, Lord, for the children whom I know.
Help me to encourage them
to listen to the thoughts and pictures
you put into their minds.
Help me to receive humbly what they tell me,
and to keep at least half an ear cocked
for your voice coming to me through them.
We pray for the youth of our own
and other lands – aimless, addicted,
creating a vacuum which tyranny could fill.
Raise up enablers and motivators.
May churches and Christian networkers
provide coaches and connecting points for young people.
We pray for conflict resolvers and trust builders
to engage in war-torn lands
and in the communities from which we come.
Help us to turn things round.

Times of trial

1105 In the place of fear,
God's strength to uphold us.
In the place of emptiness,
God's wisdom to guide us.
In the place of confusion,
God's eye for our seeing.
In the place of discord,
God's ear for our hearing.
In the place of froth,
God's word for our speaking,
to save us from false agendas
that harm our bodies or souls.

1106 Where times are dark,
where wrong parades as right,
where faith grows dim,
Christ, Light of the World,
meet us in our place of darkness.
Journey with us
and bring us to your new dawning.

1107 God, it's so unfair.
Christ, what have I done to deserve this?
Don't they realise what they do to me?
I rage, but then I think the Christian thing
is to pretend I'm all right,
that it's like water off a duck's back.
You know I can't take much more.
If I end it all they'll take notice.
Then they'll realise what they've done to me.
Why don't I? Because I haven't got the guts?
No, I could do it. I won't do it because I want to win.
If I end it now my ego will win –
it will go out with a big statement,
but my true self will be lost.
So I will stay with you, soul of my soul, despite all the pain.
I will be present to the leaf I see, the chirp I hear,
the sunray that hides behind the cloud,
the stature that waits to be revealed.

1108 Irresistible One,
    when the world falls apart, be our Centre,
    when the world turns sour, be our Sweetness,
    when we become weak, be our Strength.

1109 Lord, do not lead us into a time of fearful trial.
    But in whatever trials we have to face,
    help us to remain true to you,
    our King who saves us.

1110 Sweet Jesus, I lay before you now
    things that are needlessly bitter –
    relationships, circumstances.
    May your sweetness turn
    food into pleasure,
    tragedy into triumph
    and ugliness into beauty.

1111 Take us under your protection,
    O beloved angel of God,
    just as the Lord of grace so ordained.
    Accompany us at all times
    and protect us from worry and danger.

1112 O God, all-powerful, you are our strength.
    O Lord of the world, our lives are yours.
    Whatever be your will, may it be done.

1113 We ask for the Light of light,
    the vision of the Trinity
    and the grace of patience
    in the face of injustice.

1114 *In times of trial or terror*
    When people are in danger on the streets,
    send big angels to stand between them,
    angels from heaven or angels from Earth.
    May terror flee.
    May calm and confidence return.

1115 Jesus, you were born into a world of oppression.
 You are with us in oppression.
 Jesus, you were born into a world
 where the innocent were killed.
 You are with us when innocent ones are killed.
 Jesus, you were a refugee in Egypt.
 You are with us when we have to flee.
 Jesus, you were broken on the Cross.
 Be with us, your broken people.

1116 God of the endless force field,
 sow confusion in those
 who would use terror as a means of change.
 Stir conviction in those
 who can bring change
 by acting justly and by the sharing of love.

1117 *After a disaster or act of terror*
 In our devastation,
 reach down to us, O God.
 In our grief,
 reach down to us, O God.
 In our anger,
 reach down to us, O God.
 In our confusion,
 reach down to us, O God.

1118 May the light that shines out from your face
 flood the world with goodness
 and gather into one
 a divided and broken humanity.

1119 O Christ, the Champion of the tests,
 when the first thought strikes,
 help me to resist.
 When the first look overwhelms,
 help me to resist.
 When the first fascination takes hold,
 help me to resist.
 If I fall, save me.

1120 We pray to you for the place of desecration:
    bring forth beauty from it.
    We pray to you for the hard and barren place:
    bring forth generosity from it.
    We pray to you for the greed- and guilt-laden place:
    bring forth forgiveness from it
    and let eternal life bloom.

1121 God who weeps over the city,
    may we know the abandoned places,
    may we sense the destructive patterns,
    may we feel the suffering groups,
    may we confess the ravages and rage,
    may we embrace the hopes and despairs.

1122 Eternal Source of Life, you are the core of our being.
    Flow through our bodies like a life-giving river.
    Wash and transform the negative conditions
    in our hearts, minds, bodies and circumstances
    with light, love and grace.

Journeying, pilgrimage

1123 In our journeying this day,
    keep us, Father, in your way.
    In our play and in our work,
    guide us, Saviour, by your Word.
    May we, Spirit, hear you talk
    in our thoughts and in our walk.
    May our steps and thinking be
    in the Blessed Trinity.

1124 Lead us on our journey
    to places of resurrection,
    to dwellings of peace,
    to healings of wounds,
    to joys of discovery.

1125 May our feet follow our hearts
until we find our place of resurrection;
the place where we are in harmony with ourselves,
our neighbours, our environment and our God;
the context in which our creativity flows
and our investment of love bears eternal fruit.

1126 Make us pilgrims of the world
until we see your face in everyone we meet.
Make us pilgrims of the grail
until we see your grace in every place we visit.
Make us pilgrims of the road
until we see your prints in every chore we do.

1127 We will journey into wild places with God.
With you we shall neither faint nor fear.
The wild creatures shall become God's friends.
With you we shall neither faint nor fear.
Their Creator also created us.
With you we shall neither faint nor fear.
Give glory to the God of heaven and Earth.
Give glory to God who is in this place.

1128 Forgetting what is past,
we look to the things unseen.
We journey in your light.
The sun shall not strike us by day,
nor the moon by night.
We journey in your light.
We look not to right or left,
but straight towards your way.
We journey in your light.
The rough places shall be smoothed
and the pitfalls shall be cleared.
We journey in your light.
The proud shall be brought low
and the humble shall be raised up.
We journey in your light.

JOURNEYING, PILGRIMAGE

      The hungry shall be fed
      and the poor shall have good news.
      We journey in your light.
      No final home have we
      on this life's passing seas.
      High king of land and sea,
      wherever we go is yours.

1129 God be with us at every leap.
      Christ be with us on every steep.
      Spirit be with us in every deep.
      Each step of the journey we go.

1130 Father be with us on every road;
      Jesus be with us on every mound;
      Spirit be with us through every stream,
      headland and ridge and round.
      Be in each sea, each town, each moor,
      each lying-down, each rising-up.
      In the trough of the billows, in the wastelands of sin,
      each step of the journey we take.

1131 God be a smooth way before us,
      a guiding star above us,
      a keen eye behind us,
      that we may be a help to the weary,
      a light in the dark
      and a guide to the lost.

1132 God of the storm, God of the stillness,
      of squalls of power and of shimmering calm,
      into life's troughs and into life's billows
      come with the reach of your long right arm.

1133 We walk in the strength of the mighty Three in One:
      the Father who cares for us,
      the Saviour beside us,
      the Spirit who makes us strong.

1134 We go forward in light of sun,
     in strength of earth, in flowing of water.
     We go forth with the desert hermits
     and the holy martyrs,
     with all the holy and risen ones.
     We go forth with the word of the apostles
     and the wisdom of the seers,
     with the angels above
     and the prayers of all God's people.

1135 May we be as free as the wind,
     as soft as sheep's wool,
     as straight as an arrow,
     that we may journey ever nearer
     to the heart of God.

1136 Incomparable Guide,
     help us to travel light
     and so to know joys of discovery;
     help us to shed prejudice
     and so to be strangers no longer but pilgrims together;
     help us to stop trying to control
     and so to let things happen
     and to find you in the journeying.

1137 Into your hands, O God,
     we release the work we shall leave behind,
     the pressures that weary us,
     the problems that would pursue us,
     the things we have neglected,
     the tasks left unfinished.

1138 Call, call, call, great Chief of the high hills.
     Call, call, call, great Christ of the far paths.
     Call, call, call, great Counsellor of the near gate.
     Set our spirits free to soar wherever you climb.
     Set our feet free to trek wherever you go.
     Set our mouths free to say whatever you command.

1139 God of the elements, glory to you,
for being our radar in the ocean wide.
Your hand be on our rudder.
Your love be over the mast on the heaving foam.

1140 In the name of the sending Father,
in the name of the pilgrim Son,
in the name of the windlike Spirit,
we embrace the Three in One.

1141 High King of land and sea,
wherever we go is yours.
You led our forebears by cloud and fire.
You lead us through the days and nights.
You led St Brendan by sign and sail.
Your presence goes before us now.

1142 May the Christ who walks with wounded feet
walk with us on the road.
May the Christ who serves with wounded hands
stretch out our hands to serve.
May the Christ who loves with the wounded heart
open our hearts to love.
Echoes an anonymous prayer

1143 May the place to which we go be without regret.
May the Trinity protect us wherever we stay.
In every dealing, may shining angels be a clear presence.
May no one's poison get to us.
May the nine orders of heaven's company
favour us with their presence.
May we arrive safely at each destination.
May the time spent not be wasted.
May men, women and children welcome us.
Echoes an eighth- or ninth-century prayer

1144 God of surprises, God of the journey,
bring us
new horizons,
fresh shafts of light,

deeper understanding of the Scriptures,
growth in love, patience and humour,
empowerment of your people.

1145 Go before us
in our pilgrimage of life.
Anticipate our needs,
prevent our falling
and lead us to our destiny.

1146 Lord of the years,
may we celebrate the good life past
and not forget the Giver of that life.
God of the call,
may we contemplate the good road ahead
and walk along it
with love in our hearts,
hand in hand with you.

1147 Out of your womb we came.
To you we shall return.
Unseen, you accompany us through this amazing
and intricate journey of life on Earth.
May we not be voyeurs,
wasting our precious days,
but pilgrims on the divine train without end.

1148 Let us go forth
in the goodness of our merciful Father,
in the gentleness of our brother Jesus,
in the radiance of the Holy Spirit,
in the faith of the apostles,
in the joyful praise of the angels,
in the holiness of the saints,
in the courage of the martyrs.

1149 Let us go forth
in the wisdom of our all-seeing Father,
in the patience of our all-loving Brother,
in the truth of the all-knowing Spirit,

in the learning of the apostles,
in the gracious guidance of the angels,
in the patience of the saints,
in the self-control of the martyrs.

1150 Lord, be within us to give us strength,
over us to protect us,
beneath us to support us,
in front of us to be our guide,
behind us to prevent us falling away,
surrounding us to give us courage,
so that alone, alone
we may walk into the great unknown.

1151 You who are Heroic Love
have built adventure
into each day and into every life.
Help us to explore, to overcome,
and to step out towards this day's horizons
in the spirit of Christ the Endless Adventurer.

1152 Lord of the elements, give us a good journey through life.
Lord of the Star of the East, give us a kindly birth.
Lord of the Star of the South, give us a great love.
Lord of the Star of the West, give us a quiet age.
Lord of the Star of the North, give us a blest death.

1153 Pilgrim God,
we thank you for Brendan's drawing together
of families and friends
into communities of divine service,
and for his adventures for you on land and sea.
Awaken in us the spirit of heroic love
and lead us into the endless adventure.

1154 You who made a pilgrimage of trust on Earth,
help us to
flee from deceptive places that destroy,
walk through valleys of despair,

grow in nurseries of wisdom,
steer clear of devouring lions,
find freedom at the Cross,
convalesce after exhausting struggles,
cut through the tangles of Vanity Fair,
remain open while passing through Doubting Castle,
persevere through ups and downs
and, when the eternal city comes into view,
plunge in and willingly cross the final river.
Inspired by John Bunyan's Pilgrim's Progress

1155 Every day we travel through this life,
may we sense you in the taste of good food,
in the crying of the wind and in the message of our bodies.
May we see you in the wild flower or the playing of a child.
May we know you in the sap of our bodies
or embrace you in their disintegration,
but always travel with you.

1156 Dear Father God,
we have journeyed to this place and here we pause.
Our lives so far have brought us here.
Our future stretches further than the eye can see.
If, thus far, our journey you have shared,
accompany us now.
Give wisdom, light and always joy,
so that in thought and gift and love
our lives shall be to fellow travellers
a witness to your presence in the world.
After Ian Fosten, with permission

1157 Pilgrim God,
who accepted such humbling
in your journey of trust on Earth,
in our pilgrimage
keep us on the paths of listening and learning,
reverence and respect, simplicity and service,
that we may not stray from your authentic steps.

JOURNEYING, PILGRIMAGE

1158 Here we are at your service, O Lord;
to you belong the empires of the world.
Echoes a Muslim prayer made on arrival at a pilgrim centre

1159 Blessing of discovery be yours,
and blessing of rest.

Blessing of scenery be yours,
and blessing of saints.

Blessing of meeting be yours,
and blessing of solitude.

Blessing of friendship be yours,
and blessing of thought.

1160 Lord, for the rest of our lives
we are willing to go anywhere
and do anything for you.
Take us, shape us, lead us,
until we reach beyond this world's shores.

1161 In our journeying this day,
keep us, Father, in your way.
Guide us, Saviour, by your Word,
you alone be overheard.
May we, Spirit, with you walk
in our thoughts and in our talk.
In our friendships let us be
in the Blessed Trinity.
Sent by a friend

1162 Teach us, good Lord,
to work with all of our hearts,
until it can be said of us,
'to work is to pray'.

1163 O God, we thank you
that you have called us to travel,
no longer as strangers

but as pilgrims together
on the journey of your people on Earth.
Lead us in the paths
that are life-giving for the world.

Arriving in a new place

1164 Lord, we offer you our conflicting feelings,
our apprehensions and our aspirations,
the strange bed, the changed roles,
the fear of the unknown.

1165 Risen Christ, we acknowledge that you are in our midst.
Circle this place and make it your own.
Keep peace within, keep evil out.
May all memories, influences or powers that are not of you
flee from this place.
May the angels guard and welcome us all.

1166 We turn our eyes upon you.
Calm us and settle us.
Help us to feel at home with you and with one another,
so there is no need to pretend.
Help us to be at ease with ourselves
and to look upon these new faces as your family.

Church

1167 Grant, O Lord, that your Church in this land
may be true to its birthright.
Kindle in us the adventure of obedience,
the single eye,
the humble, generous spirit
which marked Aidan, Hilda and our national saints.

1168 Risen Christ,
you come with
searing white purity of understanding.

You come with flaming, all-seeing eyes;
you come perfectly formed,
like a burnished bronze sculpture,
and your voice is like the sound of many waters.
Come to the Church:
teach her, cleanse her, forge her.
Speak to her in many-voiced splendour
until the surrounding population
sees something of you reflected through her.

1169 God, who is present to all,
may your churches be communities of
prayer and feasting,
living and learning,
work and celebration,
hospitality and outreach;
the fire of Christ in the midst,
drawing all people to you.

1170 May our church be a seedbed of prayer
from which arise many callings.
May our church be a seedbed of hospitality
from which arise many refreshment places.
May our church be a sanctuary for the battered
from which arise many creative pursuits.
May our church be a seedbed of wisdom
from which arise many growing places.
May our church be a seedbed of the Trinity
from which arises ever-fruitful diversity in unity.

1171 May our churches bring honour to you
and healing to the people.
May they be places of hospitality and hope.
May they be seedbeds of justice and friendship.
May they be sanctuaries for those who are oppressed.
May they bring refreshment to tired traders
and work people.
May they stir us to explore the endless adventure.

1172 Bless the Church.
Through her pastors,
nourish us.
Through her teachers,
establish us.
Through her prophets,
envision us.
Through her musicians,
inspire us.
Through her saints,
sanctify us.
Through her givers,
bless us.

1173 Divine Weaver,
we bless you for the many-coloured tapestry
which is your Church.
We grieve with you that so many strands
have been torn apart.
Weave together in us
scriptural holiness and a catholic spirit,
Pentecostal callings and contemplative calm,
radical justice and sacramental grace –
that we may reflect your Body on Earth
as it is in heaven.

1174 Grant us the humility to know
that we did not create ourselves
and nor can we create your Church.
May we treasure one another as living stones,
each needed in the spiritual building
which makes up your Church on Earth,
through Christ our Lord.

1175 Triune God who mothers us all,
make whole the people through your Church.
Through her Scriptures, inform us.
Through her sacraments, nourish us.
Through her ministry, enfold us.

CHURCH

> Through her charisms, inspire us.
> Through her prophets, challenge us.
> Through her saints, sanctify us.

1176 Holy Spirit, release us, that we may be strong and free.
Sending Spirit, empower us to reach out to others.
May your Church grow in holiness and in numbers.

1177 Lord Christ, you prayed for the unity of all who believe.
May your churches rejoice in the communion of heaven
and attain communion round one table on Earth.
Lord Christ, you call us to love our neighbours.
May we and our local communities seek the common good.
Lord Christ, through bread and wine
you give us signs of your presence transforming all creation.
May artists and those in the media glimpse this vision
and reflect it to the world.

1178 Lord of the Church, Servant King,
take from us attitudes and practices
that put barriers between the Church and the people:
cultural elitism in worship,
clerical status,
looking down on people,
treating the Church as our property.
Make us a pilgrim people,
a Church without walls.

1179 Triune God who mothers us all,
call into being those who nurture
tender shoots and searching souls.
Raise up those who come alongside others.
Soak your Church in new doses
of tender loving care.
Foster fresh callings
and hold your people in your heart.

1180 Save us from being laws unto ourselves.
Save us from thinking that our church
is the centre of everything.

Grace us to listen to those
who have oversight in other parts of the Church.
Grace us with deep respect
for the Faith that has been handed down.

1181 God of the memory held in genes and stones,
help us so to connect
with the roots of our varied cultures
that fresh expressions of your Church may emerge
that are natural, true and attractive.

1182 Holy Spirit, fulfil through us
the work begun by Jesus.
Invigorate our work,
subdue our natural presumptions,
raise us to humility and generous courage.
May no personal scheming
reduce our love to petty dimensions.
May all be accomplished according to the spirit
of your Son's last prayer for his Church
and through the Spirit of love
which you send to us.
Echoes a prayer of Pope John XXII

1183 God of Hilda and the humble heart,
we confess with shame
the loss in the Church
of integrity, humility and patience;
the crushing of spontaneity;
the caging of the wild Spirit;
the breaking off of relationships;
the bruising of crushed reeds;
the arrogance of the intellect;
the pride of empire-building.
Have mercy on us and forgive us.

Nurture us in the tender mercies of our mother,
the Church.
May we
grow in her wisdom,

be stretched by her teachers,
be challenged by her prophets.
May we
be corrected by her shepherds,
be illumined by her seers,
be spurred by her pioneers.
May we
be warned by her erring ones,
be blessed by her givers.

1184 Dear God, you know that many spiritual people
regard religious groups who own property as negative
and they look for small sacred spaces that have no agenda.
You know that many are wary
of the power structures of institutions
and that others find churches
that are not committed to the Earth an outrage.
You know that many women find churches
which women are not allowed to shape destructive,
and they therefore seek movements
where they can feel at home.
You know that men who can be attracted
to the 'wild Jesus'
have no wish to be but passive recipients of words
that are not theirs in a church service.
We pray to you, who are both Defenceless Love
and Head and Source of the Church,
to inspire through us fresh expressions of church.
May your people meet in sacred places
and on common ground they do not own,
may we be committed to the Earth,
and may women and men
be offered welcoming, adventurous spaces
in which they can grow into their fullness
as human beings.

Government

1185 Help us bring to birth a civilisation inspired by love
and the values of respect and freedom,
the values of Aidan and Hilda.
Help us clear out the power and greed
that have usurped these values and torn us apart.
Raise up a new generation of God-inspired leaders.
Restore fellowship between races and religions.
Replace our barriers with hospitable space.
Inspired by trail-blazers of the past,
make us trail-blazers today.

1186 High King of heaven and Earth,
may the diverse authorities of our times
acknowledge you as the Source of our common life,
emulate you as the Servant King,
and build trust and gratitude
among their neighbours.

1187 We pray against
the Pharisee tendency in our society.
We pray for
the financial moguls who give a bit to charity
but milk the most vulnerable dry;
the media moguls
who run down struggling public servants
and destroy rivals without a blink;
celebrities who smile nicely on camera
and abuse others the rest of the day and night.
Give us clarity about what is right
and courage to confront what is wrong in others.
May we do this in such a way
that they know we care for them
and not just for those they abuse.

1188 Lord, give us the statesmanship of the humble heart,
the willingness to move out towards others.
Give us the faith to do our bit,
that we may help to build a civilisation of love.

1189 May our sons grow up strong and straight like young trees.
May our daughters have the beauty of inner serenity.
May our farms and industries overflow.
May the voice of complaining cease from our streets.
Happy are the people from whom such blessings flow
who put their trust in God.
Inspired by Psalm 144

1190 We pray for
this land,
this nurse,
this womb.

We pray for her children,
Christians and Muslims,
believers and unbelievers.

We pray for her prisoners, including prisoners of
prejudice,
pride,
poverty
and addictive substances.

We pray for
her sports people and those injured and ailing,
her extraverts and introverts,
her famous and her forgotten people.

And we pray that she may journey
from fragmentation towards wholeness.

Stillness

1191 Out of the depths of life's torrents,
we weave a prayer of stillness
and enter into God's presence.
Afloat in an ocean of need,
we weave a prayer of direction
and steer towards God's port.

1192 We are sorry for the distractions
which turn people's thoughts away from you
to selfish pursuits.
Help us to recover a sense of belonging
by returning to the Ground
from which we all come.

1193 Babe of Heaven,
strengthen us on our pilgrimage.
Your birth shows us
the simplicity of the Father's love,
the wonder of being human.
Help us to live fully human lives for you.
We quieten our souls under the stillness of sky
and we nestle with you in the Father's lap.

1194 In the silence, we become aware of you, O God.
In the silence, we adore you.
In the silence, our sins stand out and are washed away.
In the silence, our problems fall into their rightful place.
In the silence, we become grateful people.
In the silence, O Lord, we become one with you
and we catch the whispers of your heart.

1195 Eternal Now, you enter into time:
you guided Moses' people through the Red Sea;
you were born of Mary in a cowshed;
you will be present when the cosmos comes to its end.
Eternal Now, you are beyond time; you are Presence.
Eternal Now, your second coming is surely
not after the first and before a third –
could it be our coming into the Eternal Presence?
Help me to become present.
May my human nature become one with you,
as two pieces of wax become one
when they are melted together.
I pray for this second coming.

1196 Sweet All-aware One,
　　　grant me the grace to find the place
　　　where you alone suffice,
　　　where you are in the soil on which I sit
　　　and stand and lay my head,
　　　there on your face to gaze.

1197 Silent, surrendered, leaving all
　　　open to you for yourself alone,
　　　into the seething mass within,
　　　pour your calm and still our being.

Forgiveness

1198 Jesus, you were driven to the sands
　　　by the searching Spirit.
　　　Strip from us what is not of you.
　　　Forgive us for
　　　our selfish deeds,
　　　our empty speech
　　　and the words with which we have wounded.
　　　Forgive us for
　　　our false desires,
　　　our vengeful attitudes
　　　and for what we have left untended.

1199 All-forgiving One,
　　　when I meet angry people who carry centuries of hostility,
　　　neglect or mistreatment,
　　　help me to listen to their stories without judgements
　　　or interruptions;
　　　and may they know
　　　that they have met someone who has deeply listened.

1200 Forgive us for
　　　grasping at things we do not need,
　　　clinging to projects that distract us from you,
　　　accumulating worries that hold us back from your path.

Help us to acquire what no money can buy:
a free spirit,
a wise mind,
a beautiful attitude,
a serving heart.

1201 Lord, plagues new and old afflict our world
and threaten its existence.
We have brought them upon ourselves.
Have mercy and forgive.
Help us to amend our ways.
Save us, O Christ, for you surely came for this hour, too.

1202 Thrice-seeing King of Heaven,
dislodge the mote that is in my blind eye
and gently place it on my tongue
where I can spit it out.

Sorrow and loss

1203 Grant our heads the waters of lament
and our ears the tears of sorrow.
The beautiful stones of the nature you have given us
have become defaced.
The precious robe of chastity has been torn.
Devotions of love have been scattered.
Inspirations have been squandered.

Home and families

1204 *On returning home*

May our homes reflect your presence,
coming through the personalities you have given us.
Grace us to express
your peace and perfect order into them.
Remind us to acknowledge your authority
over all that will be thought, purchased and arranged.
Give us a fresh supply of truth and beauty
on which to draw as we relax, entertain, work and sleep.

HOME AND FAMILIES

1205 God bless our families.
May we be there for one another.
May we respect each one's unique personality.
May we learn to take things in our stride.
May we pray, have fun and forgive.

1206 May the Three Loves in God's heart
free us to
enjoy each other's company,
accept each other's pain,
express our needs,
forgive from our hearts,
that we may flower as people.

1207 God protect the household.
God consecrate the children.
God encompass our assets.

1208 *TV*

God make the TV
a blessing to the family.
When there's horrible stuff,
may we turn the switch off.
When there's too much choice,
may we listen to your voice.
May the people in the soap
not give up hope.
When the top spots show off,
may we say 'that's enough'.
May the world out there
also get on air.
What in heaven is seen –
may it get on our screen.

1209 *Parents*

May the Three of Limitless Love
replenish our stock of love.
May those we care for not take us for granted.

God give us grace to
listen to our loved ones,
play with our loved ones,
weep with our loved ones,
confront our loved ones,
explain things to our loved ones
and then to give them away
as a blessing to the world.

1210 God help us to
listen to our loved ones,
play with our loved ones,
laugh with our loved ones,
weep with our loved ones,
forgive our loved ones,
take responsibility for our loved ones,
be faithful to our loved ones for ever.

1211 *Fathers*

Father, give us all fatherly care.
Help fathers to reflect you
in the way they discharge their responsibilities.
May they be priests to their spouses
and to their children.

1212 *Mothers*

Mother, dear pearl of great price,
too often have we taken you for granted.
May the Holy Trinity protect you.
May the Three of Limitless Love renew you so that
an island shall you be in our seas,
a light shall you be in our nights,
a well shall you be in our deserts,
until heaven's arms enfold you.

HOME AND FAMILIES

1213 *A baby*

    May this little one
    bring love and affection to you
    and good to the world.
    May this be a day of grace for you.
    May you be a guarding one to this gift of heaven,
    along with the saints and the angels
    and the Three of Limitless Love.

Pets

1214 God care for this pet.
    Keep you well and fit.
    May your life on this Earth be blest
    and then may you go to your rest.
    Friends may we be for a while.
    Always bring to mind a smile.
    May you be kept content.
    Theft may God prevent.
    May you be a pleasure to us.
    May we bless you and not fuss.

1215 Each day and each night,
    in cold and heat,
    in light and dark,
    keep them from falling;
    keep them from road accidents;
    keep them from thieves;
    keep them from poisons;
    keep them content,
    O sweet Maker of all.

1216 [Name of pet], the eye of God be on you
    to bless you,
    to look after you,
    to give you pleasure,
    and to make you a pleasure.

Ancestors

1217 Great Spirit, as the sun rises in the east,
so our ancestors arose out of your love.
Great Spirit, as you shine like the bright North Star,
so our ancestors steered their course by you.
Great Spirit, in the dimness of memory,
this alone we know:
that as the sun goes to its rest,
so our ancestors went to their rest in you.
Great Spirit, our gene pool is yours.
As the sun completes its circle,
so our ancestors who are near to us in time,
and those who are distant,
are all encompassed in your love.

1218 Moon, you gave light to our ancestors.
Air, you gave breath to our ancestors.
Earth, you gave food to our ancestors.
Water, you gave life to our ancestors.
Creator of moon and air, earth and water,
it was you who gave our ancestors their being.
From you they came; to you they returned.
Glory to you.

1219 Keeper of kindreds,
encompass our forebears and our family
in your reconciling arms,
in your strong arms of love.
Christ of the agony,
Christ of the bleeding,
Christ racked and stretched out on the tree,
we place upon you our own agony,
we place upon you our bleeding hearts,
we place upon you our despair.
Take it,
break it,
remake it.
Your tree of death became the tree of life.
Give your blessing of life to us.

Divorce

1220 Grant us
acceptance of pain without bitterness,
grieving for loss without blame,
forgiveness for frailty without remorse,
renewal of trust without fear.

1221 Sadness and sin behind us be,
farewell to marriage, but friends let us be.
Bless our children in their hurts;
bless us as parents despite our warts.

Vehicles

1222 *Car*

May it bless the land it will travel on
and bless the earth that fuels it.
May it bless each person who enters it
and bless each person it passes:
the people on the roadside,
the people in the shops and workplaces,
the people in the public buildings and schools.
May each journey be an act of prayer –
a reflection of our journey through life.

1223 *To the owner or user of a new car*

May this be a gift of space to you,
may this be a gift of movement to you,
may this be a gift of sight to you,
may this be a gift of meeting to you.
In the name of the God
who makes and moves all things.

1224 *For a motorcyclist*

God bless your steed.
God bless your speed.
Christ meet your need.
By the Spirit be led
with angels overhead
until you reach your bed.

1225 *Mountain bike*

> God speed to you.
> Good movement to you.
> Fine balance to you.
> Power of air to you.
> Power of wheel to you.
> Power of frame to you.
> Good ups to you.
> And also good downs.

Leisure

Internet

1226 God save us from an impersonal world.
If only Facebook were really a big room
where I was not a generic product.
God, show us your face,
and slow me down until I see your face in another person.

1227 Sweet the notes of purity with which a bird tweets.
Make our tweets as pure as the divine melodies
that only the deep soul's ears may hear.

1228 May I tweet with the melody of the lark,
the wisdom of the owl
and the eye of the eagle,
in the name of the Holy Dove.

1229 *Holidays*

> Blessing of discovery be ours,
> and blessing of rest.
> Blessing of scenery be ours,
> and blessing of sleep.
> Blessing of meeting be ours,
> and blessing of solitude.
> Blessing of fun be ours,
> and blessing of thought.
> Blessing of change be ours,
> and blessing of homecoming.

1230 *Discos and parties*

>Circle us, Lord.
>Keep these graces within:
>the grace of movement,
>the grace of beauty,
>the grace of happiness,
>the grace of conversation,
>the grace of restraint,
>the grace of self-forgetfulness,
>the grace of being true to ourselves.

Loving friendships

1231 *Reunions*

>The welcome of the Father's arms be ours.
>The welcome of the Saviour's heart be ours.
>The welcome of the Spirit's call be with us.
>Deep peace of this earth to us.
>Deep peace of this sky to us.
>Deep peace of this place to us.
>The kindly eye of the Three be upon us,
>to aid us and guard us,
>to cherish and enrich us.
>May God take us in the clasp
>of his own two hands.

1232 Root of our Desire,
>thank you for the sap that rises in our bodies,
>and for the feelings of attraction between two people.

>Ocean of Mercy,
>wash through us, until distorted desire ebbs away.

>Divine Lover,
>teach us to hold each other in our hearts,
>and not to possess them,
>but to grow in tenderness as a plant grows.

1233 Beauty of friendship, grow between us,
friendship without guile,
friendship without malice,
friendship without striving.
Goodness of friendship, grow between us,
friendship with insight,
friendship with faithfulness,
friendship with the light touch.

1234 Be in the eye of each friend on our journey,
to bless and to teach each one.
The eye of the Father be upon us.
The eye of the Son be upon us.
The eye of the Spirit be upon us.
The eye of the Friendly Three
be upon us for ever.

1235 Eternal Friend,
we thank you for the countless people who,
through the human gift of friendship,
have turned into your friends.
Renew in us the gift of friendship,
and draw many folk in to the circle of your love.

God's world

Thanksgiving and praise

1236 Glorious Source, we give you greeting!
Let Sister Earth and Brother Sun praise you.
Let the fields and the forests praise you.
Let the birds and the beasts praise you.
Let everything that has breath praise you,
Mother and Father of all that has being.

1237 For the glory of creation
streaming from your heart,
we praise you.
For the air of the eternal
seeping through the physical,
we praise you.
For the everlasting glory
dipping into time,
we praise you.
For the wonder of your presence
beckoning from each leaf,
we praise you.
For setting us,
like the stars in their courses,
within the orbit of your love,
we praise you.

1238 Infinite Birther,
thank you for moments of grace
in the unfolding life of the cosmos;
for the explosion of a star
and the creation of our solar system;
for the cooling aeons and the birth of our planet;
for the seed of life and the emergence of plants;
for the evolution of creatures
and the dawning of human consciousness;
for our ability to make a fire,
a wheel and a computer.
But, far more than these all,
we thank you for yourself.

1239 Lord of the Dance, grant me joy in all things:
in the towel that rubs my body,
the steam that heats my coffee,
the street that greets my feet
and the wonder of a life.
Echoes words on a Seattle plaque

1240 We give you thanks for great moments of grace
in the evolution of the cosmos.
For the death of a star
which brought to birth planet Earth.
For the emergence of life forms.
For the emergence of minerals,
vegetables and animals.
For the cooperation,
and not just the competition,
between all that lives.
We give thanks for the moments of grace
in the life of a person;
the power of attraction and the wonder of a birth.
For the human person,
endowed with conscience, awe and intelligence,
a co-creator with you.

1241 Unto you, O Lord, be praise for
every flower that ever grew,
every bird that ever flew,
every wind that ever blew.
Unto you, O Lord, be praise for
every flake of virgin snow,
every place where humans go,
every joy and every woe.
Unto you, O Lord, be praise for
every life that shall be born,
every heart that shall be torn,
every day and every dawn.
Echoes an early Irish prayer

GOD'S WORLD

1242 Maker of all creatures, we honour you.
Friend of all creatures, we honour you.
Force of all creatures, we honour you.

1243 I thank you for the wind
that clears the fogs of life,
for chimneys that allow air and warmth
to move through our lives,
for the texture of the bricks,
tiles and wood that breathe.
I thank you for housetops and street lights
and for the sound of traffic moving.
I thank you for Internet, TV and satellite dishes
that open the world up
to people in their little dwellings.
So much energy, so much enterprise –
the friendly smiles of Sister Earth.

1244 Thank you,
Creator of the world,
for the music and medicine of flowers,
which give us a scent of heaven upon Earth;
and for their vases which enable them to give their best.
May those who look at them see your glory.

1245 Creator of our land,
our Earth, the trees,
the animals and humans:
all is for your honour.

1246 For the beauty and bounty of the world,
its seasons and its gifts;
for the wonder of life
and the Earth on which we live:
we offer you our heartfelt praise.

1247 Glory to the Birther, glory to the Son,
glory to the Spirit who makes creation one.

1248 Glory to you, the vital Force
that vibrates throughout the cosmos.
Glory to you, the infinite Mind
that understands the cosmos.
Glory to you, the fertile Birther
that conceives each element of the cosmos.
Glory to you, the purest Love
that comes to live in one small corner of the cosmos.
Glory to you, the Gatherer
of planets and peoples, space and time,
the Climax of the cosmos.

1249 Thank you for
the taste of good food,
the crying of the wind
and the pulsing of our bodies.
Thank you for the cartwheels of the heart
the playing of a child
and the diving of a fish.

Blessings

1250 God bless the earth that is beneath us,
the sky that is above us,
the life that lies before us,
your image deep within us.
Echoes a traditional Scottish blessing

1251 May the blessing of the rain be on us,
the sweet soft rain.
May it fall upon our spirits
so that all the little flowers may spring up
and shed their sweetness on the air.
May the blessing of the great rains be upon us,
that they beat upon our spirits
and wash them fair and clean,
and leave there many a shining pool
where the blue of heaven shines,
and sometimes a star.
Echoes a traditional Irish blessing

1252 God be a smooth way before you,
a guiding star above you,
a keen eye behind you.

1253 God be with you whatever you pass.
Jesus be with you whatever you climb.
Spirit be with you wherever you stay.

1254 God be with you at each stop and each sea,
at each lying down and each rising up,
in the trough of the waves, on the crest of the billows,
each step of the journey you take.

1255 God bless the path on which you go.
God bless the earth beneath your feet.
God bless your destination.

1256 May the land to which you are journeying
abound with the fruits
of what you have planted here.
May they never fail to increase
in the land to which you go.

Blessings on food

1257 May the blessing of the five loaves and the two fishes,
which God shared out among the 5000, be ours.
May the King who did the sharing bless our sharing.

1258 Bless, O Lord, this food we are about to eat;
and we pray, O God,
that it may be good for our bodies and souls;
and if there be any poor creatures hungry or thirsty
walking along the road,
send them in to us that we can share the food with them,
just as you share your gifts with all of us.

BLESSINGS ON FOOD

1259 Bless us, O God, bless our food and our drink.
Give us, O God of the nourishing meal,
well-being to the body, the frame of the soul.
Give us, O God of the honey-sweet milk,
the sap and the savour of the fragrant farms.

1260 May this food restore our strength,
give new energy to tired limbs,
new thoughts to weary minds.
May this drink restore our souls,
give new vision to dry spirits,
new warmth to cold hearts.
And, once refreshed, may we give new pleasure
to you, who give all to us.

1261 God in our in our waking, God in our speaking;
God in our cooking, God in our eating;
God in our laughing, God in our digesting;
God in our working, God in our resting.

1262 May this food so fresh and fragrant
call forth reverence for you.
As you give this strength to our perishable limbs,
so give us grace for our eternal lives.

1263 Thanks to you for the abundance of food,
for the bounty of creation,
for all that is good.

1264 In a world where so many are hungry,
may we eat this food with humble hearts.
In a world where so many are lonely,
may we share this friendship with joyful hearts.

1265 Bless you, King of the universe,
for this sign of your tender care.
Bless you, King of this eating room,
for this sign that you are here.

1266 Generous God,
>   as once you multiplied the five loaves and two fishes,
>   multiply the gifts each of us brings,
>   that from our sharing together, blessings may flow.

1267 Blessed are you, High King of the universe,
>   it is of your goodness that
>   we have this food to eat and this wine to drink.
>   Blessed be you for ever!

1268 Bless, O Lord,
>   this food which we are about to eat
>   for our bodily welfare.
>   May we be strengthened thereby
>   to do your holy will.

1269 Glory, praise and thanks to you, O God,
>   for this food and our good health.
>   We also thank you for all the food and health
>   for which we have not thanked you.

1270 A thousand thanks to you, O God,
>   who has given us this food for the body.
>   Grant us, we ask you who are so generous, eternal life.

1271 May the freshness and fragrance of the fields
>   be with us as we enjoy this meal.
>   May the freshness and fragrance of your presence
>   linger with us as we journey on.

1272 Bless you, Creator of all we eat.
>   Bless you, Saviour – you with us meet.
>   Bless you, Spirit who makes this sweet.

1273 You who put beam in golden sun,
>   you who put food in wheat and herd,
>   you who put fish in stream and sea,
>   put a grateful heart in us.

1274 The food which we are to eat
    is earth, water and sun
    coming to us through pleasing plants.
    The food which we are to eat
    is the fruit of the labour of many creatures.
    We are thankful for it.
    May it give us health, strength and joy,
    and may it increase our love.
    Echoes a Unitarian prayer

1275 The food that we are to eat comes to us
    through the labours of our sister Earth,
    her creatures,
    and our brothers and sisters
    far and near.
    May we be thankful for this gift.

1276 Risen Christ of the miraculous catching of fish
    and the perfect lakeside meal,
    be with us as we share this meal.

1277 May this food give new energy to tired limbs,
    new thoughts to weary minds,
    and new warmth to cold hearts.

After food

1278 A thousand thanks to you,
    O King of the universe.
    A thousand thanks to you,
    O Lord of grace,
    for what you have given us since our birth,
    and for what you will give us
    until the day of our death.

1279 Thanks be to you, O God,
    praise be to you, O God,
    reverence be to you, O God,
    for all you have given us.

As you have given physical life
to earn us our worldly food,
so grant us eternal life
to show forth your glory.

Garden

1280 Here,
may the earth be full of health,
may the plants be full of goodness,
may the flowers be full of colour,
may the birds be full of chirps,
may the pets be full of wags,
may the people be full of joy.

1281 There is no plant in the ground
that does not tell of your beauty, Lord.
May this garden speak to us of the fragrance of your love.
May the fruits of the Earth speak to us of your mercy.

1282 Bless the moon that is above us,
the earth that is beneath us,
the hard work to be done here,
the seedlings that shall grow here,
the neighbours we shall greet here,
and all who overlook here.

Sport

1283 God help us to
run straight,
bear failure,
be true,
make friends,
honour the other,
explore the world,
give our best,
reverence our Creator.

1284 We bless you, God, for the goodness of this day.
May the strength of the ox be yours,
the speed of a gazelle be yours,
the suppleness of a fish be yours,
the flight of a bird be yours,
the joy of the earth be yours,
the warmth of the sun be yours:
the wreath of God around your neck,
the wreath of God around your chest,
the wreath of God around your thighs,
the wreath of God around your feet
and the gold of life everlasting.

1285 Bless to me my body.
Bless to me my brain.
Bless to me my training.
Bless to me my game.

Thank you for football,
which creates a level playing field
for billionaires and street children alike.
May FIFA be a family that is free
from prejudice, bribery and ill will,
with a Rule to which all subscribe.

Money

1286 God of generosity and order,
wean us from the selfish pursuit of gain.
Inspire us to administer our money
in the power and wisdom of your Spirit for
the good of the world,
the sustaining of those who serve you without salary
and, above all, for your glory.

1287 God of the Economy – the whole created universe –
teach us to use money as a servant of the common good.
Teach us to use the market as a guide, not as a god.

Teach us to invest in what brings long-term well-being
to the planet and its people.
And teach us to combat the cheats
dressed in sheep's clothing.

1288 Beloved One,
we long to dwell always in your presence.
Help us to
speak the truth from our hearts,
keep gossip from our tongues,
do nothing but good to our friends,
bless others in our use of money,
that we grow ever more secure in you.
Echoes Psalm 15

1289 *Lottery win*

Good be on you, gift from heaven.
Restraint be on you, gift from heaven.
Wisdom be on you, gift from heaven.
Generosity be on you, gift from heaven,
lest you become a gift from hell.

1290 Vast and Giving One,
wean us from attachment to possessions.
Forgive our nations for bingeing
on loans our children must repay.
Cure our addiction to debt.
Grant us mercy as we reap what we have sown.
May we not create a spiritual famine where abundance lies,
by failing to share the gift of our lives.

1291 God bless this money for what it can make possible:
the nurturing of our bodies or minds,
a pat on the back for work well done,
the enlarging of our horizons,
expressing love to others through gifts;
for it is in giving that we shall receive
more than we can ask.

Prayers for others and the world

Caring for God's world

1292 You made the Earth, and through the long ages
planted it with every kind of plant.
You made animals to crawl and to run upon it,
birds to fly over it and fish to swim around it.
When all was prepared,
you formed humankind from the soil.
You breathed your life into them.
May we never forget that we are mortal creatures;
from earth we come, to earth we go.
We did not make ourselves.
We and the Earth need to be redeemed
through the Saviour who restores unity
between Earth and heaven.
Saviour, bless and redeem us.

1293 Creator of the land,
out of wet mud you have fashioned a wonderful world.
But now we trample upon and destroy it.
Teach us
to drink in your love through creation,
to shop and eat in grateful awareness of your providence
and to tend the world with care.

1294 Creator and Saviour, we have
exploited Earth for our selfish ends,
turned our backs on the cycles of life
and forgotten we are your stewards.
Now soils become barren,
air and water become unclean,
species disappear
and humans are diminished.
In penitence we come to you.

1295 Bestower, we have raped and spoiled your world.
Forgive us.
Salvager, we have mindlessly squandered
precious but limited fossil fuels.
Forgive us.

Spirit, we have hardened our hearts towards your creatures
who are processed for our supermarkets
without having had a life.
Forgive us.

1296 Nurturing God, bless this soil,
the soil on which we live and work
and make community.
In your mercy, may it bring forth goodness
to nourish and renew
the whole community who share it.

1297 God bless the oil
and the good things it has made possible.
God forgive us for grabbing it
and wasting it without wisdom.
God help us
as we reap the harvest of our misdeeds.
God guide us
as we seek to harness the energies
of sun and wind and water – and make us wise.

1298 We pray for the well-being of the creation,
the healthfulness of the air,
the richness of the Earth and its provisions,
and the beauty of the whole world.

1299 Help us to know
that the Earth does not belong to us;
we belong to Earth.
Help us to know
that we did not weave the web of life;
we are merely a strand in it.
Help us to know
that whatever we do to ourselves,
we do to the Earth.
Help us to know
that whatever befalls the Earth
befalls the sons and daughters of the Earth.

1300 Creator, we have raped and spoiled your world:
   forgive.
   Saviour, we have ignored your warnings
   to tend your Earth like a vineyard:
   forgive.
   Sustainer, we have tried to live without you:
   forgive.

1301 Creator God,
   help us to give all creatures their due respect.
   Teach us how to conserve, to share, to enjoy,
   to tend the earth with care,
   to develop agriculture that truly enhances,
   to guide science along wise and considerate ways,
   to restore the lands that have been ravaged
   until we, the Earth and you
   blossom in a relationship of love.

1302 You are the Rock from which all Earth is fashioned.
   May we give precious Earth its worth.
   You are the Food from which all life is fed.
   May we give precious life its worth.
   You are the Source from which all matter is forged.
   May we give precious matter its worth.

1303 Birther, the planet is pulling against you.
   It is falling apart.
   It is becoming deluged.
   You do not want this.
   So we come close to you.
   Show us what to stop doing.
   Show us what to start doing.
   Show us how to build together
   a worldwide Noah's ark for today.

1304 Dear Saviour,
   who restored unity between Earth and heaven,
   teach us to care for your Earth
   and to be good stewards of all that is in it.

May our eyes be open to see your hand in nature.
May our hands be open to cherish your gifts
in the material things around.
May we learn how to live in harmony with your laws.

1305 God forgive us
for the polluting waste
dumped by rich nations on lands of the poor,
for the lust of the few
to own and control life forms,
for turning your gifts of water and life itself
into products for gain,
for turning the sowing of seed
from a sacred duty into a crime,
for the destruction of biodiversity.
Change our hearts.

1306 Great Spirit, whose breath is felt in the soft breeze,
may we cherish the precious Earth,
the Earth of the God of life.
May we provide for those
who can neither sow nor reap
because human ills have drained them.

1307 Creator, make us co-workers with you,
that the Earth and all who live upon it
may reap a full harvest.
Show us how to reflect your rhythms
in our lives and our work,
and to conserve the world's rich resources,
that we may sustain a vibrant environment.

1308 Caring Father God,
we offer to you the fuels and forests,
the seas and soil,
the air and animals,
the technology and the textiles of the world.
May we steward your creation to your glory,
and for the benefit of future generations.

1309 May we love you in your Earth
and in every grain of sand.
May we love you in your skies
and in every ray of light.
May we love you in the animals
and in everything that breathes.
May we love you in your plants
and in every leaf that greens.
May we love you in your creation
and in the symphony of the whole.
May we love you for yourself
and in your infinite Being.

1310 This we know: the Earth does not belong to us.
The Earth is God's and so are all people.
This we know: we did not weave the web of life.
The Earth is God's and so is all that breathes on it.
Whatever befalls the Earth
befalls the sons and daughters of the Earth.
The Earth is God's and so we will serve it.

1311 For the rainforests gone,
and the deserts caused by human destruction,
for polluted seas and dirty streets,
for not being content to savour
the simple gifts of creation,
we grieve with you, O God.

God, give us cities
where street vendors don't ask us to buy,
where libraries give us free Internet use,
and where water is a gift, not a commodity.

1312 In dependence on the God of life,
may we cherish the precious Earth,
the Earth of the God of life,
the Earth of the Christ of love,
the Earth of the Spirit Holy.
In dependence on the God of life
may the Earth be our bed of hope.

The human family

1313 Caring Provider,
in you we live and move and have our being.
Sustain those who eke out the minerals,
create textiles, grow crops or rear cattle.
Give us wisdom to manage technology for the world's good.
Bless all work done today
that enables the human family
to be clothed, fed and housed in dignity,
to receive a fair return for work
and to celebrate the gift of life.

1314 Birther and Arbiter of the human family,
who delights in our diversity
but calls us to make our home in you,
teach us to live by your laws,
to find the dignity of diversity
and the love that even the oceans cannot quench.

1315 God of shepherds and angels,
as Hilda drew out the songs
that were locked in shy Caedmon's heart,
may we draw out the music
that lies buried in a thousand lives:
the music of speech and seeing,
the music of laughter and loving,
the music of craft and creating.

1316 God who dances with creation,
planting your likeness in the people,
striking the world with thunder,
send us out to fill the world with love.

1317 Teach us who live in comfort
to disarm terrorists through repentance
as well as through force of law.
Energise us with your compassion
to help the dispossessed,
to listen to those without a voice
and to reach out in friendship to all.

1318 We thank you for great people of faith
 who light up our night and urge us on to heavenly virtues.
 May we learn from those who
 overcome heroic odds with nobility of spirit,
 are gracious in defeat and magnanimous in triumph.
 Show us how to truly love,
 and be content with little things.

1319 Good God, may we never forget
 that the blessings of prosperity and peace
 come from eternal vigilance
 in the struggle against greed, neglect and injustice.
 May our nations
 be freed from the bondage of fear,
 rise above selfish ambition
 and become flexible to your direction.

 May the qualities
 that make democracy function flourish:
 homespun qualities of faithfulness, honesty and care.

1320 God bless the stranger at the door.
 God bless the baby on the floor.
 God bless the shopper, piled with goods.
 God bless teenagers masked in hoods.
 God bless the sombre city gent.
 God bless the crone, lined and bent.
 God bless us all – one family,
 love-encompassed in Trinity.

1321 Dear Father,
 what pleasure it gives you
 when we reflect in our relationships
 the love you and Jesus and the Spirit
 have for one another and for us.
 We know that we are as near to you, Father,
 as we are to the people from whom we are most divided.
 We pray for those people we are furthest from.
 In our hearts we reach out to them.
 And you are pleased.
 And we are pleased.

1322 Holy Spirit, renew in us
joy in our work,
life in our being,
love in our relationships.

Noble Christ, take from us cynicism,
control and mindless chatter.
Give to us wholeheartedness,
awareness and compassion.
May we be a sacrament of strength
to those whose hands we hold,
as your strong-fingered hands hold us.
Strengthen our resolve,
sharpen our minds, shape our wills,
grace our lands.

1323 Arbiter of the nations,
we confess that the twin evils of power and greed
have often usurped your values and torn us apart.
Humble our proud pretensions that we can sustain
a good society without you.
Replace our military walls with sacred, hospitable space.
Move us to build cities of friendship
between races and religions.
Raise up a new generation of God-inspired leaders.
Give us a soul that honours you.

1324 Almighty God,
nothing on Earth can compare to you,
nothing on Earth can contain you.
If we, your people, experience failure,
but turn again to you,
forgive us and restore us.
If there is drought or famine
and we cry to you,
send us rain and revive the crops.
If those who have warred and wasted the land
confess and say sorry to you,
hear from heaven, forgive us,
and heal our land.

Echoes a prayer of King Solomon; see 2 Chronicles 6

1325 Bind us together, Lord,
　　　bind us together,
　　　bind us together in love.
　　　We are one family of God,
　　　brothers and sisters in Christ,
　　　called to give love to the world.
　　　Draw us nearer our Head.

1326 God of Community,
　　　bring to birth a community of justice.
　　　We pray for the powerful
　　　who impose their will on the weak;
　　　may they come to know your defenceless love.
　　　We pray for those who seek revenge through acts of terror;
　　　may they come to know your defenceless love.
　　　We pray for those who have lost limbs or loved ones;
　　　may they come to know your defenceless love.

1327 Yahweh, people call you by a hundred names,
　　　but YOU ARE.
　　　Help us to be.
　　　Out of the silence of a listening heart,
　　　may compassion and rapport with others grow.
　　　Out of the sharing of our treasures,
　　　may others come to bless you,
　　　and may you have all the glory.

1328 Crucified Jesus, you lived and died a Jew,
　　　with love in your heart towards all.
　　　Risen Christ, you appeared under open skies
　　　to those who did not recognise you.
　　　Embrace your Jewish family
　　　in your heart of love,
　　　and may we do the same.

1329 Great-hearted God,
　　　who reaches out to all,
　　　inspire our every nerve and sinew
　　　to reach out to others with your love.

May we accept each person as yours.
May we include each person in our hearts.
May we find a way
to walk with those who stumble,
to watch with those who suffer
and to work with those who avoid us.

1330 Christ of the people,
who learnt lessons in your home,
in the temple and at the carpenter's bench,
make us humble to learn facts from others,
make us observant to learn goodness from others,
make us reflective to learn from others' mistakes.

1331 God bless Muslims and God bless Christians.
God bless Hindus and God bless Jews.
God bless atheists and God bless pagans.
God bless your children in Africa and your children in Asia.
God bless your children in America
and your children in Australasia.
God bless your children in Europe
and your children in the Middle East.
God bless young people and God bless old people.
And let all the people say: Amen.

1332 Creator God,
bless all the people.
Saviour God,
bless all the people.
Spirit of God,
bless all the people.
Bless our neighbours,
bless our enemies,
bless our leaders.
Change their hearts.
Change our hearts.
Change all hearts.
Help us.
Guide us.
Trust us.

1333 God save the people:
　　　save us from our hardness,
　　　save us from our deafness.
　　　God save the people:
　　　save us from our vileness,
　　　save us from our 'niceness'.
　　　God save the people:
　　　save us from our nemesis,
　　　save us from ourselves.

1334 May we make common cause with those who do right.
　　　May we not make a fuss about where good comes from.
　　　May we let God look after himself.

1335 Father, we of this day are children of confusion:
　　　restore the vision of God to us.
　　　The noise of the city deafens us to the still, small voice:
　　　restore the hearing of God to us.
　　　The pace of modern living deadens us:
　　　restore the alertness of God to us.
　　　The pride of fame and fashion enslaves us:
　　　restore the liberty of God to us.

1336 All-powerful and All-compassionate One,
　　　wean the people from the false gods
　　　of fortune, fame and fantasy.
　　　Teach our world that we have to reap what we sow.
　　　Raise up children to serve you as the living God.

1337 We bless you for your covenant with Noah.
　　　Renew our relationship with the Earth.
　　　We bless you for your covenant with Moses.
　　　Renew our relationship with the world.
　　　We bless you for your covenant with David.
　　　Renew our relationship with the Church.
　　　We bless you for your covenant with Jesus.
　　　Renew our relationship with you.

1338 High King, Creator of all,
    remind us that every human life is sacred,
    whether it belongs to a woman in a war-torn land
    or to a disabled person next door,
    to an unborn infant or a terminally ill patient.
    Remind us that, whatever a person's age, race or creed,
    each individual has been made in your likeness,
    and Christ has given his all for each one.
    This makes every person precious in your sight.

1339 We pray for those who are unable
    to find the paid work they desire;
    may they know that you will accompany them
    as they give their best from day to day.
    We pray for work and community creators;
    may they generate energy, ideas
    and possibilities of work sharing.

1340 Supreme Ruler of heaven and Earth,
    from whom all authority flows,
    may the diverse authorities of our times
    acknowledge you as the Source of life,
    emulate you as the Servant King
    and fear you as the Judge of truth.

1341 Guardian, be over the restless people,
    a covering of truth and peace.
    May the saints and the Saviour watch over us
    and keep us true in all we do.

1342 Give us wise leaders, clear vision
    and an understanding of what is right.
    Inspire in us true values.
    May we know ourselves,
    know what is good
    and know when to stop.
    May we work towards a prejudice-free,
    hate-free, fear-free world.

May we learn to celebrate with joy,
to let a thousand flowers bloom
and to delight in one another's creativity.
May our foreign policy be
to earn the trust and gratitude of our neighbours.
May we honour one another,
seek the common good
and live as fellow citizens of your eternal kingdom.

1343 Make us wise in our understanding,
open in our listening,
generous in our giving
and vulnerable in our sharing.

1344 Lord, help me
to take the time to sit in the shoes of the other person –
to start from where they are,
to listen to what they feel,
to refrain from the too-hasty judgement
or the too-ready answer,
to smile and be gentle
and yet not to collude with the slipshod,
but to prayerfully see a thing through.

1345 In our pleasures,
your kingdom come.
In our leaders,
your kingdom come.
In our gatherings,
your kingdom come.
On the roads,
your kingdom come.
In each thing we do this day,
your kingdom come.

1346 Help us to know
that the world does not belong to us,
that what we do to the world will be done to us.
May we forgo the gods of power and wealth,
and find our true greatness in listening to the world
and in serving the planet.

1347 Lord, we would like to be part of a nursery of saints.
Show us what needs to happen for this to be.
May our lives be a seedbed of prayer and of friendship
lived out in fellowship with others of like mind.

1348 May the love of the Three
give birth to a new community.
May the yielding of the Three
give birth to a new humanity.
May the life of the Three
give birth to a new creativity.
May the togetherness of the Three
give birth to a new unity.
May the glory of the Three
give birth to a new society.

1349 *A boy's first steps towards manhood*
God help you to
run straight,
speak what is true,
ask questions,
overcome fear,
learn self-control;
bear failure,
stand alone,
care for your body,
guard your soul;
honour women,
respect men,
explore the world,
give your best;
open your heart to all people,
close your heart to all pretence,
know yourself;
reverence the Creator,
walk with the Saviour,
flow with the Spirit,
enter into your eternal destiny.

1350 *A girl's first period*
> This is a blessing of the God of life,
> the blessing of mild mother Mary,
> from whose breasts our Lord suckled milk.
> May the Spirit bathe you and make you to grow wise.
>
> May God give you strength in every such time.
> May Christ give you love in every such time.
> May Spirit give you peace in every such time.
>
> Lord, place these nine choice graces in the upturned face
> of this day's wakened lass:
> the grace of deportment,
> the grace of voice,
> the grace of provision,
> the grace of goodness,
> the grace of wisdom,
> the grace of caring,
> the grace of femininity,
> the grace of a lovely personality,
> the grace of godly speech.

God's care for creation

1351 When rich nations begin to reap what they have sown,
may they learn from this to live more simply,
that others may simply live;
to produce sustainably, to invest ethically,
and to live as responsible members of a world community.

1352 May our government and civic leaders be
shepherds of their people and not self-serving,
alert to needs and not apathetic,
strategic for long-term good
and not blown off course by every wind,
friends of the whole human family
and not prejudiced or partisan.

1353 High-borne eagles and nesting birds,
       be one with God's friends on Earth.
       Speckled trout and mountain deer,
       speak without words God's praise.
       Snarling wolf and savage boar,
       lie down at sainted feet.
       Serpents of fear and fierce desire,
       uncoil and concede defeat.
       Creatures tame and creatures wild,
       show to us a living God.

1354 Generosity of God,
       spilling over into creation,
       flow into your Church that we may
       bless the air and the animals,
       tend the earth with care,
       give love to your creation
       and live a rhythm that restores
       well-being to the planet.

1355 Generosity of God,
       spilling over into creation,
       we bless you for flowers and their wealth of beauty,
       for creatures and their glorious variety,
       for seas and seasons and scents.
       May we, too, reflect your boundless generosity.

1356 God, you dance with creation,
       plant your likeness in the people
       and strike the world with thunder:
       send us out to fill the world with love.

1357 Lord, may the swirling storm clouds
       remind me that I am a creature, not Creator;
       that I am liable to suffer from the changes and chances
       of this mortal life.
       May the clouds teach me to look always to you –
       the Creator of both storm and sunshine.
       May they teach me to maintain joy when life is frowning,
       and to maintain perspective in and out of season.

1358 Earth, whose seeds and fields and food
have come to be –
may she bestow to us the finest of her yield.
Earth, whose waters, common to all,
flow faithfully through the nights and days –
may she pour on us the milk of kindness
that brings us lustre.

1359 Great Provider,
may we receive what the Earth gives us
in respect,
in simplicity,
in solidarity,
in humility,
in joy,
in service,
in vocation.

1360 Divine Birther,
may the whole world celebrate your existence.
May every race add colour to the celebration.
May every soul join with the song of creation.
May the birds sing,
may the trees clap
and may we taste and dance.

1361 You pulled the continents out of the sea.
Out of wet mud you have fashioned a wonderful world,
and what beautiful men and women!
We ask your help not to spoil it.

1362 The grace of your creation is like a cool day
between rainy seasons.
We drink in your creation with our eyes and with our ears.
How strong and good and sure your earth smells,
and everything that grows there.
We drink in your creation and cannot get enough of it.

But we forget the evil we have done.
Tear us away from our sins.
This wonderful world fades
and one day our eyes snap shut.
Then all that is not from you is over and dead.
Let the people say with joy
that you are the Lord.
Echoes a prayer from Ashanti, Ghana

All creation

1363 As the sun circles the world,
circle this land, O God.
Circle the soil, circle the waters.
Circle the crops, circle the homes.
Keep harm without, keep good within.

1364 Creator, you caused the Earth to bring forth the Saviour.
Spirit, come now and renew the face of the Earth:
all that grows on it, all who live on it.

1365 We offer you the Earth
and the vegetables that grow from it;
for all creation is yours
and we want to be enriching it.
We offer you the Earth
and the minerals that lie under it;
for all creation is yours
and we want to be enriching it.
We offer you the Earth
and the birds and beasts that move over it;
for all creation is yours
and we want to be enriching it.
We offer you ourselves
who make our home upon it;
for all creation is yours
and we want to be enriching it.

1366 Dear planet Earth,
    the Light of all light shine on you,
    the Power of all power energise you,
    the Love of all love transform you.
    Dear people,
    the Love of all love transform you.

1367 *Tsunamis and other natural disasters*
    When volcanic ash prevents air flights,
    when tsunamis wash away villages
    and when hurricanes obliterate buildings,
    teach us that our appointments
    and our achievements are in your hands.
    Let us be schooled in the Earth
    and humbled to learn from those around us.

Peace on Earth

1368 Peace to the land and all that grows on it.
    Peace to the sea and all that swims in it.
    Peace to the air and all that flies through it.
    Peace with our God who calls us to serve.

1369 Peace between believers;
    peace between neighbours;
    peace between lovers;
    in love of the King of Life.
    Peace between person and person;
    peace between wife and husband;
    peace between parents and children;
    the peace of Christ above all peace.

1370 Peace between parties,
    peace between neighbours,
    peace between lovers,
    in love of the King of Life.
    Peace between peoples,
    peace between traditions,
    peace between generations,
    in love of the Lord of all.

1371 Deep peace of the quiet earth,
deep peace of the still waters,
deep peace of the setting sun,
deep peace of the forgiving heart,
deep peace of the true call,
deep peace of the Son of Peace
be ours, today, for ever.

1372 Deep peace of the warming sun to you.
Deep peace of the pure white moon to you.
Deep peace of the shining stars to you.
Deep peace of the cleansing winds to you.
Deep peace of the quiet earth to you.
Deep peace of the knowing stones to you.
Deep peace of the forgiving heart to you.
Deep peace of the Son of Peace to you.
Deep peace.
Echoes a prayer of Fiona McLeod

1373 Deep peace of the green-blue sea,
deep peace of the rising sun,
deep peace of the shoreside Christ,
deep peace of the Risen One
be ours today.

1374 Deep peace of the setting sun,
deep peace of the forgiving heart,
deep peace of the lakeside Christ
be ours, today, for ever.

1375 Peace between victor and vanquished.
Peace between old and young.
Peace between rich and poor.
Peace between wives and husbands.
The peace of Christ above all peace.

1376 Deep peace of the Spirit to you.
Peace of the air flowing out to you.
Peace of the Son growing strong in you.

1377 Pardoner and Restorer,
    help us to listen,
    without judgement and with empathy,
    to the stories of those who are inflamed.

    Help us to stay calm and learn what we can.
    Help us to be clear about what we can achieve,
    not to promise what we cannot deliver
    and to take responsibility for what we can deliver.
    If it is possible, help us to walk a mile
    in the other's shoes and even to want the best for them,
    as for us.

1378 We pray for an end to the injustices
    which become breeding grounds of war.
    We pray for the restoration of fellowship
    and the building of integrity.
    We pray for commitment
    to the unending struggle against selfish ways
    and violation of human dignity.
    We pray for that peace
    which is the full blossoming of our life together.

1379 Lord, the nations rage
    and people around us become vengeful.
    You see it all.
    The kingdoms of this world
    will become your kingdom.
    So help us look upon what is happening
    with the calm assurance and quiet confidence
    of the Risen Christ,
    and leave the rest to you.

1380 You who order the universe,
    pour your oil on the troubled waters of our lives.
    We bring to you the troubles
    in our places of work,
    in our relationships,
    in our church
    and in the world.
    Calm us, and help us rest in you.

Unity

1381 May we eagerly desire the best for one another,
knowing that we share the same origin, the same essence,
and that we are on a journey together
away from fragmentation
and towards completion of all things in Christ.

1382 God of the rainbow, take our many colours,
temperaments, shapes and sizes and,
through rain and sunshine pouring from your Spirit,
transform us into a rainbow coalition
whose glory is beyond our imagining.

1383 Ground of all being,
all peoples come from you.
May we honour one another
and seek the common good.
Unity of the world,
from you all peace, all justice flow.
May we cherish the web of life
and respect the rule of law.

1384 Christ who holds all things together,
before you died
you prayed for the unity of all who believe.
May your churches rejoice
in the communion of heaven,
and attain communion
round one table on Earth.
May they inspire local communities
to love their neighbours as themselves.
Through bread and wine,
make us signs of your presence
that transforms all creation.

1385 You whose order rules the atom,
you whose law propels the sea,
bring the nations, drowned in discord,
closer to your harmony.

God of beauty, heal our sickness,
God of love, our fractures mend.
Foster unity that binds us,
rich to poor and foe to friend.

1386 Christ, help us to see
each member of your body as you see them.
May we support each person in their calling.
May we honour the weak.
May we relate well
to other members of the body
as we make our contribution.

1387 Holy God, Author of life,
by sharing our life on Earth,
you declare every life to be sacred.
Imbue us with deep respect for each person
and for each of the many roles
that are needed to sustain a cohesive world.

The cosmos

1388 *When humans visit another planet*

Dear planet,
the Light of all lights shine on you;
the Power of all powers energise you;
the Love of all loves win you.
May you become aware
that the Eternal Three
caress without ceasing
all forms, all realities
with graces, energies
and creative manifestations.
May you be unhindered by human egotism.
May consciousness of the One in Three
dawn upon you.
May cooperation with the One in Three
develop upon you.
May you move forward
into your divine destiny.

1389 Holy Spirit,
>	breathe upon the cosmos.
>	May it share in Christ's resurrection
>	and grow with the birth pangs of his kingdom.
>	May we, even in the middle of its groanings and pains,
>	be instruments of its healing
>	and breathe peace upon it this day.

All humanity

1390 Cherisher,
>	we place into your hands
>	the children of the streets and our broken families.
>	Grant us grace to accept that which is of you
>	in a difficult family member,
>	even though it is hidden beneath ugly traits.
>	Help us to
>	learn from failure,
>	be transparent about our fears,
>	work on our weaknesses,
>	build good communication,
>	and not expect a partner to supply everything we need.
>	May we give each other space to dance and fly
>	and hibernate and to come together again refreshed.

1391 We pray for the people:
>	their patterns and their pastimes,
>	their work and their homes,
>	their lovemaking and their conflicts,
>	their dreams and their disillusionments,
>	their hopes and their eternal hungers.

Those who are suffering

1392 Christ of the scars of love,
>	into your hands we place
>	those who have been scarred by life:
>	those who have been betrayed,
>	those who have suffered loss of limb or esteem.

Christ of the scars of love,
into your hands we place unwanted babies,
neighbours defamed, lovers spurned.
Christ of the scars of love,
into your hands we place
those who are victims of violence,
sharp practice or false accusation.

1393 Healing power of Christ,
penetrate the brittle shell
of the ones for whom we pray.
Where they are no longer present to others,
attract them to your gaze.
Where they are down and out,
grasp hold of them and raise them up.
Where they are fettered,
set them free to leap and praise.

1394 On those who harbour fear,
come, Holy Spirit.
On those whose day is drab,
come, Holy Spirit.
On those whose lives are parched,
come, Holy Spirit.

1395 We are appealing to you,
since you are the King of Heaven.
We are praying to you,
since you are the King of Good.
Lift each wasting,
each weariness and each sickness.
Lift each soreness and each discomfort.
We are keenly praying to you.
Lift each stiffness
as you separate earth from ocean.

1396 Life-giver, Pain-bearer,
we offer you our tears for those broken by abuse
and our anguish for those who rebel against you.

We offer you the pain we endure
from those who are hostile
and our burdens for the needy and poor.
May our sufferings contribute to the suffering
that your universal body needs to complete
in order to transform every last person and place on Earth.

Battered families

1397 God of tender, loving care,
bless these, your battered children.
Take the pain out of their lives.
Take the fear out of their lives.
Take the despair out of their lives.
Take the resentment out of their lives,
and fill them with your gentle, healing love.

1398 Gentle Father,
bless these battered children.
Take the hurt out of their lives.
May your gentle spirit flow
through all those who care for them.

1399 Tender Saviour,
bless these battered wives.
Take the fear out of their lives.
May your tender spirit flow
through all those who care for them.

1400 Caressing Spirit,
bless these elderly who feel battered
by their children's rejection.
Take resentment out of their lives.
May your caressing spirit flow
through all those who care for them.

1401 The Divine Gift come into your loss.
The Divine Peace come into your dread.
The Divine Hope come into your despair.
The Divine Helper come to your aid.

1402 Into your loss,
  come,
  O Being of Gift,
  O Being of Peace,
  O Being of Life eternal.
  Into your threat,
  come,
  O Being of Strength,
  O Being of Peace,
  O Being of Life eternal.
  Into your despair,
  come,
  O Being of Hope,
  O Being of Peace,
  O Being of Life eternal.
  Into your devastation,
  come,
  O Being of Love,
  O Being of Peace,
  O Being of Life eternal.

1403 Bruised?
  The blessing of acceptance be yours.
  Bitter?
  The blessing of forgiveness be yours.
  Angry?
  The blessing of gentleness be yours.
  Suicidal?
  The blessing of trust be yours.
  Broken?
  The blessing of immortality be yours.

1404 *Tragedy*
  The blessing of acceptance be yours.
  The blessing of forgiveness be yours.
  The blessing of gentleness be yours.
  The blessing of resilience be yours.
  The blessing of eternal life be yours.

Serving others

1405 *Servant King*

Give us eyes to notice the needy
and the stranger at the door.
Give us hearts to embrace the unwanted,
the homeless and the poor.
Give us minds to weave understanding
and truth to spread and store.
Give us hands to help in little things,
and to serve for evermore.

1406 May our hearts be places of royal hospitality
where cheerfulness and mercy abound.
May they unlock the song in every mind
and nourish every hungry soul.

1407 Set us free, O God,
to put ourselves in others' shoes,
to be open to others in listening,
to be sensitive to others in praying;
that we may see Christ
in the face of each person we meet,
and cross barriers for you
as you crossed barriers for us.

1408 Holy Trinity,
as you yield to one another,
may we yield to you in each person we meet.
Help us to acquire, through pain,
a deep, God-given knowing
that builds the foundation of unity.

1409 O God, who endowed Hilda
with gifts of prudence and strength
to govern as a wise mother
over a large and fractious family,
help us to sustain ordered lives,
where those of clashing views
may find shelter and understanding,
that our common life may be sustained,
and people may be excited by holiness.

1410 Increase our desire
to enter into the world's life.
Make us secure enough to be with others.
Lead us into the deep divine–human chord.

Anniversaries

1411 The joy of memory be yours today,
the joy of growth along the way.
Forgiveness be yours for failings past,
fruit be yours that will always last.
May that day when you embarked
be also a day that in heaven is marked.
The joy of that day be in your face,
the joy that made you grow in grace.

1412 On this, your anniversary,
God give you the best of memories,
Christ give you pardon for failings,
Spirit give you the fruits of friendship.

1413 *Birthday*
Joy of birth be yours today.
Joy of memory be yours today.
Joy of life be yours today.
Joy of goodness be yours today.
Joy of creation be yours today.
Joy of friendship be yours today.
Joy of giving be yours today.
Joy of maturing be yours today.
Joy of being known be yours today.
Joy of self-knowing be yours today.
Joy of Shepherd Father be yours today.
Joy of Mary's Son be yours today.
Joy of Friendly Spirit be yours today.
Joy of eternal life be yours today
and for ever.

Family members

1414 *Baby*

You are made in the likeness
of the good Birther, little one.
May good grow in you.
You are made in the likeness
of the Compassionate Saviour, little one.
May compassion grow in you.
You are made in the likeness
of the creative Spirit, little one.
May creativity grow in you.
You are made in the likeness
of the Three's Eternal Dance, little one.
May fun and laughter grow in you.

1415 *Stepchildren*

The family of God draw round you,
the family of God to welcome you,
the family of God to listen to you,
the family of God to cherish you,
the family of God to heal you.
Mary, the mother of our Lord,
Joseph at his work,
the saints of heaven,
your guardian angels
and we, your new loved ones.
May heaven's gate of welcome open wide;
may our heart of welcome open wide;
may your heart of welcome open wide,
this day and always.

1416 A family of friends to draw round you.
A family to cherish you and introduce you to new things.
The family of God to draw round you –
Mary, the mother of Jesus,
Joseph in his workplace –
opening heaven's gates to welcome you.

1417 *Toddler*
The three palmfuls of the Sacred Three
to preserve you from every envy or evil eye:
the palmful of the Father of life,
the palmful of the Christ of love,
the palmful of the Spirit of peace,
the God of threefold love.

1418 Wisdom of years be yours.
Joy of friendships be yours.
Wealth of memories be yours.
Fruit of endeavour be yours.
Hope of heaven be yours.
Peace of God's child be yours.

When away from home

1419 We release into your hands, O Lord,
our homes,
those for whom we love and care,
any who are dependent on us
who may feel vulnerable without us.
Lord, you love those whom we love.
We release into your hands, O Lord,
those for whom we have responsibilities,
those who are in need at this time,
those we have supported.
Lord, you care for all those for whom we care.
We release into your hands, O Lord,
our work,
the pressures that weary us,
the problems that would pursue us,
the things we have forgotten,
the tasks left unfinished.
Lord, you rule over all things.

1420 *Blessing*

> Into the Sacred Three we immerse you.
> Into their power and peace we place you.
> May their breath be ours to live,
> may their love be ours to give.
> Into the Sacred Three we immerse you.

Personal prayers

Computer

1421 Creator God, bless the surge
that brings this computer alive.
Saviour God, edit out the trash
and save that which is good.
Spirit of God,
give to me ordered records,
creative thoughts and life-giving words.

1422 Dear Lord,
every single evening
as I'm lying here in bed,
this tiny little prayer
keeps running through my head:
God bless all my family,
wherever they may be;
keep them warm and safe from harm
for they're so close to me.

Dear God,
there's one more thing
I wish that you could do.
Hope you don't mind me asking:
please bless my computer too.
Now I know that it's unusual
to bless a motherboard,
but listen just a second
while I explain it to you, Lord.

You see, that little metal box
holds more than odds and ends;
inside those small compartments
rest so many of my friends.
I know so much about them
by the kindness that they give,
and this little scrap of metal
takes me in to where they live.

By faith is how I know them,
much the same as you,
we share in what life brings us
and from that our friendships grew.

Please take an extra minute
from your duties up above,
to bless those in my address book
that's filled with so much love.

Wherever else this prayer may reach,
to each and every friend,
bless each email inbox
and each person who hits 'send'.
When you update your heavenly list
on your own Great CD-ROM,
bless everyone who says this prayer
sent up to GOD.com.

Journeys

1423 Bless the car to me, O Lord,
bless me to my car.
Be in my driving,
be in my concentration,
be in my decisions.

1424 Bless this journey to me, O Lord.
It is a small reflection of my journey through life,
my life given to you,
my way chosen by you;
a journey with you,
a journey to you,
a journey to knowing myself,
a journey to knowing you,
a journey of being saved and healed.

The ordinary and the extraordinary

1425 *Hope and fear*
O God of Life, darken not to me your light.
O God of Life, close not to me your joy.
O God of Life, shut not to me your door.
O God of Life, crown me with your gladness.

PERSONAL PRAYERS

1426 *Gifts of God*

Father, fill me with love for you
and a desire to praise you.
In Jesus' name, stir up the Holy Spirit in me
to pray in another language.
Remove all obstacles in the way of receiving this gift.
May I pray in tongues daily for several minutes.
Thank you.

1427 *The tongue*

Guardian of Truth, God of Love,
when my tongue runs away with me,
run after it and bring it back.
When my tongue runs others down,
pick it up and put it in its place.
When my tongue blesses others,
bless it to me.

1428 *Exams*

Open my eyes to see how this subject
reflects something of you.
I bless this exam
in the name of the Designer of truth.
I bless this exam
in the name of the Protector from ill.
I bless this exam
in the name of the Spirit who guides.
Aid me to understand this subject
with my heart as well as with my head.
Give me
wisdom to know the nub of things,
strength to recall what is useful,
peace to leave the result to you.

1429 *Questionnaires*

God, save me from questionnaires
that are much ado about nothing.
Give me grace to refuse them,
or humour if I have to complete them.

God bless the questionnaires
that will help others to serve the world better.
Give me grace to fill it in with attentive answers,
or at least the strength to send it off with love.

1430 *Purse*

God, take my purse
and be its nurse.
God, take my card
and be its guard.
God, take me in hand.
I'll understand.

1431 *Room*

God bless the room in which I sleep.
May it not be an untidy heap.
Give something of beauty for my eyes to see.
Clean outside and inside, please let it be.

1432 *Neighbours*

I don't know much about next door,
and I'm not sure I like what I know.
But in the name of Jesus I will bless you.
Some time, may a smile replace that sour face;
some day, may the garden start to look happy.
Whatever goes on inside,
may God somehow get inside you.

1433 *Animals*

Father, bless the pet;
also bless the vet.
Saviour, bless the flock;
also bless the cock.
Spirit, bless the horse;
also bless my course.

1434 *Gym*

God bless the gym
and every limb.

God bless the pool;
make it not too cool.
God bless my body;
may it not be shoddy.

1435 *Crisis*

Dear Father, Mother, Source of my being,
the precious robe with which you birthed me
is torn into shreds.
Love has been scattered.
Yet I long for you, and you long to gather together
the fragments of my life.
You know who I am.
Snatch me from the maze.
Restore me to my right mind.
Heal my wounds.
Return me to fellowship with the human family
and make me one with you.

Retreats

1436 Boundless Nourisher,
help me to retreat in order to advance;
to move out of tram lines and
reorientate my life with you.
Help me to relax and listen,
to observe and receive;
perhaps to walk in the steps of saints,
or to read and reflect and renew my mind.
Above all, may I stop running away,
and learn to wonder as I wander with you.

1437 I will come apart with you, Lord,
that you may still my heart.
I will come apart with you, Lord,
that you may stock my mind.
I will come apart with you, Lord,
that you may steel my will.
I will retreat with you, Lord,
that together we may advance.

1438 Lead me, Lord, into a place of prayer,
to live simply, silently and alone with you,
so that I may die to myself quicker
and Christ may grow in me faster;
so that you may give more of him
to the world that hungers for him.
Echoes words of Catherine Doherty

1439 You, Lord, burn in this place.
Your presence fills it.
Strip from me all that is not of you.
Call me to whatever you will.
Lead me wherever you will.

1440 God, make my heart a little cell.
Keep harm without, keep peace within.
God, make my heart an altar
where I may gaze into your face.
God, make my heart your home
where I am content to be with you.

Self and others

1441 When I say 'don't', would you say it like that, Lord?
When I say 'them', would you say it like that, Lord?
When I say 'I', would you,
who called yourself 'I Am',
strain and push like that, Lord?
Break my brittle shell, Lord,
and make me as human as you.

1442 I pray for my sister; Lord, let me take the strain.
I pray for my brother; Lord, may he rest his brain.
I pray for the folk who've lost a bit of heart.
Give them the oomph to make a new start.
I pray for the people at the bottom of the pile.
May you and I together take their loads for a while.

1443 Lord, sometimes I feel beaten and battered
like that man in the story,
and I ask you to fill more of your people
with compassion,
so that one of them will come alongside me.
Lord, each day, if you open my eyes,
I see someone in need:
a child on a bus, bullied or excluded,
someone at work, suffering or mistreated,
a stranger in the street.
Teach me to be generous,
to give and not to count the cost.

Circling prayers

CIRCLING PRAYERS

1444 Circle this place by day and by night.
Keep far from it all that harms.
Bring to it all that is good.
May this place be fragrant with the presence of the Lord.
God's peace be always here
and in those who dwell here.

1445 Circle us, Lord.
Keep love within, keep strife without.
Keep hope within, keep despair without.
Keep peace within, keep harm without.

1446 Circle the world, Lord.
Keep love within, keep strife without.
Keep hope within, keep despair without.
Keep peace within, keep harm without.

1447 Circle us, Lord.
Keep strife without, keep peace within.
Keep fear without, keep hope within.
Keep pride without, keep trust within.
Keep harm without, keep good within.

1448 Circle the world, Lord.
Keep grudges without, keep friendship within.
Circle the world, Lord.
Keep wrangling without, keep trust within.

1449 Circle them, Lord,
keep love within, keep hate without.
Circle them, Lord,
keep light within, keep dark without.
Circle them, Lord,
keep faith within, keep mistrust without.

1450 The Holy Three encircle you.
The Saving Three release you.
The Eternal Three keep you.
May the Loving Three caress you
and work in you,

in your loved ones,
in those you have lost,
in your dark,
in your day,
in your pain,
in your seeing,
in your journey,
in eternity.

1451 Circle us, Lord.
Keep harm without, keep good within.
Circle us, Lord.
Keep falsehood without, keep truth within.
Circle us, Lord.
Keep fear without, keep faith within.
Circle us, Lord.
Keep rage without, keep peace within.

1452 Circle this house, Lord, by day and by night,
in winter's dark and summer's light.
Keep joy within, keep blame without;
keep love within, keep shame without.

1453 Circle this place by day and by night,
in winter's cold and summer's light.
Keep within Christ's healing balm;
keep without all that would harm.

1454 Circle us, Lord.
Keep trust within, keep fear without.
Keep love within, keep hate without.
Keep hope within, keep despair without.
Keep goodness within, keep evil without.

1455 Circle us, Lord.
Keep these evils without:
the evil of fear,
the evil of boasting,
the evil of pretence,
the evil of excess,
the evil of abuse.

1456 Circle this place, O God,
    and keep these good things within:
    eagerness to learn,
    flowering of talents,
    experience of beauty,
    warmth of friendship,
    respect for all,
    care for the planet.

    Circle this place, O God,
    and keep these bad things without:
    low self-esteem,
    confusion,
    prejudice,
    pride,
    stealing,
    fear.

Seasons

Spring

1457 O Monarch of the Tree of Life,
   may the blossoms bring forth the sweetest fruit,
   may the birds sing out the highest praise,
   may your Spirit's gentle breath cover all.

1458 Life-giver,
   bring buds to flower,
   bring rain to the earth,
   bring songs to our hearts.
   Renewer,
   may gardens become green,
   may beauty emerge,
   may dreams come to pass.

1459 Today, darkness and light are equal partners.
   As the sun crosses over the equator
   may we cross over
   from dark to light,
   from complaining to appreciation,
   from dithering to boldness,
   from stagnation to creativity,
   from coldness to love,
   from us to you.

1460 We arise today in the promise of the rising seed.
   We arise today in the goodness of creation's life.

1461 With fresh shoots and buds of promise,
   may we be glad in the God of life.
   With first ears of corn and winged arrivals,
   may we be glad in the God of life.

1462 Great Spirit, the birds sing:
   what song do you wish to awake in our hearts?
   The clouds open:
   what do you wish to open in our hearts?
   The stones know:
   what do you wish us to know in our minds?

The plants come into bloom:
what do you wish to bring to flower in our time?

1463 The face of nature laughs in the springtime.
Restore laughter to our lives.
Her breath is fresh, and her eyes are clearest blue.
Restore freshness to our lives.
The call of the birds is wild and free.
Restore lightness to our lives.
Waterfalls splash with joy.
Restore joy to our lives.
Meadows light up with the colours of flowers.
Restore colour to our lives.
The breeze is nature's harp, playing a song of love.
Restore love song to our lives.
Men are strong, women pretty,
and the world is in love with its Creator.
Restore strength and beauty to our lives.

1464 Birther,
make seeds fertile,
make thoughts fruitful,
make waste places flourish.

Renewing God, spring has bounced into our midst.
May we spring into action as Christ's athletes,
and let your seeds in us sprout.
Sweep away the cobwebs
and let the innate beauty
with which you dignified our souls be profligate.

Summer

1465 Farewell season of sowing and hidden striving;
now toil will bear its fruit.
Beauty, once hidden,
will come forth like a bride.

SEASONS

1466 The sun rides high and long,
a sign of blessing from our God.
Everything that breathes cries 'Yes!'
At day's fading we cry 'Yes' to Christ,
the eternal Sun.

1467 A blessing on the season of growth,
on all that is done and felt,
the blessing of the fertile Creator,
the blessing of the virile Son,
the blessing of the Spirit, the sustaining One.

1468 We give thanks for the growth of sunlit days.
We offer you the first of our crops
and the best of our lives –
all that we have, all that we are –
for all things come from you,
and of your own do we give you.

1469 As we enter this season of creativity,
may we think your thoughts after you.
As we explore new realms of life,
may we sense your Spirit after you.
As we enter our beds of hope,
may we dream your dreams after you.

1470 God of the summer,
may this be for us
a season of growth and friendship,
a season of activity and celebration.
May vigour and chivalrous love
flow strongly in our veins.
May heroes and holy ones
urge us on to give our all.

1471 Life of Jesus, Sun of suns,
filling every part of us,
life be in our speech,
sense in what we say.

Love be in our deeds
till you come back again.
Love of Jesus, Sun of suns,
filling every heart for us,
love be in our deeds,
thought be in our words.
Care be in our mien
till you come back again.

1472 To the Sun of suns, come,
singing Jesus is Lord.
Earth, come to the sun's king,
singing Jesus is Lord.
Sky, come to the sun's king,
singing Jesus is Lord.
Spirits, come to the sun's king,
singing Jesus is Lord.
Birther, Saviour,
lighting Spirit, you are the Lord.

1473 Sun shines,
sap rises,
buds burst,
lambs frolic,
birds sing,
people play.
Glory to God
who sustains and nurtures us all.

1474 God of the rising green,
God of the sweeping blue,
God of the long, bright day,
may we, too, give glory to you.
God, eternally awake,
may your energies flow through us.
God of the rising sap,
may we be your sap today.

1475 We thank you, Divine Radiance,
for these amazing days;
for the leaping greenery and the arching blue sky.
Everything that breathes seems to cry 'Yes!'
May our whole being cry 'Yes' to you.

1476 Rejoice, you earth of sunlit days,
pointing us to Christ, the Sun of rays.
Rejoice, you spirits of earth and air,
saluting Christ who climbs heaven's stair.
Rejoice, you folk in darkened thrall,
Christ scatters darkness, and shines on all.

1477 God of the long day,
you who are eternally awake,
I offer you my eternal 'Yes' –
the flower of my humanity,
the energy and awareness of my days,
the creativity of my life,
the beauty of form
and the hope of future potential.

1478 *Midsummer*

God of the longest day,
may our lives be a long day for you,
always reflecting your light;
open, awake.

Autumn

1479 The sheaves and the green leaves fall.
Generous be our hearts.
Open be our hands.
Justice be our benchmark.
Thanksgiving be our call.
For the sake of your great giving,
O Christ who was ground like flour,
our Bread of Life,
feed and nourish us evermore.

1480 The seed is Christ's, the granary is Christ's.
In the granary of God may we be gathered.
The sea is Christ's, the fishes are Christ's.
In the nets of God may we all meet.

1481 Harvester God, as autumn light ripens the grain,
ripen too our souls.
As brown leaves fall and sheaves are stored,
help us to leave behind summer's ways
and go forward in deepening compassion,
thankful to heaven.

1482 Great Spirit, bring to harvest the fragments of our lives
and crown our year with goodness.
Penetrate the storehouse of our memories,
making them whole and holy.

1483 O sacred season of autumn, be our teacher,
for we wish to learn the virtue of contentment.
As we gaze upon your full-coloured beauty,
we sense all about you an at-homeness
with your amber riches.
You are the season of retirement,
of full barns and harvested fields.
The cycle of growth has ceased,
and the busy work of giving life
is now completed.
We sense in you no regrets;
for you have lived a full life.

1484 Bountiful God, seed-time has ripened into harvest,
your Earth has yielded fruits.
Winter's cleansing cold gave way to spring's gentle warmth,
and now summer's full sun has offered us autumn gifts.
We savour your presence with grateful hearts.

1485 God of goodness,
the wonders of your creation,
the splendour of the heavens,
the order and richness of nature
speak to us of your glory.

The coming of your Son,
the presence of your Spirit,
the fellowship of your Church
show us the marvel of your love.
The patterns of the year,
the beauty of the Earth,
the ripening gifts of harvest
call us to worship and adore you.
Hear our heartfelt 'Amen'.

1486 Thank you for harvest's boundless store,
and the fruits of the Earth
which sustain and gladden us.
Thank you for those who work the land
or are part of the food chain that reaches to our door.
Thank you for comforts of life
and the power to help others.
Thank you for your creation
and the One you sent to restore us
when we fell away from your plan.

1487 May this season of mellow fruitfulness
enrich and bless us.
May we harvest relationships of trust,
forgiveness and generosity.
And, until we meet again,
may we be kept in the hollow of God's hand.

1488 Thank you for a roof over our head,
for firm earth under our tread,
for supplies to fill our hunger,
for friends to assuage our anger.

1489 As the trees are stripped of foliage,
may we be stripped of clutter.
As the leaves fall to the ground,
may we fall into your lap.
As the crops ready for harvest are gathered,
may the wisdom of our days be garnered.

1490 *Samhain*
> Star Kindler,
> be our light in the darkness that lies ahead.
> Weaver of wonder,
> weave in us your patterns in the winter that lies ahead.
> Gatherer of souls,
> encompass those whom we see no longer.
> Rock of our salvation,
> when dark cares loom large, be our firm foundation.
> We draw near to you.

Winter

1491 Christ at the yearly turning,
Christ at every bend.
Christ at each beginning,
Christ at every end.
Christ in dark's deep shadows,
Christ in shades of death.
Christ in primeval history,
Christ in wintry earth.

1492 In the chill of wintry wind,
in the depths of uncertain thoughts,
sing to us the story of the universe,
visit us as Saviour of our being.

1493 Star Kindler and Weaver of wonder,
as winter stars light up the darkness of night,
reveal to us fresh sources of hope.

1494 Hold us, O God of the cold, dark days,
secure in the knowledge
that from its wintry depths
the Earth brings forth a Saviour.

SEASONS

1495 Creator God,
    whose power and beauty are never spent,
    in wintry earth waken us
    to the mystery of your presence.

1496 We arise today
    in the deep formation of winter,
    in the transforming power of ice,
    in the cleansing work of frost.
    We arise today
    in the simplicity of the bare earth,
    in the strength of the fierce elements,
    in the beauty and brilliance of snow.

1497 Stripped of inessentials we stand, rooted in you.
    In the anticipation of gathering strength,
    you sustain our well-being.
    In the stillness of the bare earth,
    we invite you to do your work in us.

1498 We bind to ourselves this day
    the strength of rock,
    the silence of earth,
    the sharpness of cold.
    We bind to ourselves this day
    the longevity of stars,
    the integrity of sky,
    the sobering of dark.

1499 Creating and Sustaining God,
    as this cold, dark season encroaches,
    give to us the stability of the deep earth
    and the hope of heaven.

1500 Thank you for leading us to the time of briefest light,
    secure in the trust that you embrace the encircling gloom,
    held by the dark which you encompass in your arms,
    content to rest in you like a baby in the womb.

1501 Counsellor, quicken our souls' progress
in this winter season.
Kindle in our hearts fires of welcome and love,
in the presence of the Holy Trinity,
in the presence of the angels without envy,
in the presence of the saints without fear.

1502 When cold night draws near,
we draw near to you.
When dark cares loom large,
we draw near to you.
In our hard place of need,
we draw near to you.

1503 The world is not dead;
it is sleeping.
Its life draws in;
it is keeping.
The Earth is gathering energy
for a new burst of life.
We breathe in the mystic air
that we may breathe out care.
Your presence supports us through the night
so we can hail the coming source of Light.
Shine through the mists, the deadening heavy clod,
gladdening Light of Christ our Lord.

1504 Lord of the seasons, on this day of briefest light,
help us to be at home with the treasures of the dark.
As the days have drawn in,
draw near to us with your everlasting light.
As shadows lengthen,
help us to embrace the shadow side of life.
As the dark swallows up the created sun,
help us to store up riches for the long days ahead.

SEASONS

1505 *New and full moons*

    Mellow moon, sheen light of the night,
    your gentle gift to us.
    Calm us under its faithful watch.
    Bathe us in its mysterious light.
    Encompass us in the mystery of its gloaming.
    You who give this light,
    descend through thick clouds on every child on Earth,
    and rest on us as we sleep.

1506 *Equinoxes*

    Divine Companion of day and night,
    you have accompanied us to this day
    when light and dark are equally balanced.
    Now the days grow shorter,
    the dark grows deeper,
    the cold comes sharper,
    accompany us still;
    warm us in your love and brighten us with your light.

Indexes

Index of first lines

A blessing on the season of growth	1467
A family of friends to draw round you	1416
A little drop of your Creator	374
A little drop of your Creator, precious one	412
A prayer for parents who are married	378
A thousand thanks to you	1278
A thousand thanks to you, O God	1270
Alive to you through her calling of prayer	727
All that moves on the Earth	262
All-advancing God, help us	743
All-aware One	758
All-compassionate One	799
All-embracing One,	39
All-forgiving God, thank you for Wenceslas	751
All-forgiving One,	1199
All-knowing God, make fruitful our learning	1074
All-knowing God, parents-in-God picture	4
All-merciful One, you hold the poor	986
All-powerful and All-compassionate One	1336
All-powerful God, circle the places	198
All-powerful One	118
All-powerful One, we seem so powerless and puny	682
All-seeing God, be our vision	1049
All-seeing God, who has given to us	1064
All-seeing Restrainer	924
All-wise God, who raised up Illtyd	695
Almighty Father, Victorious Saviour	390
Almighty God . . . your servant Hilda	1026
Almighty God of the invincible force field	977
Almighty God, nothing on Earth can compare	1324
Almighty One, who out of your love	178
Among the hungry	10
An eye was seeing you	428
And now we give you thanks	308
And now we give you thanks	315
Angel of God, sent from the Fragrant Father	184
Angels' Lord, who for nine months	33
Anointing Spirit, distribute among us	940
Arbiter of the nations	1323
As Christ removed the sleep	426
As Comgall's monks transformed	653

INDEX OF FIRST LINES

As Cuthbert stormed the gates of heaven	980
As fish live in water, may we live in you	1096
As in the night vision Caedmon's soul	643
As it began to be in the time of David	661
As it was in the stillness of the morning	576
As moon circles Earth	413
As nature laughs in spring	860
As once you changed water into wine	57
As the grain once scattered on the fields	289
As the grains of wheat	167
As the press of work pauses at noon	490
As the sun circles the world	1363
As the sun sets in the west	533
As the trees are stripped of foliage	1489
As we bless you for Mary	343
As we eat and drink,	295
As we enter into sleep	158
As we enter this season of creativity	1469
As we gaze into your light	864
As we lay down our clothes	588
As we pour out this wine	291
As we share this foretaste of the heavenly feast	282
As we thank you for Piran's faith	739
As your trial drew near, you looked upon	79
Ascended Lord, you have made us living stones	111
At creation the angels sang in delight	169
At midsummer, creation says yes	622
At the drawing in of the day	530
At the start of Beltane	318
At this time of briefest light	417
Awaken us to your glory	444
Babe of Heaven	1193
Babe of heaven, Defenceless Love	25
Baptising God	636
Baptising God, who impelled your saints	654
Bathe us in your cleansing rivers	897
Be in the eye of each friend on our journey	1234
Be in the humdrum	812
Be in the interruptions and the setbacks	818
Be with us now, Lord	196
Be with us today	452
Bearer of pain and Maker of love	73
Beautiful Christ	107
Beauty of friendship, grow between us	1233
Before your Cross, O Christ	843

Beloved One, we long to dwell	1288
Bend our minds to holy learning	1082
Bend our wills to the holy yoke of obedience	1002
Bestower, we have raped and spoiled your world	1295
Bind us together, Lord	1325
Birther and Arbiter of the human family	1314
Birther, Father, Mother of the cosmos	43
Birther, make seeds fertile	1464
Birther of the human race	461
Birther, the planet is pulling against you	1303
Birther who brought worlds into being	151
Bless all work done today	815
Bless, O Lord, this Christmas tree	38
Bless, O Lord, this food	1268
Bless, O Lord, this food we are about to eat	1258
Bless the car to me, O Lord	1423
Bless the Church	1172
Bless the moon that is above us	1282
Bless this journey to me, O Lord	1424
Bless this little space	826
Bless this room	382
Bless to me my body	1285
Bless to us, O God	817
Bless to us, O God	828
Bless to us, O God	948
Bless to us this time of threshold	48
Bless us now, Lord, in the middle of the day	493
Bless us, O God, bless our food and our drink	1259
Bless you, Creator of all we eat	1272
Bless you, King of the universe	1265
Blessed are you, God of pain, God of mercy	351
Blessed are you, God of the planet	303
Blessed are You, High King of the universe	1267
Blessed are you, King of all creation	293
Blessing of discovery be ours	1229
Blessing of discovery be yours	1159
Blest are those women	746
Blest are you, Sacred One, for those who	206
Blest be all creation	544
Blest be God the giver of light	582
Boundless Nourisher, help me to retreat	1436
Bountiful God, seed-time has ripened into harvest	1484
Break in us the drive to manipulate others	1014
Break the ties that bind us to our past	1022
Breath of God, blow away all that is unclean	119

INDEX OF FIRST LINES

Bring to flower in your children	1033
Bruised?	1403
Builder of planets and of paradise	633
Call, call, call, great Chief of the high hills	1138
Call forth life within us	947
Call forth this night bearers	583
Calm us to wait for the gift of Christ	1
Candlelighter Lord	231
Caressing Spirit	1400
Caring Father God	1308
Caring Provider, in you we live and move	1313
Carpenter Christ, give us common sense	1042
Carpenter Christ, who learned your craft	655
Champion, save us from being fair-weather Christians	668
Cherisher, we place into your hands	1390
Child of Glory, Child of Mary	39
Child of Glory, Child of Mary	42
Child of Heaven, Defenceless Love	1009
Christ at the yearly turning	1491
Christ be in the work and each thing we do	813
Christ be within us	789
Christ, born of the loveliest Mary	768
Christ forsaken	271
Christ, help us to see	1386
Christ Jesus, in the light of your risen presence	100
Christ, Light of the world	9
Christ, linking us across the shores	192
Christ of fearless love	1071
Christ of the gentle heart	962
Christ of the Journey	1098
Christ of the loving heart	991
Christ of the people	1330
Christ of the scars	71
Christ of the scars of love	1392
Christ, save us from a cheap Easter	74
Christ, splendour of the Father's glory	60
Christ, the peace of things above	926
Christ, wake us to your summons, urgent in our midst	2
Christ who comes with justice and peace	272
Christ who holds all things together	1384
Christ who stilled the storm	911
Christ, you are the refined molten metal	70
Circle her/him, Lord, keep peace within	376
Circle the world, Lord. Keep grudges without	1448
Circle the world, Lord. Keep love within	1446

Circle them, Lord, keep love within	1449
Circle this house, Lord, by day and by night	1452
Circle this place by day and by night	392
Circle this place by day and by night	1444
Circle this place by day and by night	1453
Circle this place, O God . . . good things	1456
Circle us, Lord. Keep harm without	1451
Circle us, Lord. Keep love within	1445
Circle us, Lord. Keep strife without	1447
Circle us, Lord. Keep these evils without	1455
Circle us, Lord. Keep these graces within	1230
Circle us, Lord. Keep trust within	1454
Circle us, O God for the rest	501
Come and put a glory in our work today	825
Come, Creator Spirit	438
Come, Guardian of heaven and Earth	584
Come, Holy Spirit	942
Come, Holy Spirit, from heaven shine forth	131
Come like fire and warm our hearts	950
Come like the fire and kindle love in our hearts	132
Come, O Holy Flame	116
Come, O Spirit of Love	123
Come to us, Wisdom	11
Come to us with your anointing power	138
Comforting Spirit	936
Counsellor, quicken our souls' progress	1501
Craftsperson of the heavens	890
Creating and Sustaining God	1499
Creator and Saviour	258
Creator and Saviour, we have exploited earth	1294
Creator God	189
Creator God, bless all the people	1332
Creator God, bless the surge	1421
Creator God, help us to give all creatures	1301
Creator God, the raw materials are yours	476
Creator God, whose power and beauty	1495
Creator, make us co-workers with you	1307
Creator of light	436
Creator of love	1046
Creator of our land	1245
Creator of the land, out of wet mud	1293
Creator Spirit, come	140
Creator Spirit, may air and elements praise you	266
Creator Spirit, wellspring of life	579
Creator, we have raped and spoiled your world	255

INDEX OF FIRST LINES

Creator, we have raped and spoiled your world	1300
Creator, you caused the Earth	314
Creator, you caused the Earth to bring forth the Saviour	1364
Creator, you give us grain and grape	298
Crucified Christ, Son of the Father	86
Crucified Jesus, you lived and died a Jew	1328
Day by day, dear God	782
Dear Father God, we have journeyed	1156
Dear Father, Mother, Source of my being	1435
Dear Father, what pleasure it gives you	1321
Dear God, help us make a church	609
Dear God, I am sorry	406
Dear God, if you came to church	600
Dear God, we've come to the end of our school years	612
Dear God, when we wake up	597
Dear God, you know that many spiritual people	1184
Dear Jesus, some people don't notice	595
Dear Jesus, the Church is your world family	607
Dear Jesus, there is a good voice	602
Dear Lord, every single evening	1422
Dear Lord Jesus, kind and loving Friend	411
Dear Lord, may all that is here	389
Dear planet	1388
Dear planet Earth	1366
Dear Saviour, who restored unity	1304
Dear Son of Mary	955
Dearest Christ, you have given love	85
Dearest Christ, you have given love	800
Deep peace of the Creator	139
Deep peace of the green-blue sea	1373
Deep peace of the quiet earth	1371
Deep peace of the setting sun	1374
Deep peace of the Spirit to you	1376
Deep peace of the warming sun to you	1372
Delayer, if you were not patient	988
Desire of every nation	15
Discipler of souls	701
Divine artist, the world is your canvas	946
Divine Artist, you endow us with gifts	669
Divine Artist, you uniquely shape	943
Divine Benefactor, whose desire	811
Divine Birther, may the whole world	1360
Divine Companion of day and night	1506
Divine Dream-weaver	1039
Divine Fashioner of Forms	895

Divine Father, help us to affirm	1021
Divine Friend, who called Herbert	687
Divine Light encompassing us	865
Divine Restorer, aid us	1004
Divine Saviour, your birth in the stable	982
Divine Source of Truth	1078
Divine Upbringer	209
Divine Weaver, we bless you	1173
Each day and each night, in cold and heat	1215
Each of us has some work to do	824
Earth Maker, by whose life	675
Earth, teach us stillness	901
Earth, whose seeds and fields and food	1358
Earth-maker God	880
Ebb tide, full tide, praise	263
Eternal Creator of day and night	237
Eternal Creator of the weeks and years	592
Eternal Fire, who lit up the cold stable	744
Eternal Friend, as we thank you	754
Eternal Friend, we thank you	1235
Eternal God, who drew aside heaven's curtain	667
Eternal God, who mothers us all	220
Eternal Guide	916
Eternal Light, shine into our hearts	339
Eternal Light, shine into our hearts	788
Eternal Love Maker	159
Eternal Mind, thank you for the minds	1010
Eternal Now, you enter into time	1195
Eternal Source of Life, you are the core of our being	1122
Eternal Spouse, who ever woos	670
Eternal Truth, grant us humility	1070
Eternal Wisdom, first-born of creation	364
Eternal Word of God	1065
Ever-shielding Father	854
Every day we travel through this life	1155
Exalted One, as haze rises	115
Examine us, O God, and know our thoughts	1081
Faithful God, David worked	659
Faithful God, from Christ's first fruits	647
Faithful God, teach me that defeat	1089
Faithful God, thank you for the glorious company	1102
Faithful God, who through Adomnan's	617
Farewell season of sowing and hidden striving	1465
Father, all love comes from you	292
Father, as Hilda shone	689

INDEX OF FIRST LINES

Father be with us on every road	1130
Father, bless the pet	1433
Father, fill me with love for you	1426
Father, free us to enjoy and not possess another	863
Father, give us all fatherly care	1211
Father, look upon your family	88
Father, may [name] and [name] be to each other	378
Father, Mother	1048
Father, Mother God	809
Father, Mother of us all	547
Father of love	377
Father of peoples	666
Father of the poor	325
Father, the birth of the Virgin Mary's Son	342
Father, the good things of your Earth	252
Father, we of this day	1335
Father, you affirmed your Son at his baptism	737
Father, you appointed Joseph	713
Father, you call us	1094
Father, you give us many gifts	1099
Fill this moment, Lord	766
Fill this room with a spirit of hospitality	386
Fire of God	180
Fire of God, may the flame	1018
First, I wish to say	407
Fisher of souls, we thank you that Gall	679
Flame of love, light us up	396
Flame of love, reach into our inmost heart	395
For earth and sea and sky	259
For living in our comfort zones	242
For our shield this day we call	148
For our shield today we call to us	195
For putting personal preferment	241
For the beauty and bounty of the world	1246
For the glory of creation	1237
For the rainforests gone	254
For the rainforests gone	1311
For the ways we have marred your image	245
Forgetting what is past	1128
Forgive our nations	848
Forgive us for grasping at things	1200
Forgive us when we grumble	368
Fount of Life, as Fechin	674
Fountain of goodness	235
Free me, Immense Spirit	1027

From false desires and selfish deeds	250
From today and always, may we	776
Gatherer of souls	186
Generosity of God . . . flow into your Church	1354
Generosity of God . . . we bless you for flowers	1355
Generous God, as once you multiplied	1266
Gentle Christ of Bodmin Moor	738
Gentle Father, bless these battered children	1398
Gentle God, in Bega	630
Gentle God, reveal to us	1101
Give me the ambition	907
Give to us thoughts greater than our own thoughts	867
Give us courage to journey, like Kevin	714
Give us eyes to notice the needy	1405
Give us faith that heeds your call to heal	842
Give us, Lord, the love that does not fail	651
Give us sorrow for our sins against	560
Give us the eye of the eagle	938
Give us wise leaders, clear vision	1342
Give us your firelight, Holy Spirit	939
Give your counsel to our government	994
Glad Bringer of brightness	453
Glorious Source, we give you greeting!	1236
Glorious Three	856
Glory be to you	723
Glory, praise and thanks to you, O God	1269
Glory to the Birther	154
Glory to the Birther, glory to the Son	1247
Glory to you, Christ our King	477
Glory to you, the vital Force	1248
Go back! go back! go back!	420
Go before us	1145
Go to your eternal home of welcome	397
God above us	153
God be a smooth way before us	1131
God be a smooth way before you	1252
God be in our day and in our sleeping	763
God be with us at every leap	1129
God be with us on our journey towards Christmas	19
God be with you at each stop and each sea	1254
God be with you whatever you pass	1253
God bless Muslims and God bless Christians	1331
God bless our families	1205
God bless the air	605
God bless the earth that is beneath us	468

INDEX OF FIRST LINES

God bless the earth that is beneath us	1250
God bless the gym	1434
God bless the oil	1297
God bless the path on which you go	1255
God bless the room in which I sleep	1431
God bless the stranger at the door	1320
God bless this money	1291
God, bless to us our bodies	473
God bless to us this year	44
God bless to you this loss	829
God bless your steed	1224
God care for this pet	1214
God direct our hours	785
God, eternally True	879
God, fill your people with your Spirit	855
God forgive us for the polluting waste	1305
God give you delight and tenderness	385
God help us to listen to our loved ones	1210
God help us to run straight	1283
God help you to run straight	1349
God in our in our waking, God in our speaking	1261
God in our rising and lying down	771
God is great	505
God, it's so unfair	1107
God, make my heart a little cell	1440
God make the TV	1208
God make us fit for purpose	963
God make us holy	286
God of a hundred names	700
God of a thousand places	715
God of Aidan of the gentle touch	619
God of all peoples . . . life of Ruth	740
God of Beauty, so ancient yet so fresh	626
God of Community	506
God of Community	506
God of compassion, who graced Barnabas	628
God of Covenant	624
God of covenant . . . by Isaac's example	698
God of covenant . . . with Jacob	703
God of creation, make us aware	884
God of creation, your Spirit brooded	888
God of destiny	882
God of eternity	224
God of fair play	623
God of generosity and order	1286

God of gods, establish your presence among us	767
God of good order	631
God of goodness	1485
God of heroic love	680
God of Hilda and the humble heart	1183
God of insight, who called Matthew	724
God of justice, God of peace	504
God of Life . . . of Indract's death	696
God of life, you summon the day to dawn	446
God of love	307
God of Monday and of Sunday	1031
God of Order and Beauty	1035
God of order born of love	735
God of our forebears, rock of their lives	629
God of outpouring mercy	808
God of prophecy . . . John the Baptist	709
God of Providence	621
God of Providence	993
God of rest	971
God of shepherds and angels	1315
God of signs and wonders	756
God of surprises, God of the journey	1144
God of tender, loving care	1397
God of the ages, God of the ancestors	197
God of the call	523
God of the Call	1025
God of the call, who led Abraham	616
God of the compassionate heart	699
God of the Economy – the whole created universe	1287
God of the elements, glory to you	1139
God of the endless force field	1116
God of the fray	247
God of the generations	705
God of the journey . . . from Finbarr	676
God of the journey . . . scholar Fursey	678
God of the long bright day	415
God of the long day	1477
God of the longest day	1478
God of the memory held in genes and stones	1181
God of the oceans	638
God of the prophet Moses	1051
God of the rainbow	1382
God of the rising green	1474
God of the seas and fisherfolk	637
God of the storm, God of the stillness	1132

INDEX OF FIRST LINES

God of the summer	1470
God of the thunder	764
God of the years	46
God of time	203
God of time; God of eternity	217
God of time, God of the saints	197
God of turbulent cities	684
God of Unity	748
God of vision, whose servant Hildegaard	693
God of wholeness	850
God of wisdom	1053
God of Wisdom, teach us	1073
God our Champion	681
God our Creator, in giving us this child	375
God our Eternal Treasure	635
God our Provider	712
God, our vision	690
God, our Vision	1054
God our Wisdom	1030
God protect the household	1207
God, save me from questionnaires	1429
God save the people	1333
God save us from an impersonal world	1226
God, Source of our Being	837
God speed to you	1225
God, take my purse	1430
God to enfold you	546
God who dances with creation	1316
God who has made us to live in rhythm	774
God who is One	144
God who is One	970
God, who is present to all	1169
God who walks with your people	673
God who weeps over the city	1121
God whose breath gives energy for struggle	130
God whose speech is glorious	706
God with us. Be in my waking and working	904
God with us lying down	557
God, you dance with creation	1356
God's blessing be upon you in this new office	827
God's own presence with you stay	360
Good angels, messengers of God	172
Good be on you, gift from heaven	1289
Good God, be with us in every experience of life	498
Good God, from you flows	1057

Good God, may we never forget	1319
Good morning, God	596
Good morning, God. My moans	463
Gracious God, may your glory be seen	931
Gracious God of faithful Edith	671
Grant, O Lord, that your Church in this land	1167
Grant our heads the waters of lament	1203
Grant to us, O Lord	711
Grant us acceptance of pain without bitterness	1220
Grant us grace to	966
Grant us the humility to know	1174
Gratitude for the sun	480
Great and awesome God	979
Great Creator of the deep red moon and falling stars	761
Great Creator of the gleaming moon	1052
Great Creator of the glowing moon	893
Great Creator, we are made in your likeness	1005
Great Creator, whose glory is seen	697
Great God	61
Great God, as the haze rises from mountaintops	587
Great God, as you brought Christ	543
Great God, give us light	590
Great God of mercy	1015
Great God, thank you for Martin	720
Great God, who called Martin	719
Great God, who called your servant David	665
Great God who mothers us all	804
Great God who mothers us all	1019
Great-hearted God	211
Great-hearted God, we thank you for Cedd	646
Great-hearted, who reaches out to all	1329
Great Provider, may we receive	1359
Great Spirit, as fish live in water	663
Great Spirit, as the sun rises in the east	1217
Great Spirit, bring to harvest the fragments of our lives	1482
Great Spirit, encouraged by your cloud	755
Great Spirit, help us to relax into your plan for us	853
Great Spirit, out of your love	471
Great Spirit, swirling in the elements	13
Great Spirit, the birds sing	1462
Great Spirit, water the world	949
Great Spirit, who broods over the sleeping world	552
Great Spirit who broods over the world	834
Great Spirit, whose breath is felt	496
Great Spirit, whose breath is felt	1306

INDEX OF FIRST LINES

Great Spirit, whose breath is felt in the soft breeze	470
Great Spirit, Wild Goose of the Almighty	124
Great Spirit, you nod and beckon	898
Ground of all being	1383
Guard for us our eyes	327
Guardian and Friend . . . Maedoc befriended	716
Guardian, be over the restless people	512
Guardian, be over the restless people	1341
Guardian of the dark night of death	225
Guardian of the planets	569
Guardian of Truth, God of Love	1427
Guardian, Source of Order	539
Guide us, good and great Redeemer	1097
Guide us, our great Mentor	851
Harvester God, as autumn light ripens the grain	1481
Have mercy on little ones abused	175
Have mercy on us, O God, for our sins	170
Have mercy this night	585
Healing Christ, you walk the world	573
Healing power of Christ	1393
Heavenly Father, we offer you our praise and thanksgiving	367
Heavenly Father, we offer you our souls and bodies	370
Help me conquer anger by gentleness	959
Help me to be true to myself	910
Help me to listen	759
Help me to put my best into my work	814
Help us bring to birth a civilisation	1185
Help us, God of the whole created world	871
Help us, Great Spirit	777
Help us, Lord, to guard our words	928
Help us, Lord, to respond	872
Help us, Lord, to trade with the gifts	1029
Help us, O God, to lay aside the cares	182
Help us, O Healing One	846
Help us pluck out by the roots	1077
Help us to breathe in step with you	1084
Help us to follow you	914
Help us to grow today	1056
Help us to know	1299
Help us to know	1346
Help us to know and accept our limits	1075
Help us to live simply, that others	985
Help us to prepare a way for you . . . creatures	7
Help us to prepare a way for you . . . others	6
Help us to sense your presence among us	778

Help us to tell our story	1011
Help us to tread in the steps of Christ	66
Here, may the earth be full of health	1280
Here we are at your service, O Lord	1158
Heroic Love	1008
High-borne eagles and nesting birds	1353
High King, Creator of all	1338
High King of heaven	734
High King of heaven and Earth	1186
High King of land and sea	1141
High King of the universe	1060
Hold us, O God of the cold, dark days	1494
Holy and Immortal God	685
Holy and loving God	618
Holy Father, Holy Jesus, Holy Guide	51
Holy God, Author of life	1387
Holy God, help us to live	983
Holy God, holy and immortal	311
Holy God, holy and mighty	400
Holy God, holy and mighty	694
Holy God, holy and mighty	710
Holy God, holy and mighty	951
Holy God, holy and mighty	1091
Holy God of Cuthbert	657
Holy God, source of friendship	645
Holy God, strong and patient	742
Holy God, who led your servant Nectan	729
Holy God, who speaks words of life	1043
Holy God, whose glory fills the Earth	702
Holy Jesus, hanged on a tree	251
Holy Raphael	181
Holy Spirit, breathe upon the cosmos	1389
Holy Spirit, come as a gentle breeze	120
Holy Spirit, come as a gentle breeze	489
Holy Spirit, free us to be just and true	996
Holy Spirit, fulfil through us	1182
Holy Spirit of God	141
Holy Spirit, refine us	459
Holy Spirit, refine us, that we may be true	128
Holy Spirit, release us	1176
Holy Spirit, renew in us joy in our work	1322
Holy Spirit, you have anointed your servants	941
Holy Three, help us to live	912
Holy Trinity, as you yield to one another	1408
Holy True and Real One	1072

INDEX OF FIRST LINES

Homemaker God	22
Humility of God	69
I arise today in the strength of the Birther	465
I commend you, [name]	427
I don't know much about next door	1432
I pray for my sister; Lord, let me take the strain	1442
I pray, Lord, for the children whom I know	1104
I see to the fridge in the presence	797
I thank you for the wind	1243
I will come apart with you, Lord	1437
Illumine our hearts, O Lord	455
I'm not in a fit state to pray, Lord	593
Immerse us in your pure water	952
Immortal God,	187
Immortal God, we remember before you	222
Impart to us imagination	1012
In a world where so many are hungry	1264
In dependence on the God of life	1312
In each hidden thought our minds	838
In God is our strength	511
In Ninian there was nothing of fear	733
In our baptism, O Lord Christ	98
In our devastation	1117
In our journeying this day	1161
In our journeying this day	1123
In our pleasures	1345
In our tiredness be our rest	562
In silence I become aware of you, O God	795
In the beginning, O God	394
In the chill of wintry wind	1492
In the darkness of this passing age	204
In the flavour of a fruit	885
In the little things we do	662
In the middle of bustle	925
In the midst of dark powers	177
In the name of the angelic force	176
In the name of the crucified and risen Christ	391
In the name of the eternal Father	384
In the name of the God of wholeness	572
In the name of the sending Father	1140
In the place of fear	1105
In the silence, we become aware of you, O God	1194
In the strength of the Warrior of God	987
In the wasteland may the Glory shine	3
In the whirling wheels of the world	499

In this Eucharist you have become	284
In your presence we affirm	944
Incomparable Guide,	1136
Increase our desire	1410
Infant Jesus	58
Infinite Birther, thank you for moments	1238
Infinite One of the wise heart	1063
Inflaming Spirit, come	121
Intimate, merciful Saviour God	236
Into our place of darkness	93
Into the life of the Father I immerse you	372
Into the Sacred Three we immerse you	157
Into the Sacred Three we immerse you	1420
Into your hands, O God	1137
Into your hands, O Lord	519
Into your loss	1402
Irresistible One	1108
Jesus, bless our eyes	604
Jesus, born in a stable	21
Jesus, broken on the cross	270
Jesus, by your cross you have redeemed us	346
Jesus Christ, Son of glory	37
Jesus, Master Carpenter of Nazareth	773
Jesus, may we journey with you	1093
Jesus, Mediator between Earth and heaven	221
Jesus, Pattern of goodness,	780
Jesus, proclaimed by angels	31
Jesus, tender Lamb of the tears	287
Jesus, they call you God's Expert Carpenter	348
Jesus – truly God, truly human	769
Jesus, we will follow you	1092
Jesus, when we are weak,	849
Jesus, who stopped the wind and stilled the waves	96
Jesus, you are the glory of eternity	234
Jesus, you are the glory of eternity shining among us	32
Jesus, you healed a mother of her sickness	847
Jesus, you helped your dad	594
Jesus, you were born into a world of oppression	1115
Jesus, you were driven to the sands	1198
Joseph of Arimathea gave you,	333
Joy of birth be yours today	1413
Keep us worthy of our calling	218
Keeper of eternity	796
Keeper of kindreds	1219
Kind Father, faithful Saviour	84

INDEX OF FIRST LINES

Kindle in our hearts, O God	555
Kindle in us the adventure of obedience	615
Kindle our imaginations	877
Kindle the memory of love	332
Kindling Spirit, come	933
Lamb of God, Defenceless Victor	294
Lead me, Lord, into a place of prayer	1438
Lead us from death to life	492
Lead us from that which binds	915
Lead us from that which is partial	919
Lead us from wasting time	918
Lead us into the desert of purging	65
Lead us on our journey	1124
Leaving what is past	1095
Let the cares of the past grow dim	30
Let the light fade and the work be done	514
Let there be	998
Let us go forth in the goodness	1148
Let us go forth in the wisdom	1149
Life of Jesus, Sun of suns	481
Life of Jesus, Sun of suns	1471
Life-giver, bring buds to flower	1458
Life-giver, Pain-bearer	1396
Life-giver, Pain-bearer, Being of Love	844
Life-giving God, the world lies open before you	435
Lift from us our anguish	589
Light up the fire in us, O Lord	213
Light-bringer, we have buried	958
Light-creator, evil cannot make its home	216
Lighten our darkness at the end of the day	568
Like Patrick, Father	736
Living God, change these elements	278
Living God, we thank you for your gifts	634
Lord Christ, you prayed for the unity	1177
Lord help me never to pretend	902
Lord in your mercy . . . may the grains	336
Lord, a thousand voices shout at us this day	474
Lord, as you were there	230
Lord, be within us to give us strength	1150
Lord, before you left this Earth	112
Lord, by your cross and precious death	559
Lord, circle this school	610
Lord, do not lead us into a time of fearful trial	1109
Lord, do you really call us to be awake and aware	450
Lord, for the rest of our lives	1160

Lord, give us that love	783
Lord, give us the statesmanship	1188
Lord, grant me the strength	1062
Lord, help me to take the time to sit	1344
Lord, help me to understand my own story	835
Lord, help us to think things through	1079
Lord, human extremity is your opportunity	642
Lord Jesus, as we think of your teaching	820
Lord Jesus, at this hour you hung on the cross	507
Lord Jesus Christ	193
Lord Jesus Christ, Light of the World	803
Lord Jesus Christ, who at this hour lay in the tomb	538
Lord Jesus, in the midst of mockery and madness	509
Lord Jesus, in your name we break the power	410
Lord Jesus, simplicity and a deep love	620
Lord Jesus, take my gaze away	792
Lord Jesus, you have taught us	313
Lord Jesus, you taught that your apostles	821
Lord Jesus, you taught that your chosen people	81
Lord, I crave the approval of others	906
Lord, I don't feel alive, but I thank you for the gift of life	449
Lord, in our hour of need, come to us	858
Lord, inspired by David and the Watermen	664
Lord, keep united in the cross	349
Lord, make our lives an open book	870
Lord, make us true like arrows	862
Lord, may the swirling storm clouds	1357
Lord, may these graces flower	909
Lord of Earth and heaven	984
Lord of the church, Servant King	1178
Lord of the Dance, grant me joy in all things	1239
Lord of the elements, give us a good journey	1152
Lord of the Great Passage	399
Lord of the holy and risen ones	328
Lord of the seasons, on this day of briefest light	1504
Lord of the solstice	416
Lord of the year behind us	47
Lord of the years	45
Lord of the years, may we celebrate	1146
Lord of time and eternity	28
Lord, plagues new and old afflict our world	1201
Lord, show us how to pray like this	968
Lord, sometimes I feel beaten and battered	1443
Lord Spirit, show me the things	246
Lord, summer ripens	329

INDEX OF FIRST LINES

Lord, thank you for sending John	323
Lord, thank you for your Spirit	321
Lord, the nations rage	1379
Lord, though we may laugh	5
Lord, today may the needs of our bodies	969
Lord, unlock the treasures of wisdom	1086
Lord, we have not much faith	866
Lord, we leave behind with you	965
Lord, we mourn	244
Lord, we offer you all we are	454
Lord, we offer you, like the women	95
Lord, we offer you our conflicting feelings	1164
Lord, we offer you this day's troubles	524
Lord, we would like to be part of a nursery of saints	1347
Lord, when we are insulted	859
Lord, when we cry out to you	1020
Lord, with joy and for love of you	49
Lord, with joy we pledge our love of you	875
Lord, you are our island	896
Lord, you come to us at the breaking of the day	309
Lord, you keep us waiting for signs of hope	16
Lord, you know each of us by name	1038
Lord, you remember us	1066
Lord, you were tested by the evil one	522
Lord, your body was broken on the cross for us	350
Lord, your table gives us life	344
Lover of souls	708
Lover of the poor	707
Majestic God, whose servant Benedict	632
Make us attentive to the lap of the waves	883
Make us attentive to your clear commands	1069
Make us aware, dear God	500
Make us eager to align our wills with yours	861
Make us patient in our observing	1007
Make us pilgrims of the world	1126
Make us rich in your eyes, dear God	945
Make us sensitive, Lord	1068
Make us true	903
Make us wise in our understanding	1343
Make whole the leisure and activity of this day	437
Maker of all creatures, we honour you	1242
Mary, you nurtured the precious life	345
Mary's Son, our friend, come and bless our kitchens	640
May all who bathe their bodies here	387
May Christ rise in glory	102

May desks and treetops praise you	261
May each land find its well-being	989
May each thing we do be without regret	1037
May every lone parent and child	29
May failures be forgiven	836
May fears of day recede	551
May flowers of a thousand colours	320
May God heal you, my dear one	425
May God search them, may God remove them	421
May God who clothes the flowers	165
May heaven's peacekeepers	529
May I do my rounds today	822
May I tweet with the melody of the lark	1228
May illness depart from our eyes	841
May it bless the land it will travel on	1222
May our church be a seedbed of prayer	1170
May our churches bring honour to you	1171
May our feet follow our hearts	1125
May our government and civic leaders	1352
May our hearts be places of royal hospitality	1406
May our homes, like Brigid's	639
May our homes reflect your presence	1204
May our nation find your will as her destiny	922
May our sons grow up strong	1189
May our work be faithful	819
May smiling faces welcome you	611
May the blessing of the five loaves and the two fishes	1257
May the blessing of the rain be on us	1251
May the Christ who walks with wounded feet	1142
May the Creator, the Saviour	317
May the Creator who fathers	1100
May the cross of Christ	373
May the Divine Father	831
May the Eternal Glory shine upon us	113
May the Eternal Glory shine upon us	502
May the Father take you	356
May the Father take you in his fragrant clasp of love	359
May the fire of the Spirit	937
May the freshness and fragrance of the fields	1271
May the fruits God gave Brigid lie on us	641
May the God of gentleness be with you	275
May the land to which you are journeying	1256
May the life of the Three	152
May the life that came through Mary	302
May the Light of lights come to our dark hearts	518

INDEX OF FIRST LINES

May the light that shines out from your face	1118
May the love of the Three	1348
May the loving Father God	383
May the media develop	887
May the place to which we go be without regret	1143
May the Spirit pour upon us as we sleep	135
May the strong Lord of life	423
May the Sun of suns shine upon us	930
May the Three Loves in God's heart	1206
May the Three of Limitless Love	494
May the Three of Limitless Love	1209
May this be a day of resurrection	482
May this be a gift of space to you	1223
May this food give new energy to tired limbs	1277
May this food restore our strength	1260
May this food so fresh and fragrant	1262
May this house be built upon the Rock of Christ	380
May this little one	1213
May this place be fragrant	393
May this season of mellow fruitfulness	1487
May this water be for your healing	429
May those who are bereft of loved ones	900
May we be as free as the wind	1135
May we be lit by the glory of God	833
May we be mindful in our speaking	873
May we be real like the elements	892
May we carry your cross	82
May we do on Earth	212
May we do this day on Earth	466
May we eagerly desire	1381
May we journey with you	23
May we, like Agatha Christie's	956
May we love you in your Earth	1309
May we make common cause with those who do right	1334
May we rest this night	578
May we rise from the holy table	285
May we see the face of Christ	458
May we walk in the hope of your kingdom	456
May you be	63
May you be bound	358
May you be honoured in our hearts	765
May you be like an oak tree of wisdom	1040
May you have truth in your hearts	830
May you respect one another	379
May you share hopes and dreams	361

May you who were baptised	398
May your cloud of witnesses	200
May your cross come between	199
May your presence draw people across the world	55
May your tender love burn inside us	1023
Mellow moon, sheen light of the night	1505
Mentor and Seeker of souls	672
Merciful God, send now, in kindness	279
Merciful One, may your compassion	805
Mighty Anchor in our storms	920
Mighty God, Columba's voice	650
Mighty God, you sheltered Tudwal	750
Mighty Provider, you remind us through Haggai	686
Mighty Restorer, who brings back all	927
Moon, you gave light to our ancestors	1218
Most merciful God, thank you for David	660
Most merciful God, we confess to you	249
Most powerful Spirit of God	355
Mother, dear pearl of great price	1212
Mr Sun, you settle down	599
[Name of pet], the eye of God be on you	1216
Nature's breath and eyes are clearest blue	565
Noble Christ, may we not become tortured souls	76
Now, dear Jesus	409
Now is born Christ the king of greatness	26
Now let us praise the Maker of Heaven	260
Now we give you thanks for work completed	567
Nurturing God, bless this soil	1296
O angel guardian of our right hands	171
O Being of life!	510
O Being of truth	852
O bright, beautiful angel	185
O Christ, like the seed that falls into the ground	91
O Christ, may the benefits of your passion	229
O Christ, Son of the living God	532
O Christ, the Champion of the tests	1119
O Christ who at this evening hour	561
O Christ, who called your disciples	625
O Christ, who chose as a brother	704
O Christ, whose presence was revealed	283
O Christ, you entered the stream of human life	59
O Christ, you had compassion on the crowds	806
O Christ, you laid your life down for us	1003
O Christ, you remembered those	94
O Christ, you took the tree in your hands	64

INDEX OF FIRST LINES

O God, all-powerful, you are our strength	1112
O God, Eternal Love, Courage and Wisdom	1083
O God of Life, darken not to me your light	1425
O God our Desire	721
O God, we confess our ingratitude	369
O God, we see your story	134
O God, we thank you . . . called us to travel	1163
O God, when the ride is bumpy	77
O God, who endowed Hilda	1409
O God, you called all life into being	497
O God, you called Caedmon	305
O God, you have prepared for those	807
O Holy Fire	67
O Holy One, I could run	319
O King of the Friday	87
O King of the Tree of life	129
O loving Christ, hanged on a tree	479
O Mighty One, may I put no one on a pedestal	1090
O Monarch of the Tree of Life	1457
O our Lord . . . true and honest	876
O Radiant Dawn, splendour of eternal light	580
O sacred season of autumn, be our teacher	1483
O Saviour Christ	40
O Saviour of the human race	648
O Son of God, change our hearts	467
O Spirit be free in us	405
O Trinity of Love	591
O Yahweh, I Am	762
On these long, bright days	322
On this day of remembrance	352
On this day of the saints of life	205
On this, your anniversary	1412
On those who harbour fear	1394
On those whose day is drab	460
On your world, Lord	486
On your world, Lord	553
Open my eyes to see how this subject	1428
Open our eyes to see you reflected	147
Open our eyes to the poisons of our time	1076
Open our eyes to your presence	233
Open our eyes to your presence	354
Our Father in heaven	179
Our Father in heaven	487
Our Father in heaven	608
Our society is ever restless	881

Out of the depths of life's torrents	1191
Out of your womb we came	1147
Overarching God	749
Pardoner and Restorer	1377
Parent of orphans	731
Peace and blessing from the Spirit	787
Peace be upon our breath	570
Peace between believers	1369
Peace between parties	1370
Peace between victor and vanquished	353
Peace between victor and vanquished	1375
Peace come into this swelling	424
Peace to the land and all that grows on it	1368
Perfect Comforter! Wonderful Refreshment!	503
Permeating Spirit	722
Pilgrim God, we thank you for Brendan's	1153
Pilgrim God, who accepted such humbling	1157
Pilgrim God, who through the prophet Nathan	728
Pour, King of life	422
Power of powers	155
Power of powers	974
Praise the God of all the people	264
Promised Spirit	114
Protect us through the hours of this night	545
Protecting Father, stalwart Steersman	268
Provider God, as autumn light ripens the grain	166
Purify our lives like gold	54
Purity, wisdom and prophecy	649
Rejoice, you earth of sunlit days	1476
Release in us the power of your Spirit	127
Remove the clutter from our lives, Lord	981
Renew us, O Risen Christ	513
Renew us this night, Lord	541
Restore to us, O God	1028
Risen Christ, as we read this passage	1067
Risen Christ, as you appeared to your disciples	105
Risen Christ, bring newness of life	957
Risen Christ, give us your resurrection eyes	786
Risen Christ of the miraculous catching of fish	1276
Risen Christ, scatter the sin from our souls	457
Risen Christ, we acknowledge that you	1165
Risen Christ, we welcome you	277
Risen Christ, you burned in the hearts of two walkers	564
Risen Christ, you burst from the grave	97
Risen Christ, you called Peter to love you	104

INDEX OF FIRST LINES

Risen Christ, you come with searing white	1168
Risen Christ, you come with us	1168
Risen Christ, you embraced our humanity	109
Risen Christ, you have entered into darkness	563
Risen Christ, you turned Mary's tears into joy	101
Risen Lord, you revealed yourself	99
Rock of ages, who called Baldred	627
Root of our Desire	1232
Rugged and real was your servant Malo	717
Sacred Three, as we thank you	692
Sadness and sin behind us be	1221
Saint Fursey saw four fires	214
Save us from being laws unto ourselves	1180
Save us from the arrogance of self-sufficiency	975
Saving God	72
Saviour God, as we	191
Saviour of us and the saints	208
Search out in us, O God	973
Servant King	908
Servant King, who called Gregory	683
Set us free, O God	1407
Shadows darken this day	558
Shed light upon our brow	62
Shine on us, Lord	340
Show us, Lord, that for which the time	1047
Silent, surrendered, at your feet	793
Silent, surrendered, leaving all	1197
Silently the Earth yields her fruits	775
Since it was you, O Christ	226
Sleep in peace	527
So much of the media	921
Son of the elements, Son of the heavens	36
Son of the prophets, on our longings	17
Sorry Lord for the shabbiness of my living	239
Sorry, Lord, for the shabbiness of our living	240
Sorry, Lord, for the sins	238
Source of Creativity	961
Source of Love, God of Tender Beauty	418
Source of our being	363
Source of Peace	923
Sovereign of seas and stars	223
Sovereign of the universe	106
Spacious God, though Neot	730
Speak, Lord, in stillness or storm	1050
Spirit, kindle in our hearts	801

Spirit of God, among the wheels of industry	125
Spirit of God as fresh as the dawn	935
Spirit of God, be wild and free in me	142
Spirit of God, be wild and free in us	932
Spirit of God, rest on your people	122
Spirit of God, the breath of creation	137
Spirit of the living God	126
Spirit of the living God, present with us now	840
Spirit of the quiet earth	133
Spirit of the Risen Christ	515
Spirit of Truth, look down	571
Spouse of Heaven	747
Star Kindler and Weaver of wonder	1493
Star Kindler, be our light	1490
Still is the earth	574
Stop! It's the middle of the day	598
Stop us, dear God	1055
Strength-giver, may your fibre grow in us	403
Stretch our hearts, Lord	1045
Strip from us, Lord	312
Stripped of inessentials we stand, rooted in you	1497
Sun shines	1473
Support us, Lord	556
Supreme Ruler of heaven and Earth	1340
Sweet All-aware One	1196
Sweet Jesus flowing into us	296
Sweet Jesus, I lay before you now	1110
Sweet Saviour, who made Modan	725
Sweet the notes of purity with which a bird tweets	1227
Take from me, O God	905
Take our hands, dear Christ	802
Take us under your protection	1111
Teach me when to be silent and when to speak	1059
Teach us, dear God	601
Teach us, dear God	868
Teach us, dear God, to know your ways	1085
Teach us, good Lord	1162
Teach us, O Christ	677
Teach us to dance like clouds that play	603
Teach us to forgo vengeance at all times	304
Teach us to leave behind	1032
Teach us to leave behind prejudice and meanness of spirit	68
Teach us who live in comfort	1317
Tender Father, who called Cuthbert	656
Tender Saviour, bless these battered wives	1399

Tender Saviour, who enjoyed the cosiness	718
Thank you, Creator of the world	1244
Thank you, Father, for your free gift of fire	784
Thank you for a roof over our head	1488
Thank you for bringing us	488
Thank you for harvest's boundless store	1486
Thank you for leading us to the time of briefest light	1500
Thank you for Mungo's mother	726
Thank you for the countless numbers	1006
Thank you for the gift of a good soul friend	1103
Thank you for the gift of sleep	485
Thank you for the holy family	27
Thank you for the life of this place	430
Thank you for the little trinities	150
Thank you for the taste	1249
Thank you for those who have made covenant with you	874
Thank you for your love for us, strong and nurturing	525
Thank you, Jesus, for your love for us	1000
Thank you, Lord, that even if we are difficult	1061
Thank you that you are a God who speaks	1044
Thanks be to you, O God	1279
Thanks to you for the abundance of food	1263
The almighty and merciful Three circle us	535
The angel passed over the homes of the Godfollowers	89
The angels delight to do your will	174
The blessing of acceptance be yours	1404
The blessing of the perfect Spirit be ours	136
The blessing of the Three be upon you	162
The Creator who brought order out of chaos	521
The day slips away	526
The Divine Gift come into your loss	1401
The dying martyr Stephen	745
The Earth gave you a cave	34
The Earth is becoming a wasteland	8
The elements bear your Creator's stamp	894
The eternal Creator keep us	273
The face of nature laughs in the springtime	1463
The family of God draw round you	1415
The food that we are to eat	1275
The food which we are to eat	1274
The glorious company of the holy and risen ones	210
The glory of God in our working	967
The God of life go with us	202
The God of life go with us	300
The grace of your creation is like a cool day	1362

The Holy Three encircle you	1450
The joy of memory be yours today	1411
The Lord renew his place in your lives	371
The love and affection of God	357
The love that Mary gave her Son	35
The Magi searched for an infant king	53
The One who created us	78
The peace of Christ be there at the ingathering	228
The peace of the Spirit be ours this night	550
The seed is Christ's, the granary is Christ's	1480
The sheaves and the green leaves fall	1479
The shield of Christ be over us	201
The sun rides high and long	1466
The sun rises daily	469
The sun rises daily because you	414
The three palmfuls of the Sacred Three	1417
The Three who are over our head	156
The Three who are over our head	772
The welcome of the Father's arms be ours	1231
The world is not dead	1503
There is no plant in the ground	891
There is no plant in the ground	1281
This is a blessing of the God of life	1350
This is the Saving Sacrifice	297
This night, O Victor over death	540
This precious nectar is our delight	280
This we know: the Earth does not belong to us	1310
Three of forgiving love	243
Three of Limitless Love, may I fall into your lap	913
Thrice holy God	160
Thrice holy God	462
Thrice-holy God	306
Thrice-holy God, eternal Three-in-One	326
Thrice-seeing King of Heaven	1202
Through the resurrection of your Son you overcame	103
To [name the affected organ]	419
To the Sun of suns come singing	1472
To those who were snatched from Earth	188
Today, darkness and light are equal partners	1459
Today, O Lord	41
Toughen me, Lord	1088
Train us	1087
Triune God, Forgiving One	1017
Triune God who mothers us all, call into being	1179
Triune God who mothers us all, make whole	1175

INDEX OF FIRST LINES

Triune God, you are neither monochrome	164
Uncreated Beauty	276
Uncreated Beauty	899
Unfold to us	999
Universal Child	24
Universal God, you have a plan	1058
Unto you, O Lord, be praise for	1241
Vast and Giving One	1290
Victor in the race	110
Warm-winged Spirit, brooding over creation	365
Watch over your weeping ones	341
We adore you who puts life in soil and seed	334
We are appealing to you	1395
We are mortal	401
We are sorry for the distractions	1192
We are sorry, God of goodness	257
We are sorry that we have not given time	794
We are the Body of Christ	267
We are the race that helped make the wood	347
We arise today	215
We arise today	402
We arise today in a mighty force	146
We arise today in a Mighty Power	976
We arise today in joy of being alive	439
We arise today in the brilliance of the sun	441
We arise today in the deep formation	1496
We arise today in the Eternal Flow of Mercy	442
We arise today in the fullness of our humanity	433
We arise today in the glorious company	613
We arise today in the goodness of creation	445
We arise today in the power of the great Father	434
We arise today in the promise of the rising seed	1460
We arise today in the simplicity of the empty soil	447
We arise today in the vast might of the Trinity	163
We arise today in the wisdom of the One	440
We arise today, the sun to encircle us	443
We arise today through the strength	448
We arise today with the legions of God	978
We ask for the Light of light	1113
We believe, O God of all gods	464
We bind to ourselves this day	1498
We bind to ourselves today	770
We bless you for Mary	90
We bless you for the sun	149
We bless you for your covenant with Noah	1337

We bless you, giver of light	330
We bless you, God, for the goodness of this day	1284
We bless you, High King of creation	288
We bless you, Lord	299
We bless you, Lord, that Samson's birth	741
We bless you, O God, and forget not all your benefits	520
We bring to you, Healer of our souls	432
We bring to you the child that craves affection	798
We come into the presence of the creating Father	491
We come into the presence of the sending Father	757
We come into your presence	232
We come to God as we are	845
We come to you, God of surprises	791
We confess on behalf of [name place]	431
We confess that we wound one another	839
We confess with shame	248
We consecrate this kitchen to you	381
We draw aside in the midst of the day	990
We give ourselves to you, Lord	1001
We give thanks for the gift of sleep	586
We give thanks for the growth of sunlit days	1468
We give thanks for your saints	753
We give you thanks because Earth's life	472
We give you thanks for great moments of grace	1240
We give you thanks for your ancient promise	316
We give you thanks, Kindly Light	917
We give you thanks that you are always present	517
We give you worship with our whole life	869
We go forward in light of sun	1134
We go in the sign of the cross of Christ	301
We grieve that we who are made to	145
We invite you, generous Healer	832
We know that night is not dark with you	577
We lie down in peace, knowing our sins are forgiven	531
We lie down this night with God	534
We lie down this night with the nine angels	183
We love you, Lord, and we lift our voices	953
We make the sign of the Cross of Christ	790
We of this day are children of confusion	972
We offer to you, Lord, the troubles of this day	516
We offer you ourselves	117
We offer you the Earth	1365
We place into your hands	388
We place our souls and bodies	536
We place our souls and bodies	964

INDEX OF FIRST LINES

We pray against the Pharisee tendency	1187
We pray for an end to the injustices	1378
We pray for believers	269
We pray for children	194
We pray for flour mills	331
We pray for modern Ninians	732
We pray for the cleansing of our perceptions	1080
We pray for the people	1391
We pray for the well-being of the creation	1298
We pray for this land	1190
We pray for those	995
We pray for those who are unable	1339
We pray for those whose tasks are backbreaking	508
We pray to you for the place of desecration	1120
We raise our hands	1024
We recall the things that stain our memories	256
We release . . . into your hands	408
We release into your hands, O Lord	1419
We remember the waste of life and wit and learning	190
We rise up clothed in the strength of Christ	484
We swear by peace and love to stand	929
We thank you, Divine Radiance	1475
We thank you for Canice	644
We thank you for great people of faith	1318
We thank you for Joseph	92
We thank you for Polycarp's rapport	310
We thank you for revealing yourself	161
We thank you for those who give their all	207
We thank you for your presence through the day	554
We thank you that in your saints	219
We thank you that in your saints	614
We turn our eyes upon you	1166
We wait in the darkness expectantly, longingly	566
We wait in the darkness, expectantly, longingly	18
We walk in the strength of the mighty Three in One	1133
We weave this day	451
We welcome the light that burns	483
We welcome your light that glints in the rising sun	52
We will journey into wild places with God	1127
We will sing to you, Almighty God	265
We will start this day	173
We wrap our souls and our bodies	575
When a person sails by with eyes all glazed	1013
When all was prepared	886
When cold night draws near	1502

When I say 'don't', would you say it like that, Lord?	1441
When in decrepitude I awake	478
When people are in danger	1114
When rich nations begin to reap what they have sown	1351
When shadows lengthen and the departed	227
When the ride is bumpy	760
When volcanic ash prevents air flights	1367
When we are still we can sense you, our Maker	548
When we eat our food	606
When we have buried your insight	362
When your blood was spilled on the soil	281
Where crooks exploit asylum seekers for money	324
Where people long for an end to injustice	997
Where times are dark	1106
Wide-winged Spirit	658
Wind of Heaven	475
Wind, wind blow on me	143
Wisdom, breathing through all creation	366
Wisdom, come in to the storehouse of our memories	528
Wisdom of years be yours	1418
Wisdom on High	691
Wisdom, permeating creation and informing all peoples	12
With Abraham and Moses	20
With Christ, to whom the spirits were subject	752
With fresh shoots and buds of promise	1461
With these hands we bless the lonely	274
With this bread we offer to you	290
Word of God	1041
Word of God, rays from you	1016
Worker Christ, as we enter our workplace	816
Yahweh, people call you by a hundred names	1327
You are here, Lord, in this place	779
You are holy, you are whole	14
You are made in the likeness	1414
You are our Saviour and Lord	537
You are the Food from which all souls are fed	168
You are the refined molten forge	878
You are the Rock from which all Earth is fashioned	1302
You are the Vine	960
You are the well of heaven	954
You began your last week on Earth	75
You called humans to tend	253
You came down	108
You created the world out of love	549
You created the world out of love	581

You fell asleep in mortal flesh, O God	542
You give us well-being in the midst of the day	495
You have given your all to us	50
You led your people by a cloud	404
You, Lord, burn in this place	1439
You made Hilda to shine	688
You made the Earth, and through the long ages	1292
You pulled the continents out of the sea	1361
You revealed your ways through Moses	338
You saw a widow give what she had	80
You warm our hearts at your table	337
You who are Heroic Love	1034
You who are Heroic Love	1151
You who are our Perpetual Light	652
You who became poor to make many rich	56
You who became poor to make many rich	934
You who lift the lowly and strengthen the frail	83
You who made a pilgrimage of trust on Earth	1154
You who order the universe	1380
You who put beam in golden sun	1273
You who put beam in moon and sun	889
You who put ear in wheat and lamb	335
You who shaped the coastlines	781
You whose Heroic Love comes in a thousand ways	1036
You whose order rules the atom	1385
Your glory be seen	823
Your glory be seen in work	810
Your kingdom come, your will be done	992
Zeal of God, fill our being	857

Subject index

Topic	Prayer number
Abortion	176, 406, 410
Abuse	270, 365, 630, 1396–1400
Addictions	699
Adventure	638, 1034, 1045, 1151, 1153
Aidan	619–21
Air	258, 544, 605
Ancestors	222, 1217–19
Angels	169–85, 1039
Animals	389, 739, 1214–16, 1353, 1433
Anniversaries	1411–13
Armed services	830
Arts	632, 669, 855, 946
Athletes of Christ	625, 1283–85
Authenticity	906–910, 985, 1072, 1166
Autumn	1479–90
Awareness	1155
Babies/infants	374–6, 1213, 1414, 1418
Balance	1035, 1357
Baptism	98, 372–3
Beauty	626, 899
Being	1195, 1327
Beltane	318
Bicycles	1225
Birds	129, 389, 467, 565, 603, 726, 777, 961, 1096, 1236, 1280, 1353, 1360, 1457, 1462, 1473
Birth	43, 768, 1011, 1152, 1278, 1413
Blessings	63, 374–96, 413–17, 1142, 1159, 1250–79, 1316, 1320, 1420
Bodies, our	944, 963, 964, 966, 969
Boozers	118, 593
Boys	1349
Brendan, Saint	638, 1153
Brigid, Saint	302–4, 639–41
Britain	325
Britanny	750
Broken people	71, 243, 271
Bunyan, John	1154
Candle-lighting	231
Candlemas	302

SUBJECT INDEX

Cars	1222–3, 1423
Celebration	609, 894, 1360
Church planting	642, 644
Churches	269, 523, 607, 1167–84, 1386
Circling	198, 376, 392, 1165, 1363, 1444–56
Cities and towns	684, 726, 1243, 1311, 1323
Cleansing	1122
Commerce	125
Communities and community	152, 192, 268, 269, 454, 506, 638, 650, 732, 837, 970, 1169, 1177, 1296, 1326, 1348, 1384
Community of Aidan & Hilda	96, 914, 970, 1167
Compassion	166, 799–807
Computer	1421–2
Conception	41
Confessions	4, 19, 88, 145, 174, 216, 233, 235–58, 338, 347, 368, 369, 406, 407, 471, 516, 622, 648, 659, 686, 700, 733, 843, 848, 979, 986, 1094, 1183, 1198–1202, 1294, 1295, 1300, 1305, 1324
Conflict resolution	1199, 1377
Connecting	1012, 1021, 1321
Consumer society	585, 712, 848, 881, 1290
Contemplation	1, 687
Cornish saints	654, 729–30, 739
Cosmology	1238, 1248, 1388–9
Courage	932
Covenant	49, 89, 698, 874, 875, 929, 1337
Crafts	635, 655, 669
Creation	1353–67
Creativity	126, 127, 152, 290, 600, 961, 1005
Crime	125, 324
Crisis	1379, 1435
Cross, the	69, 82, 83, 86, 87, 95, 199, 235, 301, 346–51, 373, 507, 575, 639, 790, 843, 1077
Cross-cultural mission	1016, 1328
Darkness	18, 31, 61, 93, 193, 246, 274, 325, 330, 537, 558, 566, 568, 569, 571, 582, 604, 651, 652, 708, 788, 803, 920, 1106, 1490
Death	397–412, 540, 584, 1097
Dedication	454, 525, 869, 1003, 1025, 1060, 1092, 1160
Democracy	1319
Deserts	27c, 65, 254, 645, 1134
Devotion	95
Disability	508, 707
Discernment	938, 1042–63, 1078–81
Disease	257
Diversity	1314

Divorce	1220–21
Dreams	18, 134, 135, 566, 882, 1039
Dying	84, 175, 397–9, 745, 1060
Earth	258, 447, 544, 880, 901, 1218, 1236, 1240, 1245, 1246, 1292, 1307, 1309–12, 1358–9, 1363–8
Ecology	336, 675, 871, 1292–1314, 1354
Economy, the	1287, 1290
Empathy	1344
Empowerment	1033, 1315
Encouragers	628, 688, 1442–3
England	680, 734
Envy	327
Equinoxes	1506
Eschatology	2, 702, 1195
Examen	433
Exams	1428
Exploitation	324
Facebook	1226
Fair trade	992
Families	27, 1204–13, 1390
Fashion	1004
Fathers	713, 1210–11
FIFA	1285
Finance	324, 994
Fire	213, 214, 395, 396, 544, 744, 784, 1018
Fitness	963, 1283–5, 1322, 1434
Flowers	109, 319, 892, 1244, 1355
Free spirits	328, 1027, 1032, 1135, 1138
Friendship	611, 618, 716, 718, 1233–5
Fun	603, 609
Gardens	389, 675, 1280–2
Generosity	58, 68, 686
Gentleness	275
Girls	1189, 1350
Gossip	327, 608, 1288
Governments and civil authorities	993–4, 1185–6, 1340, 1342, 1345, 1352
Greed	724, 1077
Growth	900, 1349, 1350
Guidance	51, 917
Halloween	194–203
Hands	71, 82, 117, 171, 274, 387, 519, 802, 1024, 1142

SUBJECT INDEX

Healing	32, 1393
Healing the land	1120–21, 1199, 1324
Heaven	177
Heroes	613, 680, 1318
Hilda, Saint	688–92, 1026, 1029–30, 1315
Holidays	1229, 1419
Holy Communion	277–99, 1384,
Homeless people	29, 37
Honesty	608, 728
Hospitality	164, 328, 386, 482, 639, 1169–71
House blessings	108, 1204, 1431
Households	388, 1204–7
Human rights	270
Humility	69, 78, 647
Hunger	980, 995
Imbolc	See *Spring* and *Light*
Immersion	157, 372
Inner healing	418, 426, 428, 577, 798, 832, 844, 939
Integrity	679, 878, 879, 892, 902, 903, 906
Inter faith	616, 1327–31
Internet	496, 904, 1226
Jews	616, 1328, 1331
Joseph of Arimathea	92
Journey	23, 66, 77, 637, 760, 1092–8, 1123–66
Joy	123, 880, 1000
Justice	325, 617, 990, 1187, 1319, 1326, 1378
Kindness	123, 725
Kitchens	381, 640, 797
Lament	145, 235–58, 1203
Laptops	514, 794, 1421–2
Laughter	453, 603, 860, 961
Leadership	751, 1340
Learning	601, 623, 672, 691, 695, 782, 868, 1029, 1063, 1070–4, 1082, 1085–7, 1330
Leisure	437, 894, 1226–30
Light	52, 61, 483, 651, 652
Lindisfarne	263
Listening	451, 474, 602, 756, 972, 1038, 1041–50, 1335
Lone parents	29
Loss and sorrow	1401–2
Lottery	1289

Lovemaking	150, 159, 1232
Lughnasadh	See *Summer*
Manhood	1349
Mary, Virgin	342–5, 722, 723
Meal blessings	984, 1257–79
Media	887, 1208
Memory	332
Midsummer	318–20, 322, 1478
Mindfulness	6, 7, 606, 791, 871, 873, 883–5, 1009, 1015, 1037, 1069
Miscarriage	411
Mission	736, 999
Money	1286–91, 1430
Monks and nuns	670
Moons, full and new	413, 1505
Mothers	40, 1212
Motorcycles	1224
Multi-cultural communities	1382–3
Music	159, 643, 693, 1315
Muslims	27c, 616, 1190, 1331
Nations	922, 979, 989, 1190, 1351, 1385
Nature	1236–7, 1241, 1309, 1355
Neighbours	1432
Networks	487
Obedience	615, 631, 981, 1002
Office	826, 827
Oil	1297
Old age	673
Openness	435, 862, 1008, 1072
Oppressed people	364, 519
Overcoming	208, 682, 696, 709, 752, 782, 1089, 1105, 1110, 1119
Pain	310
Parents	377, 378, 1090, 1209
Parties and discos	609, 1230
Peace	521, 540, 926, 1368–83
Pets	1214–16, 1433
Pilgrimage	25, 1123–1166
Places	430–2, 694, 727, 1120, 1143, 1156, 1164–5
Plants	89
Poverty	986
Praise	1236–7
Presence	491, 499, 500, 756–98, 1115

SUBJECT INDEX

Pride and prejudice	905, 986, 991
Prophecy	634, 1051
Protection	1111, 1150
Purging	65, 70
Purity	257, 715, 981, 1168
Questionnaires	1429
Race	81, 159, 704, 740, 1185
Rain	1251
Rape	726
Reaching out	1009, 1023, 1321, 1329
Reconciliation	39, 272, 688, 924, 974
Refugees	1115
Relinquishment	1137
Renewal	10, 460, 552, 579, 741, 996, 1394–5
Renunciation	965
Repentance	979
Respect	928, 998
Rest	489, 490, 503
Restoration	997
Resurrection, place of	1124–5
Retreats	1436–40
Reunions	1231
Revival	127, 138
Rhythm	259, 446, 774, 782, 914, 969, 1028, 1031, 1075, 1084, 1307
Rising prayers	146, 163, 215, 402, 433, 434, 440–3, 448, 978
Rogation	314
Sabbath	794
Saints	613–755, 1148–9
Saints in order of their day	302–53
Samhain	1489 and see *Winter*
Sanctity of life	1338, 1387
Santa Claus	731
Schedules	962
School	610–12
Scripture	914, 1064–8
Sea of troubles	268, 621, 1380
Seafarers	738
Service/servant leadership	683, 1405–10
Shield	148, 195
Silence and stillness	323, 451, 793, 795, 1041, 1191–4
Simplicity	620, 646, 914, 981–5
Sleep	158, 287, 526–93

Shops	262
Society	152, 1185, 1187–90, 1290, 1323, 1342, 1346, 1390
Song	643
Soul friend	687, 914, 1017, 1019, 1098–1104, 1347
Speech	761
Spiritual warfare	67, 72, 176, 685, 976–8, 1022, 1076
Sport	134, 894, 1283–5, 1434
Spring	1457–64
Stars, planets	569, 890, 1152
Stepchildren/parents	1415–16
Stewards	914, 1308
Storytelling	1011
Suicidal thoughts	1107
Summer	1465–78
Summer solstice	320, 414, 415
Sun	149, 480, 481
Talents	689, 1029
Tears	75, 79, 257, 660
Tenderness	345
Terror, acts of	900, 1114–17, 1317
Thanksgivings	1006, 1010, 1249
Toilet	387
Tongue, the	1427
Tongues	1426
Transformation	56, 1052, 1122, 1332–3, 1441
Travel	1419, 1423–4
Tree of Life	129
Trees	64
Trials and temptations	1105–14, 1119
TV	1208
Twitter	1227–28
Unborn babies	321
Unemployment	828, 829
Unity	656, 658, 974, 1325, 1381–7
Valentine's Day	306–8
Victims of neglect, violence and war	1392, 1401–4
Villages of God/colonies of heaven	653, 719, 732, 735
Violence	270
Vocations	138, 523
Voyages	1139
Vulnerability	75, 522, 1036, 1071, 1343, 1396

SUBJECT INDEX

Waiting	20, 85, 115, 793, 931, 941
Wales	659–65
Water	149, 258, 336, 429, 544, 897
Welcome	1013, 1024
Wild goose	124
Wildness	142, 627, 714, 932, 1127
Wind	119, 127, 143
Winter	1491–1506
Winter solstice	416, 417
Wisdom	11, 12, 901, 933, 1030, 1040, 1083
Witchcraft	176, 194
Witness	1011
Women	692
Work	476, 497, 611, 810–25, 1162, 1339
Wounded memory	838
Writing	1043
Young people	27d

www.ingramcontent.com/pod-product-compliance
Lightning Source LLC
Chambersburg PA
CBHW020349080526
44584CB00014B/946